Collins

INTERNATIONAL PRIMARY ENGLISH

Teacher's Guide 4

William Collins' dream of knowledge for all began with the publication of his first book in 1819.
A self-educated mill worker, he not only enriched millions of lives, but also founded a flourishing publishing house. Today, staying true to this spirit, Collins books are packed with inspiration, innovation and practical expertise. They place you at the centre of a world of possibility and give you exactly what you need to explore it.

Collins. Freedom to teach.

An imprint of HarperCollins*Publishers*
The News Building
1 London Bridge Street
London SE1 9GF

Browse the complete Collins catalogue at
www.collins.co.uk

© HarperCollins*Publishers* Limited 2016

10 9 8 7

ISBN 978-0-00-814771-6

Catherine Baker asserts her moral rights to be identified as the author of this work.

All rights reserved. No part of this publication may be reproduced, stored in a retrieval system, or transmitted in any form by any means, electronic, mechanical, photocopying, recording or otherwise, without the prior written permission of the Publisher or a licence permitting restricted copying in the United Kingdom issues by the Copyright Licensing Agency Ltd., 90 Tottenham Court Road, London W1T 4LP.

British Library Cataloguing in Publication Data
A catalogue record for this publication is available from the British Library.

Publisher Celia Wigley
Publishing manager Karen Jamieson
Commissioning editor Lucy Cooper
Series editor Karen Morrison
Managing editor Caroline Green
Editor Amanda Redstone
Project managed by Emily Hooton
Edited by Karen Williams
Proofread by Gaynor Spry and Cassie Fox
Cover design by Amparo Barrera
Cover artwork by Priyankar Gupta
Internal design by Ken Vail Graphic Design
Typesetting by Ken Vail Graphic Design and Contentra Technologies India Private Limited
Illustrations by Ken Vail Graphic Design, Priyankar Gupta, Advocate Art and Beehive Illustration
Production by Robin Forrester and Lyndsey Rogers

Printed and bound by CPI Group (UK) Ltd, Croydon, CR0 4YY

Text acknowledgements
The publishers gratefully acknowledge the permissions granted to reproduce copyright material in the book. Every effort has been made to contact the holders of copyright material, but if any have been inadvertently overlooked, the Publisher will be pleased to make the necessary arrangements at the first opportunity.

HarperCollins*Publishers* Limited for an extract and artwork from *Let's Go to Mars* by Janice Marriott, illustrated by Mark Ruffle, text copyright © Janie Marriott; for an extract and artwork from *The Brave Baby* by Malachy Doyle, illustrated by Richard Johnson. Text reproduced by permission of HarperCollins*Publishers*; The Catchpole Agency. HarperCollins*Publishers* for an extract and artwork from *I've Just had a Bright Idea*, written and illustrated by Scoular Anderson, text copyright © Scoular Anderson; for an extract and artwork from *Peter and the Wolf* by Diane Redmond, illustrated by John Bendall-Brunello, text copyright © Diane Redmond. Text reproduced by permission of HarperCollins*Publishers*; Ed Victor Ltd.

David Higham Associates for an extract from "Street Child" by Berlie Doherty published in *Collins Primary Literacy Pupil Book 4*, pp.4-5. Reproduced with permission; Ann Webley for material adapted from *Collins Primary Literacy Pupil Book 4*, pp.50-51, 90. Reproduced with permission; David Higham Associates for the poems "Old Man Ocean" and "The Crow" by Russell Hoban published in *The Pedalling Man*, Heinemann, 1991 © The Trustees of the Russell Hoban Trust; Bloomsbury and Peters Fraser & Dunlop for the poems 'The Youngest' and 'Last One Into Bed' by Michael Rosen, published in *Mustard, Custard, Grumble Belly and Gravy*, Bloomsbury Publishing Plc. Reprinted by permission of Bloomsbury and Peters Fraser & Dunlop (www.petersfraserdunlop.com) on behalf of Michael Rosen; David Higham Associates for an extract from *Goggle Eyes* by Anne Fine, Penguin; and *Kamla and Kate* by Jamila Gavin, Mammoth. Reproduced with permission; First News for Schools for extracts from 'Malala's Award' and ' Mini Mars Mission', www.firstnews.co.uk. Reproduced with permission; Solo Syndication for an extract from "An Alien? Fat Chance!", *Daily Mail*, 14/01/1998, copyright © Solo Syndication, 1998; Irene Rawnsley for the poem "A Good Idea" published in *Dog's Dinner* by Irene Rawnsley, Methuen Children's Books, 1990. Reproduced by kind permission of the author; Chris Baker for an extract from *Sheetal's First Landing*, copyright © Chris Baker, 2015. Reproduced by kind permission of the author; Judith Nicholls for the poem "The Last Dragon" published in *Storm's Eye*, Oxford University Press; 1994, copyright © Judith Nicholls. Reproduced by kind permission of the author; Brian Moses for the poem "Lost Magic" published in *Behind the Staffroom Door*, Macmillan Children's Books, 2007. Reproduced by kind permission of the author; and George Szirtes for the poem "The bicycle's wrists" published in *In the Land of Giants*, Salt Publishing, 2012. Reproduced by kind permission of the author.

Photo acknowledgements
The publishers wish to thank the following for permission to reproduce photographs. Every effort has been made to trace copyright holders and to obtain their permission for the use of copyright materials. The publishers will gladly receive any information enabling them to rectify any error or omission at the first opportunity.

(t = top, c = centre, b = bottom, r = right, l = left)

Cover & p1 Priyankar Gupta
PCM 1 Peter Higginbotham Collection/Mary Evans Picture Library, PCM 10 Frances Linzee Gordon/Getty Images.

Contents

Section 1 Introduction

About Collins International Primary English	5
Assessment in primary English	7
Formal written assessment	7
Learning objectives matching grid	8

Section 2 Unit-by-Unit Support

Unit 1: Stories of the past
Unit overview	23
Curriculum focus	23
Related resources	24
Week 1	24
Week 2	29
Week 3	31

Unit 2: Mars: the trip of a lifetime!
Unit overview	33
Curriculum focus	33
Related resources	34
Week 1	34
Week 2	38
Week 3	42

Unit 3: The power of the sea
Unit overview	44
Curriculum focus	44
Related resources	45
Week 1	45
Week 2	48
Week 3	50

Unit 4: Other people, other places
Unit overview	53
Curriculum focus	53
Related resources	54
Week 1	54
Week 2	57
Week 3	60

Unit 5: The only problem is …
Unit overview	62
Curriculum focus	62
Related resources	63
Week 1	63
Week 2	66
Week 3	68

Unit 6: Making the headlines
Unit overview	71
Curriculum focus	71
Related resources	72
Week 1	72
Week 2	75
Week 3	76

Unit 7: Inventions
Unit overview	80
Curriculum focus	80
Related resources	81
Week 1	81
Week 2	83
Week 3	86

Unit 8: Putting on a show
Unit overview	88
Curriculum focus	88
Related resources	89
Week 1	89
Week 2	91
Week 3	94

Unit 9: Imaginary worlds
Unit overview	96
Curriculum focus	96
Related resources	97
Week 1	97
Week 2	101
Week 3	103

Section 3 Photocopiable masters (PCMs)

PCM 1–23	**106**
Formal assessment 1	**132**
Formal assessment 2	**136**
Formal assessment 3	**140**

Introduction

About Collins International Primary English

Collins International Primary English is specifically written to fully meet the requirements of the Cambridge Primary English curriculum framework, and the material has been carefully developed to meet the needs of primary English learners and teachers in a range of international contexts.

The course materials are supplemented and enhanced by a range of print and electronic resources, including photocopiable (printable) master sheets for support, extension and assessment of classroom based activities (you can find these on pages 106 to 131 of this Teacher's Guide as well as on the digital resource) and a range of interactive digital activities to add interest and excitement to learning. Reading texts are supported by audio files.

Components of the course

For each of Stages 1–6 as detailed in the Cambridge Primary English curriculum framework, we offer:

- a full colour, highly illustrated Student's Book with integral reading texts
- a write-in Workbook linked to the Student's Book
- this comprehensive Teacher's Guide with clear instructions for using the materials
- an interactive digital package, which includes warm-up presentations, audio files of readings, interactive activities and record keeping for teacher use only.

Approach

The course is designed with learner-centred learning at its heart. Learners work through a range of contextualised reading, writing, speaking and listening activities with guidance and support from their teacher. Plenty of opportunity is provided for learners to consolidate and apply what they have learnt and to relate what they are learning both to other contexts and the environment in which they live.

Much of learners' work is conducted in pairs or small groups in line with international best practice. The tasks and activities are designed to be engaging for learners and to support teachers in their assessment of learner progress and achievement. Each set of lessons is planned to support clear learning objectives, and the activities within each unit provide opportunities for oral and written feedback by the teacher as well as self- and peer-assessment options.

Throughout the course, there is a wide variety of learning experiences on offer. The materials are organised so that they do not impose a rigid structure, but rather allow for a range of options linked to the learning objectives.

Differentiation

Differentiation in the form of support and extension ideas is built into the unit-by-unit teaching support in this Teacher's Guide.

Achievement levels are likely to vary from learner to learner, so we have included a graded set of assessment criteria in each weekly review section. The square, circle and triangle assessment criteria indicate what learners at varying levels might be expected to have achieved each week. The square indicates what can be expected of almost all learners. The circle indicates what might be expected of most learners, and the triangle indicates what level of achievement might be expected from more able learners. Levels will vary as some learners may find some topics more interesting and/or easier; similarly, some may excel at speaking activities rather than written ones.

Teacher's Guide

The Teacher's Guide offers detailed guidance for covering each unit. Each unit is designed to cover three teaching weeks. The teacher knows their class and context best, so they should feel free to vary the pace and the amount of work covered each week to suit their circumstances. Each unit has a clear structure, with an introduction, suggestions for introducing the unit, learning objectives and a resource list of supporting materials that can be used in the unit.

Student's Book

The Student's Book offers a clear structure and easy-to-follow design to help learners to navigate the course. The following features are found at all levels:

- A range of fiction, non-fiction, poetry, playscripts and transactional texts are provided to use as a starting point for contextualised learning.
- Skills-based headers allow teachers to locate activities within the curriculum framework and indicate to learners what skills are being focussed on in each task.
- Clear instruction rubrics are provided for each activity. The rubrics allow learners to develop more and more independent learning as they begin to master and understand instructive text. The rubrics also model assessment type tasks and prepare them for formal assessment at all levels.
- Icons indicate where there is an audio-visual support for the text. Teachers can play these to the class and learners can use these themselves if they need to listen to the text again.
- Grammar and language boxes provide teaching text and examples to show the language feature in use. These are colour coded so that learners can easily recognise them as they work through the course.
- The notepad feature contains reminders, hints and interesting facts.
- The 'Thinking deeper' boxes contain additional information and encourage learners to apply what they have been learning in different contexts or in more challenging ways. These are clearly signposted in the text.

Workbook

The Workbook is clearly linked to the Student's Book. The activities here contain structured spaces for learners to record answers. The activities can be used as classroom tasks, for homework, or for assessment purposes. The completed Workbook tasks give the teacher an opportunity to check work and give written feedback and/or grades. Learners have a consolidated record of their work and parents can see what kind of activities learners are doing in class.

Digital resources

The digital resources are offered online by subscription. You can access these at Collins Connect. These resources can be used to introduce topics and support learning and assessment.

The interactive activities include:
- drag-and-drop activities
- matching activities
- look-cover-say-spell activities
- cloze procedure (fill in the missing words)
- labelling diagrams
- and many more.

Learners receive instant feedback when they complete the activities and the responses are randomised so learners can complete the tasks they enjoy more than once, getting a different arrangement of items each time.

Some materials can be printed out for use in the classroom. These include a set of additional activity sheets that can be used for support, extension and/or homework as well as an additional assessment task for each unit. (These tasks are teacher marked.)

Collins Connect offers an easy and accessible method of keeping records. Teachers can compile class lists and keep track of progress in an easy-to-use and well-supported system.

Using the audio files in the classroom

All of the reading and listening texts in the course have been recorded and are supplied with the digital subscription as audio recordings. The audio recordings offer a range of voices, pace and expression and they will enhance the classroom experience by introducing variety and making it easier for the teacher to observe learners as they listen to, and follow texts. The audio files can also be accessed in the student-only view so learners who are struggling with reading can listen to these on their own as many times as they like.

We suggest that you use the audio recordings as you introduce each reading text. Learners can either listen only or follow in their books as they listen to the text. Following and listening allows them to hear the words and the correct pronunciation and also to get a sense of where to pause, where to change expression and how to pace themselves when reading aloud.

Assessment in primary English

In the primary English programme, assessment is a continuous, planned process that involves collecting information about learner progress and learning in order to provide constructive feedback to both learners and parents and also to guide planning and the next teaching steps.

The Cambridge Primary English curriculum framework makes it clear what learners are expected to learn and achieve at each level. Our task as teachers is to assess whether or not learners have achieved the stated goals using clearly-focused, varied, reliable and flexible methods of assessment.

In the Collins International Primary English course, assessment is continuous and in-built. It applies the principles of international best practice and ensures that assessment:

- is ongoing and regular
- supports individual achievement and allows for learners to reflect on their learning and set targets for themselves
- provides feedback and encouragement to learners
- allows for integration of assessment into the activities and classroom teaching by combining different assessment methods, including observations, questioning, self-assessment and formal and informal tasks/tests
- uses strategies that cater for a variety of learner needs in the classroom (language, physical, emotional and cultural), and acknowledges that learners do not all need to be assessed at the same time, or in the same way
- allows for, and prepares learners for, more formal summative assessment including controlled activities, tasks and tests.

Formal written assessment

The Collins International Primary English course offers a set of assessment sheets that teachers can use to formally assess learning and to award marks if necessary. These sheets test the skills and competencies developed in a cumulative manner. In some cases, learners will use the same texts as context. In other cases, they will be expected to read and make sense of an unseen text and to answer a range of contextualised questions based on that.

At Stage 4, there is an end of unit review (test) at the end of units 3, 6 and 9. These are accompanied by a mark scheme.

In addition to the materials supplied in the course, schools may opt for their learners to take standardised Cambridge Primary progression tests at Stages 3, 4, 5 and 6. These tests are developed by Cambridge Assessment International Education but they are written and marked in schools. Teachers download tests and administer them in their own classrooms. Cambridge International provides a mark scheme and you can upload learners' test results and then analyse the results and print reports. You can also compare a learner's results against their class, school or other schools around the world and on a year-by-year basis.

Learning objectives matching grid

The types of reading texts and the objectives covered in each unit are listed here by strand for easy reference. These same objectives are listed at the beginning of each unit in the unit-by-unit support section of this guide.

Unit 1	Reading	Writing	Listening and speaking
Stories of the past Texts: *Ragged Schools* (listening text, historical non-fiction) *Street Child* (historical fiction) *Hope for destitute children* (newspaper report)	4R01 Extend the range of reading; 4R02 Explore the different processes of reading silently and reading aloud; 4R04 Use knowledge of punctuation and grammar to read with fluency, understanding and expression; 4R05 Identify all the punctuation marks and respond to them when reading; 4R06 Apply phonic/spelling, graphic, grammatical and contextual knowledge in reading unfamiliar words; 4R08 Express a personal response to a text, and link characters and settings to personal experience; 4Rx1 Retell or paraphrase events from the text in response to questions; 4Rx4 Explore explicit meanings within a text; 4Ri1 Investigate how settings and characters are built up from details and identify key words and phrases; 4Rw7 Understand the main stages in a story from introduction to resolution;	4W04 Look for alternatives for overused words and expressions; 4W05 Make short notes from a text and use these to aid writing; 4W07 Reread own writing aloud to check punctuation and grammatical sense; 4Wa1 Write character profiles, using detail to capture the reader's imagination; 4Wa3 Choose and compare words to strengthen the impact of writing, including some powerful verbs; 4Wa4 Use more powerful verbs, e.g. 'rushed' instead of 'went'; 4Wa5 Explore degrees of intensity in adjectives, e.g. 'cold', 'tepid', 'warm', 'hot'; 4Wa8 Show awareness of the reader by adopting an appropriate style or viewpoint; 4Wa11 Summarise a sentence or a paragraph in a limited number of words; 4Wt1 Explore different ways of planning stories, and write longer stories from plans; 4Wt2 Begin to use paragraphs more consistently to organise and sequence ideas;	4SL1 Organise ideas in a longer speaking turn to help the listener; 4SL5 Listen carefully in discussion, contributing relevant comments and questions.

	4Rw9 Understand how paragraphs and chapters are used to organise ideas;	4Wp1 Use a wider variety of connectives in an increasing range of sentences;	
	4Rw8 Explore narrative order and the focus on significant events;	4Wp2 Practise using commas to mark out meaning within sentences;	
	4Rv2 Read newspaper reports and consider how they engage the reader.	4Wp5 Confirm all parts of the verb 'to be' and know when to use each one;	
		4Wp6 Use a range of end-of-sentence punctuation with accuracy;	
		4Wp7 Use speech marks and begin to use other associated punctuation;	
		4Wp8 Learn the use of the apostrophe to show possession, e.g. girl's, girls';	
		4Ws1 Extend knowledge and use of spelling patterns, e.g. vowel phonemes, double consonants, silent letters, common prefixes and suffixes;	
		4Ws2 Investigate spelling patterns; generate and test rules that govern them;	
		4Ws3 Check and correct spellings and Identify words that need to be learnt;	
		4Ws5 Revise rules for spelling words with common inflections, e.g. –ing, –ed, –s.	
Unit 2	**Reading**	**Writing**	**Listening and speaking**
Mars: the trip of a lifetime! Texts:	4R01 Extend the range of reading; 4R02 Explore the different processes of reading silently and reading aloud;	4W05 Make short notes from a text and use these to aid writing; 4W06 Collect and present information from non-fiction texts;	4SL1 Organise ideas in a longer speaking turn to help the listener; 4SL2 Vary use of vocabulary and level of detail according to purpose;

Listening text: *Information about Mars* (non-fiction)	4R04 Use knowledge of punctuation and grammar to read with fluency, understanding and expression;	4W07 Reread own writing aloud to check punctuation and grammatical sense;	4SL3 Understand the gist of an account or the significant points and respond to main ideas with relevant suggestions and comments;
Visit Mars – for the trip of a lifetime! (non-fiction advertisement, persuasive)	4R05 Identify all the punctuation marks and respond to them when reading;	4Wa2 Adopt a viewpoint as a writer, expressing opinions about characters or places;	4SL6 Adapt the pace and loudness of speaking appropriately when performing or reading aloud;
	4R06 Apply phonic/spelling, graphic, grammatical and contextual knowledge in reading unfamiliar words;	4Wa4 Use more powerful verbs, e.g. 'rushed' instead of 'went';	4SL7 Adapt speech and gesture to create a character in drama.
The Incredible Robo (non-fiction advertisement, persuasive)	4R08 Express a personal response to a text, and link characters and settings to personal experience;	4Wa5 Explore degrees of intensity in adjectives, e.g. 'cold', 'tepid', 'warm', 'hot';	
Don't send humans to Mars! (non-fiction persuasive report)	4Rx1 Retell or paraphrase events from the text in response to questions;	4Wa6 Elaborate on basic information with some detail;	
	4Rx2 Note key words and phrases to identify the main points in a passage;	4Wa8 Show awareness of the reader by adopting an appropriate style or viewpoint;	
	4Rx3 Distinguish between fact and opinion in print and IT sources;	4Wa9 Present an explanation or a point of view in ordered points, e.g. in a letter;	
	4Rx4 Explore explicit meanings within a text;	4Wa11 Summarise a sentence or a paragraph in a limited number of words;	
	4Ri2 Explore implicit meanings within a text;	4Wt1 Explore different ways of planning stories, and write longer stories from plans;	
	4Rw3 Understand how expressive and descriptive language creates mood;	4Wt2 Begin to use paragraphs more consistently to organise and sequence ideas;	
	4Rw5 Understand the use of connectives to structure an argument, e.g. 'if', 'although';	4Wp1 Use a wider variety of connectives in an increasing range of sentences;	
	4Rw6 Understand how points are ordered to make a coherent argument;	4Wp2 Practise using commas to mark out meaning within sentences;	
	4Rw11 Investigate the grammar of different sentences: statements, questions and orders.	4Wp6 Use a range of end-of-sentence punctuation with accuracy;	

		4Rv1 Identify different types of non-fiction text and their known key features; 4Rv3 Understand how persuasive writing is used to convince a reader.	4Ws1 Extend knowledge and use of spelling patterns, e.g. vowel phonemes, double consonants, silent letters, common prefixes and suffixes; 4Ws2 Investigate spelling patterns; generate and test rules that govern them; 4Ws3 Check and correct spellings and identify words that need to be learnt; 4Ws6 Extend earlier work on prefixes and suffixes.	
Unit 3		**Reading**	**Writing**	**Listening and speaking**
The power of the sea *Old Man Ocean, Sea Haiku, Tanka* (poems) *Tsunami* (non-fiction explanation) *How sand is made* (non-fiction explanation)		4R01 Extend the range of reading; 4R03 Read further stories or poems by a favourite writer, and compare them; 4R04 Use knowledge of punctuation and grammar to read with fluency, understanding and expression; 4R05 Identify all the punctuation marks and respond to them when reading; 4R06 Apply phonic/spelling, graphic, grammatical and contextual knowledge in reading unfamiliar words; 4R08 Express a personal response to a text, and link characters and settings to personal experience; 4Rx1 Retell or paraphrase events from the text in response to questions; 4Rx2 Note key words and phrases to identify	4W01 Identify syllabic patterns in multisyllabic words; 4W02 Explore the layout and presentation of writing, in the context of helping it to fit its purpose; 4W07 Reread own writing aloud to check punctuation and grammatical sense; 4Wa3 Choose and compare words to strengthen the impact of writing, including some powerful verbs; 4Wa4 Use more powerful verbs, e.g. 'rushed' instead of 'went'; 4Wa5 Explore degrees of intensity in adjectives, e.g. 'cold', 'tepid', 'warm', 'hot'; 4Wa6 Elaborate on basic information with some detail; 4Wa8 Show awareness of the reader by adopting an appropriate style or viewpoint;	4SL2 Vary use of vocabulary and level of detail according to purpose; 4SL5 Listen carefully in discussion, contributing relevant comments and questions; 4SL6 Adapt the pace and loudness of speaking appropriately when performing or reading aloud.

	the main points in a passage; 4Rx4 Explore explicit meanings within a text; 4Ri1 Investigate how settings and characters are built up from details and identify key words and phrases; 4Ri2 Explore implicit meanings within a text; 4Rw1 Recognise meaning in figurative language; 4Rw3 Understand how expressive and descriptive language creates mood; 4Rw4 Identify adverbs and their impact on meaning; 4Rw6 Understand how points are ordered to make a coherent argument; 4Rw9 Understand how paragraphs and chapters are used to organise ideas; 4Rw10 Compare and contrast poems and investigate poetic features; 4Rv1 Identify different types of non-fiction text and their known key features.	4Wa9 Present an explanation or a point of view in ordered points, e.g. in a letter; 4Wa11 Summarise a sentence or a paragraph in a limited number of words; 4Wt1 Explore different ways of planning stories, and write longer stories from plans; 4Wt2 Begin to use paragraphs more consistently to organise and sequence ideas; 4Wp1 Use a wider variety of connectives in an increasing range of sentences; 4Wp2 Practise using commas to mark out meaning within sentences; 4Wp4 Investigate past and present tenses and future forms of verbs; 4Wp5 Confirm all parts of the verb 'to be' and know when to use each one; 4Wp6 Use a range of end-of-sentence punctuation with accuracy; 4Ws3 Check and correct spellings and identify words that need to be learnt; 4Ws9 Build words from other words with similar meanings, e.g. 'medical', 'medicine'; 4Ws10 Collect and classify words with common roots, e.g. 'invent', 'prevent'.	

Unit 4	Reading	Writing	Listening and speaking
Other people, other places Texts: Listening text: *The Clever Farmer* (stories set in other cultures) *Abunuwasi's House* (fiction, stories set in other cultures) *The Brave Baby* (fiction, stories set in other cultures)	4R01 Extend the range of reading; 4R02 Explore the different processes of reading silently and reading aloud; 4R03 Read further stories or poems by a favourite writer, and compare them; 4R04 Use knowledge of punctuation and grammar to read with fluency, understanding and expression; 4R05 Identify all the punctuation marks and respond to them when reading; 4R06 Apply phonic/spelling, graphic, grammatical and contextual knowledge in reading unfamiliar words; 4R07 Read and perform play scripts, exploring how scenes are built up; 4R08 Express a personal response to a text, and link characters and settings to personal experience; 4Rx1 Retell or paraphrase events from the text in response to questions; 4Rx4 Explore explicit meanings within a text; 4Ri1 Investigate how settings and characters are built up from details and identify key words and phrases; 4Ri2 Explore implicit meanings within a text;	4W01 Identify syllabic patterns in multisyllabic words; 4W05 Make short notes from a text and use these to aid writing; 4W07 Reread own writing aloud to check punctuation and grammatical sense; 4Wa1 Write character profiles, using detail to capture the reader's imagination; 4Wa2 Adopt a viewpoint as a writer, expressing opinions about characters or places; 4Wa3 Choose and compare words to strengthen the impact of writing, including some powerful verbs; 4Wa4 Use more powerful verbs, e.g. 'rushed' instead of 'went'; 4Wa5 Explore degrees of intensity in adjectives, e.g. 'cold', 'tepid', 'warm', 'hot'; 4Wa6 Elaborate on basic information with some detail; 4Wa10 Explore alternative openings and endings for stories; 4Wa11 Summarise a sentence or a paragraph in a limited number of words; 4Wt1 Explore different ways of planning stories, and write longer stories from plans;	4SL1 Organise ideas in a longer speaking turn to help the listener; 4SL2 Vary use of vocabulary and level of detail according to purpose; 4SL3 Understand the gist of an account or the significant points and respond to main ideas with relevant suggestions and comments; 4SL5 Listen carefully in discussion, contributing relevant comments and questions; 4SL6 Adapt the pace and loudness of speaking appropriately when performing or reading aloud; 4SL7 Adapt speech and gesture to create a character in drama; 4SL8 Comment on different ways that meaning can be expressed in own and others' talk.

	4Rw1 Recognise meaning in figurative language;	4Wp3 Experiment with varying tenses within texts, e.g. in dialogue;	
	4Rw2 Understand the impact of imagery and figurative language in poetry, including alliteration and simile, e.g. 'as ... as a ...';	4Wp4 Investigate past and present tenses and future forms of verbs;	
	4Rw3 Understand how expressive and descriptive language creates mood;	4Wp5 Confirm all parts of the verb 'to be' and know when to use each one;	
	4Rw7 Understand the main stages in a story from introduction to resolution;	4Wp7 Use speech marks and begin to use other associated punctuation;	
	4Rw8 Explore narrative order and the focus on significant events.	4Wp8 Learn the use of the apostrophe to show possession, e.g. girl's, girls';	
		4Ws1 Extend knowledge and use of spelling patterns, e.g. vowel phonemes, double consonants, silent letters, common prefixes and suffixes;	
		4Ws2 Investigate spelling patterns; generate and test rules that govern them;	
		4Ws3 Check and correct spellings and identify words that need to be learnt;	
		4Ws5 Revise rules for spelling words with common inflections, e.g. *–ing, –ed, –s*;	
		4Ws6 Extend earlier work on prefixes and suffixes;	
		4Ws7 Match spelling to meaning when words sound the same (homophones), e.g. 'to'/'two'/'too', 'right'/'write'.	

Unit 5	Reading	Writing	Listening and speaking
The only problem is … Texts: *The Youngest* (poem) *Meeting Mr Faulkner* (fiction, real-life story dealing with issues) *Last one into bed* (poem) *The New Boy* (fiction, real-life story dealing with issues)	4R01 Extend the range of reading; 4R02 Explore the different processes of reading silently and reading aloud; 4R03 Read further stories or poems by a favourite writer, and compare them; 4R04 Use knowledge of punctuation and grammar to read with fluency, understanding and expression; 4R05 Identify all the punctuation marks and respond to them when reading; 4R06 Apply phonic/spelling, graphic, grammatical and contextual knowledge in reading unfamiliar words; 4R07 Read and perform play scripts, exploring how scenes are built up; 4R08 Express a personal response to a text, and link characters and settings to personal experience; 4Rx1 Retell or paraphrase events from the text in response to questions; 4Rx4 Explore explicit meanings within a text; 4Ri1 Investigate how settings and characters are built up from details and identify key words and phrases.	4W01 Identify syllabic patterns in multisyllabic words; 4W05 Make short notes from a text and use these to aid writing; 4W07 Reread own writing aloud to check punctuation and grammatical sense; 4Wa1 Write character profiles, using detail to capture the reader's imagination; 4Wa2 Adopt a viewpoint as a writer, expressing opinions about characters or places; 4Wa3 Choose and compare words to strengthen the impact of writing, including some powerful verbs; 4Wa4 Use more powerful verbs, e.g. 'rushed' instead of 'went'; 4Wa5 Explore degrees of intensity in adjectives, e.g. 'cold', 'tepid', 'warm', 'hot'; 4Wa6 Elaborate on basic information with some detail; 4Wa10 Explore alternative openings and endings for stories; 4Wa11 Summarise a sentence or a paragraph in a limited number of words; 4Wt1 Explore different ways of planning stories, and write longer stories from plans; 4Wp3 Experiment with varying tenses within texts, e.g. in dialogue;	4SL1 Organise ideas in a longer speaking turn to help the listener; 4SL2 Vary use of vocabulary and level of detail according to purpose; 4SL3 Understand the gist of an account or the significant points and respond to main ideas with relevant suggestions and comments; 4SL5 Listen carefully in discussion, contributing relevant comments and questions; 4SL6 Adapt the pace and loudness of speaking appropriately when performing or reading aloud; 4SL7 Adapt speech and gesture to create a character in drama; 4SL8 Comment on different ways that meaning can be expressed in own and others' talk.

	4Ri2 Explore implicit meanings within a text;

4Rw1 Recognise meaning in figurative language;

4Rw2 Understand the impact of imagery and figurative language in poetry, including alliteration and simile, e.g. 'as ... as a ...';

4Rw3 Understand how expressive and descriptive language creates mood;

4Rw7 Understand the main stages in a story from introduction to resolution;

4Rw8 Explore narrative order and the focus on significant events. | 4Wp4 Investigate past and present tenses and future forms of verbs;

4Wp5 Confirm all parts of the verb 'to be' and know when to use each one'

4Wp7 Use speech marks and begin to use other associated punctuation;

4Wp8 Learn the use of the apostrophe to show possession, e.g. girl's, girls';

4Ws1 Extend knowledge and use of spelling patterns, e.g. vowel phonemes, double consonants, silent letters, common prefixes and suffixes;

4Ws2 Investigate spelling patterns; generate and test rules that govern them;

4Ws3 Check and correct spellings and identify words that need to be learnt;

4Ws5 Revise rules for spelling words with common inflections, e.g. –ing, –ed, –s;

4Ws6 Extend earlier work on prefixes and suffixes;

4Ws7 Match spelling to meaning when words sound the same (homophones), e.g. 'to'/'two'/'too', 'right'/'write'. | |
| **Unit 6** | **Reading** | **Writing** | **Listening and speaking** |
| **Making the headlines**

Texts:

Malala's award (non-fiction, newspaper report) | 4R01 Extend the range of reading.;

4R02 Explore the different processes of reading silently and reading aloud;

4R04 Use knowledge of punctuation and | 4W02 Explore the layout and presentation of writing, in the context of helping it to fit its purpose;

4W05 Make short notes from a text and | 4SL4 Deal politely with opposing points of view;

4SL5 Listen carefully in discussion, contributing relevant comments and questions. |

Mini Mars mission (non-fiction, newspaper report) *Fossil Hunt* (non-fiction, magazine article) *Make your own fossil!* (non-fiction, magazine article with instructions)	grammar to read with fluency, understanding and expression; 4R05 Identify all the punctuation marks and respond to them when reading; 4R06 Apply phonic/spelling, graphic, grammatical and contextual knowledge in reading unfamiliar words; 4R08 Express a personal response to a text, and link characters and settings to personal experience; 4Rx1 Retell or paraphrase events from the text in response to questions; 4Rx2 Note key words and phrases to identify the main points in a passage; 4Rx3 Distinguish between fact and opinion in print and IT sources; 4Rx4 Explore explicit meanings within a text; 4Ri2 Explore implicit meanings within a text; 4Rw5 Understand the use of connectives to structure an argument, e.g. 'if', 'although'; 4Rv1 Identify different types of non-fiction text and their known key features; 4Rv2 Read newspaper reports and consider how they engage the reader.	use these to aid writing; 4W06 Collect and present information from non-fiction texts; 4W07 Reread own writing aloud to check punctuation and grammatical sense; 4Wa2 Adopt a viewpoint as a writer, expressing opinions about characters or places; 4Wa7 Write newspaper-style reports, instructions and non-chronological reports; 4Wa8 Show awareness of the reader by adopting an appropriate style or viewpoint; 4Wt2 Begin to use paragraphs more consistently to organise and sequence ideas; 4Wp1 Use a wider variety of connectives in an increasing range of sentences; 4Wp2 Practise using commas to mark out meaning within sentences; 4Wp6 Use a range of end-of-sentence punctuation with accuracy; 4Ws1 Extend knowledge and use of spelling patterns, e.g. vowel phonemes, double consonants, silent letters, common prefixes and suffixes; 4Ws2 Investigate spelling patterns; generate and test rules that govern them;	

		4Ws3 Check and correct spellings and identify words that need to be learnt; 4Ws5 Revise rules for spelling words with common inflections, e.g. –ing, –ed, –s.	
Unit 7	**Reading**	**Writing**	**Listening and speaking**
Inventions Texts: *Encyclopaedia of Inventions* (non-fiction, reference) *A Good Idea* (poem) *I'm bored with walking to school* (poem) *How do zips work?* (non-fiction, reference) *Velcro* (non-fiction, reference)	4R01 Extend the range of reading; 4R04 Use knowledge of punctuation and grammar to read with fluency, understanding and expression; 4R05 Identify all the punctuation marks and respond to them when reading; 4R06 Apply phonic/spelling, graphic, grammatical and contextual knowledge in reading unfamiliar words; 4R08 Express a personal response to a text, and link characters and settings to personal experience; 4Rx1 Retell or paraphrase events from the text in response to questions; 4Rx2 Note key words and phrases to identify the main points in a passage; 4Rx4 Explore explicit meanings within a text; 4Ri2 Explore implicit meanings within a text; 4Rw5 Understand the use of connectives to structure an argument, e.g. 'if', 'although'; 4Rw6 Understand how points are ordered to make a coherent argument;	4W02 Explore the layout and presentation of writing, in the context of helping it to fit its purpose; 4W05 Make short notes from a text and use these to aid writing; 4W06 Collect and present information from non-fiction texts; 4W07 Reread own writing aloud to check punctuation and grammatical sense; 4Wa2 Adopt a viewpoint as a writer, expressing opinions about characters or places; 4Wa6 Elaborate on basic information with some detail; 4Wa8 Show awareness of the reader by adopting an appropriate style or viewpoint; 4Wa9 Present an explanation or a point of view in ordered points, e.g. in a letter; 4Wa11 Summarise a sentence or a paragraph in a limited number of words; 4Wt2 Begin to use paragraphs more consistently to organise and sequence ideas;	4SL1 Organise ideas in a longer speaking turn to help the listener; 4SL2 Vary use of vocabulary and level of detail according to purpose; 4SL4 Deal politely with opposing points of view; 4SL5 Listen carefully in discussion, contributing relevant comments and questions; 4SL6 Adapt the pace and loudness of speaking appropriately when performing or reading aloud.

	4Rv1 Identify different types of non-fiction text and their known key features; 4Rv3 Understand how persuasive writing is used to convince a reader.	4Wp1 Use a wider variety of connectives in an increasing range of sentences; 4Wp3 Experiment with varying tenses within texts, e.g. in dialogue; 4Wp4 Investigate past and present tenses and future forms of verbs; 4Wp5 Confirm all parts of the verb 'to be' and know when to use each one; 4Wp6 Use a range of end-of-sentence punctuation with accuracy; 4Ws3 Check and correct spellings and identify words that need to be learnt; 4Ws8 Use all the letters in sequence for alphabetical ordering; 4Ws9 Build words from other words with similar meanings, e.g. 'medical', 'medicine'; 4Ws10 Collect and classify words with common roots, e.g. 'invent', 'prevent'.	
Unit 8	**Reading**	**Writing**	**Listening and speaking**
Putting on a show Texts: Listening text: *Peter and the Wolf* (playscript) *Peter and the Wolf* (playscript) *A Difficult Decision* (fiction, real-life story with dilemma and playscript of same story)	4R01 Extend the range of reading; 4R02 Explore the different processes of reading silently and reading aloud; 4R04 Use knowledge of punctuation and grammar to read with fluency, understanding and expression; 4R05 Identify all the punctuation marks and respond to them when reading;	4W02 Explore the layout and presentation of writing, in the context of helping it to fit its purpose; 4W04 Look for alternatives for overused words and expressions; 4W07 Reread own writing aloud to check punctuation and grammatical sense; 4W08 Write sentences, dictated by	4SL1 Organise ideas in a longer speaking turn to help the listener; 4SL2 Vary use of vocabulary and level of detail according to purpose; 4SL3 Understand the gist of an account or the significant points and respond to main ideas with relevant suggestions and comments; 4SL5 Listen carefully in discussion, contributing

	4R06 Apply phonic/spelling, graphic, grammatical and contextual knowledge in reading unfamiliar words; 4R07 Read and perform play scripts, exploring how scenes are built up; 4R08 Express a personal response to a text, and link characters and settings to personal experience; 4Rx1 Retell or paraphrase events from the text in response to questions; 4Rx4 Explore explicit meanings within a text; 4Ri1 Investigate how settings and characters are built up from details and identify key words and phrases; 4Ri2 Explore implicit meanings within a text; 4Rw1 Recognise meaning in figurative language; 4Rw2 Understand the impact of imagery and figurative language in poetry, including alliteration and simile, e.g. 'as ... as a ...'; 4Rw3 Understand how expressive and descriptive language creates mood; 4Rw4 Identify adverbs and their impact on meaning.	the teacher, from memory; 4Wa1 Write character profiles, using detail to capture the reader's imagination; 4Wa2 Adopt a viewpoint as a writer, expressing opinions about characters or places; 4Wa3 Choose and compare words to strengthen the impact of writing, including some powerful verbs; 4Wa4 Use more powerful verbs, e.g. 'rushed' instead of 'went'. 4Wa8 Show awareness of the reader by adopting an appropriate style or viewpoint; 4Wt1 Explore different ways of planning stories, and write longer stories from plans; 4Wp3 Experiment with varying tenses within texts, e.g. in dialogue; 4Wp4 Investigate past and present tenses and future forms of verbs; 4Ws1 Extend knowledge and use of spelling patterns, e.g. vowel phonemes, double consonants, silent letters, common prefixes and suffixes; 4Ws2 Investigate spelling patterns; generate and test rules that govern them; 4Ws3 Check and correct spellings and identify words that need to be learnt;	relevant comments and questions; 4SL6 Adapt the pace and loudness of speaking appropriately when performing or reading aloud; 4SL7 Adapt speech and gesture to create a character in drama; 4SL8 Comment on different ways that meaning can be expressed in own and others' talk.

		4Ws6 Extend earlier work on prefixes and suffixes; 4Ws8 Use all the letters in sequence for alphabetical ordering.	
Unit 9	**Reading**	**Writing**	**Listening and speaking**
Imaginary worlds Texts: Listening text: *Sheetal's First Landing* (story set in imaginary world) *Sheetal's First Landing* (story set in imaginary world) *The Last Dragon* (poem) *Lost Magic* (poem)	4R01 Extend the range of reading; 4R02 Explore the different processes of reading silently and reading aloud; 4R04 Use knowledge of punctuation and grammar to read with fluency, understanding and expression; 4R05 Identify all the punctuation marks and respond to them when reading; 4R06 Apply phonic/spelling, graphic, grammatical and contextual knowledge in reading unfamiliar words; 4R08 Express a personal response to a text, and link characters and settings to personal experience; 4Rx1 Retell or paraphrase events from the text in response to questions; 4Rx2 Note key words and phrases to identify the main points in a passage; 4Rx4 Explore explicit meanings within a text; 4Ri2 Explore implicit meanings within a text; 4Ri1 Investigate how settings and characters are built up from details and identify key words and phrases; 4Rw1 Recognise meaning in figurative language;	4W04 Look for alternatives for overused words and expressions; 4W05 Make short notes from a text and use these to aid writing; 4W07 Reread own writing aloud to check punctuation and grammatical sense; 4W08 Write sentences, dictated by the teacher, from memory; 4Wa2 Adopt a viewpoint as a writer, expressing opinions about characters or places; 4Wa3 Choose and compare words to strengthen the impact of writing, including some powerful verbs; 4Wa4 Use more powerful verbs, e.g. 'rushed' instead of 'went'; 4Wa5 Explore degrees of intensity in adjectives, e.g. 'cold', 'tepid', 'warm', 'hot'; 4Wa8 Show awareness of the reader by adopting an appropriate style or viewpoint; 4Wa10 Explore alternative openings and endings for stories; 4Wa11 Summarise a sentence or a paragraph in a limited number of words;	4SL1 Organise ideas in a longer speaking turn to help the listener; 4SL3 Understand the gist of an account or the significant points and respond to main ideas with relevant suggestions and comments; 4SL4 Deal politely with opposing points of view; 4SL5 Listen carefully in discussion, contributing relevant comments and questions; 4SL7 Adapt speech and gesture to create a character in drama.

	4Rw3 Understand how expressive and descriptive language creates mood;	4Wt1 Explore different ways of planning stories, and write longer stories from plans;	
	4Rw4 Identify adverbs and their impact on meaning;	4Wp3 Experiment with varying tenses within texts, e.g. in dialogue;	
	4Rw7 Understand the main stages in a story from introduction to resolution;	4Wp4 Investigate past and present tenses and future forms of verbs;	
	4Rw8 Explore narrative order and the focus on significant events;	4Wp6 Use a range of end-of-sentence punctuation with accuracy;	
	4Rw10 Compare and contrast poems and investigate poetic features.	4Wp7 Use speech marks and begin to use other associated punctuation.	
		4Ws1 Extend knowledge and use of spelling patterns, e.g. vowel phonemes, double consonants, silent letters, common prefixes and suffixes;	
		4Ws2 Investigate spelling patterns; generate and test rules that govern them;	
		4Ws3 Check and correct spellings and identify words that need to be learnt;	
		4Ws4 Spell words with common letter strings but different pronunciations, e.g. 'tough', 'through', 'trough', 'plough';	
		4Ws7 Match spelling to meaning when words sound the same (homophones), e.g. 'to'/'two'/'too', 'right'/'write'.	

Handwriting is not taught explicitly in this course although objective '4W03 Use joined-up handwriting in all writing' is implicitly covered in the activities and supporting notes in the Teacher's Guide. We recommend that teachers choose a structured and suitable course for teaching additional handwriting skills at Stage 4 level. *Collins Primary Focus: Handwriting,* by Sue Peet, is a useful resource for this as the series progresses from introduction of fine motor movements, through pre-cursive and cursive styles at the early stages, progressing to different handwriting styles, calligraphy and links to computer fonts at the higher levels.

Unit 1 Stories of the past

Unit overview

In this unit, learners will read a historical story and a newspaper article that gives additional information about the period in which the story is set. They will answer comprehension questions and practise identifying the main idea in a paragraph. They will plan and write their own newspaper article and historical story, using background information from the unit.

Reading	Writing	Listening and speaking
4R01 Extend the range of reading;	4W04 Look for alternatives for overused words and expressions;	4SL1 Organise ideas in a longer speaking turn to help the listener;
4R02 Explore the different processes of reading silently and reading aloud;	4W05 Make short notes from a text and use these to aid writing;	SL5 Listen carefully in discussion, contributing relevant comments and questions.
4R04 Use knowledge of punctuation and grammar to read with fluency, understanding and expression;	4W07 Reread own writing aloud to check punctuation and grammatical sense;	
4R05 Identify all the punctuation marks and respond to them when reading;	4Wa1 Write character profiles, using detail to capture the reader's imagination;	
4R06 Apply phonic/spelling, graphic, grammatical and contextual knowledge in reading unfamiliar words;	4Wa3 Choose and compare words to strengthen the impact of writing, including some powerful verbs;	
4R08 Express a personal response to a text, and link characters and settings to personal experience;	4Wa4 Use more powerful verbs, e.g. 'rushed' instead of 'went';	
4Rx1 Retell or paraphrase events from the text in response to questions;	4Wa5 Explore degrees of intensity in adjectives, e.g. 'cold', 'tepid', 'warm', 'hot';	
4Rx4 Explore explicit meanings within a text;	4Wa8 Show awareness of the reader by adopting an appropriate style or viewpoint;	
4Ri1 Investigate how settings and characters are built up from details and identify key words and phrases;	4Wa11 Summarise a sentence or a paragraph in a limited number of words;	
4Rw7 Understand the main stages in a story from introduction to resolution;	4Wt1 Explore different ways of planning stories, and write longer stories from plans;	
4Rw9 Understand how paragraphs and chapters are used to organise ideas;	4Wt2 Begin to use paragraphs more consistently to organise and sequence ideas;	
4Rw8 Explore narrative order and the focus on significant events;	4Wp1 Use a wider variety of connectives in an increasing range of sentences;	
	4Wp2 Practise using commas to mark out meaning within sentences;	
	4Wp5 Confirm all parts of the verb 'to be' and know when to use each one.	
	4Wp6 Use a range of end-of-sentence punctuation with accuracy;	

4Rv2 Read newspaper reports and consider how they engage the reader.	4Wp7 Use speech marks and begin to use other associated punctuation;	
	4Wp8 Learn the use of the apostrophe to show possession, e.g. girl's, girls';	
	4Ws1 Extend knowledge and use of spelling patterns, e.g. vowel phonemes, double consonants, silent letters, common prefixes and suffixes.	
	4Ws2 Investigate spelling patterns; generate and test rules that govern them;	
	4Ws3 Check and correct spellings and identify words that need to be learnt;	
	4Ws5 Revise rules for spelling words with common inflections, e.g. –ing, –ed, –s.	

Related resources

- Audio files: *Ragged Schools*; *Street Child*
- PCM 1: Punctuate the story
- PCM 2: Reading newspaper reports
- PCM 3: Newspaper report
- PCM 4: Notes for a historical story
- PCM 5: Paragraph plan for a story

Resource books or websites about life for children in Victorian Britain

Introducing the unit

Talk with the class about what life might have been like in your community 150 years ago. What differences might learners notice if they could time-travel back to about 1860 or 1870? Record learners' ideas on the whiteboard. Prompt them to think about changes in education in particular. For example, did most children go to school in 1860? What might they have done instead of going to school? Discuss whether learners think life would have been better or worse for children in their community 150 years ago.

Introduce the idea that, at that time, most children had no access to schooling, and many children had to work for a living.

Week 1

Student's Book pages 1–6

Workbook pages 1–6

Student's Book page 1

Listening and speaking

Explain to the class that they are going to listen to some information about the Ragged Schools which were set up in the 19th century to help poor children get an education. Prompt learners to think about the advantages and disadvantages of Ragged Schools as they listen. Then play the recording, or read the text to the class. You may need to repeat the reading a second time.

1 Listening text

Over 150 years ago, many children in Britain didn't go to school. Often, this was because their families were poor, so the children had to work hard to earn money for their families to live on. Poor families couldn't send their children to school, because going to school was too expensive. Also, if a child was in school, they wouldn't be able to earn very much money. Then their family might have to go without essential things such as food and clothes.

'Ragged Schools' were set up to help the very poorest children to get an education. The schools got their name because the children who went there were so poor that they only had ragged clothes to wear.

Unlike most schools at that time, the Ragged Schools didn't charge any money. They taught children to read and write and do basic maths, and they also trained the children in some of the skills they would need in adult life. For example, children who went to Ragged Schools often learnt about how to look after their money and make it go further. Many of the children were also taught the basic skills they would need to do a job. As well as educating children, many Ragged Schools gave them food to eat.

It wasn't always much fun being a pupil in a Ragged School. The teachers could be very strict, and children were often made to do boring tasks such as writing a sentence out 100 times. If they didn't pay attention or didn't learn their lessons quickly, children could be punished or hit by the teacher. But some teachers were much kinder and tried to look after the children well, and prepare them for life in the adult world.

2 Organise learners into pairs, and discuss paired work rules with them. Write the rules on the board.

Paired work rules

- Take turns to speak.
- Do not interrupt when the other person is speaking.
- Listen to the other person's point of view and respond politely.
- Ask each other questions to find out more about what you both think.
- Decide how you will report back to the class. Both of you need to contribute to this.

Remind the pairs to use the discussion prompt in the Student's Book. Give them about five minutes to discuss the advantages and disadvantages of attending a Ragged School, and then invite each pair to report their views back to the class. Encourage the other learners to listen to each pair carefully, ask appropriate questions and make constructive comments.

A range of responses are possible, but prompt learners to consider the following if necessary:

- Plus: Ragged Schools gave poor children an education which they couldn't otherwise afford, and this would help them to get better jobs and do better in adult life.
- Plus: Ragged Schools gave children food at a time when many poor children became ill or even died because of malnutrition.
- Plus: Ragged Schools were free, so in theory even the poorest children could afford to go.
- Minus: If poor children attended school instead of working, they couldn't earn so much money, and their family might suffer as a result.
- Minus: The schools could be boring, and sometimes there were tough physical punishments.

When all the pairs have reported back, review the range of opinion in the class. Did all the pairs agree? If not, you could have a vote to decide on the issue.

3 In their pairs or in larger groups, learners should look at the two pictures on page 1 of the Student's Book. Encourage them to discuss the questions together, and record their answers in their notebooks.

Answers
Answers will vary, but could include:
a   In the picture of the Ragged School, children are using various different types of equipment and machinery. It looks as if they are all boys. One boy is climbing a ladder to reach some equipment. A teacher is sitting at a desk and writing.
b   The children in the Ragged School are probably learning how to use equipment they will need in their jobs later on.
c   The class in the Ragged School is much more active than that in the modern primary school. It is also quite crowded, and it looks as though it could be dangerous. In the modern primary school all the children are sitting at desks and they have books and paper in front of them, so it looks as if they will be learning to read and write. There are girls as well as boys in the class. They are dressed smartly and look ready to learn.
d   Both classes contain a lot of children, and the children are a similar age.
e   Learners' own answers.

Student's Book pages 2–3

Reading and comprehension

1 Learners work individually, reading the text silently. Tell them to put up their hands if they find a word they don't know, and write these words, with their meanings, on the board. At the end of the lesson make sure that learners record any words they don't know in their personal dictionaries.

2 Move around the classroom while the reading is in progress, assisting where necessary and reminding learners to read silently if necessary.

3 Learners should then discuss and write the answers to the comprehension questions in pairs.

Many of the questions are open, but even for more closed questions, always allow learners their own variations in the answers, as long as the sense of the answer is correct, and the language used is correct.

Answers
3 a The setting for the first part of the extract is Barnie's study.
b This is an open question, so accept any answers which use good descriptive vocabulary and show an understanding of the text.
c This is an open question; learners may feel that Barnie is worried about the boys and wants to find out more.
d Jim is worried that Barnie might tell the police because if he did so, Jim and the other boys might end up in the workhouse.
e The advantages for Jim, if he takes Barnie to see the other boys, are that he will get some hot coffee and a safe place to sleep. Perhaps it will also help Jim himself and the other boys to have a safer and happier life. The disadvantages are that he doesn't yet know if he can trust Barnie not to tell the police, and perhaps the other boys will be angry with him.
f This is an open question; accept any sensible answer that is in keeping with the text, and includes some reasons for the learner's view.

Workbook page 1
Reading
Ask learners to do activities 1 and 2 in their Workbooks for homework, so you can see how well they have understood the passage and the character of Barnie. If necessary, explain beforehand how to fill in the speech bubble, using full sentences to describe Barnie's thoughts, and how to fill in the spider diagram using brief words and phrases.

Extension and support
Ask learners to research children's charities that operate in your local area.
- More able learners could work individually; they may choose to interview someone connected with their chosen charity, and they could choose their own format in which to report back their findings (a written report, computer presentation or oral presentation).
- Less able learners could work in groups or pairs, and you could suggest a charity for them to research. If necessary, give them a sheet with headings to help them structure their notes, for example 'Name of charity', 'What the charity does', 'Why people should support the charity'. They could give a brief oral presentation of their findings, using their notes.

Student's Book page 4
Grammar
Revise the correct forms of the verb 'to have' and 'to be' before learners tackle this question, so that you can check they know the standard English versions of these verbs. Then introduce the dialect word 'ain't' and ask learners to locate it in the story text.

Ask learners to answer the questions, and then share their answers.

Answers
a "I haven't got a mother."
b "I haven't got a father."
c "I am not telling you any lies."

More able learners could tackle the questions in the 'Thinking deeper' box. They may feel that the use of dialect makes Jim's language more vivid and allows us to picture him more clearly, but accept any sensible and well-reasoned answer.

Workbook page 2
Follow up this activity with Workbook Grammar questions 1, 2 and 3, which can be done as individual activities either for homework or in class.

Answers
1
Present: You **are**; We **are**; They **are**
Past: I **was**; He **was**; They **were**
Future: I **will be**; It **will be**; We **will be**
2
a Present: I **am** the fastest runner in my class.
b Present: Amira **is** my sister's best friend.
c Past: Dad **was** very good at maths when he **was** my age.
d Past: Jon's favourite meal **was** chicken st*ir*-fry.
e Future: We **will be** at Grandma's house this weekend.
f Future: Sahar says she **will be** an astronaut when she grows up.

3 This question 3 is open; look for grammatical and well-punctuated answers that make sense in the context.

Student's Book pages 4–5

Grammar

Introduce the idea of powerful verbs by talking about the verb 'went' in sentences like 'He went down the road'. Can learners think of other verbs that could be used instead, to give a clearer picture of how the person moved? Discuss some alternatives, for example: 'charged', 'sprinted', 'tiptoed', 'thundered', 'sidled', 'crept', 'plodded' etc.

Learners could do question 1 as a class or paired activity. Question 2 should be done individually, so you have an opportunity to assess learners' vocabulary choices and grasp of grammar.

Answers
1 a insisted **b** stared **c** spitting **d** creeping
2 Open questions; look for appropriate powerful verbs that add detail to the sentences.

Workbook page 3

Grammar

Finish this section with exercises 1 and 2, which learners can complete individually or in pairs, in class or for homework. The answers are open, but look for interesting vocabulary choices that fit with the sentence grammar and make sense in context.

Student's Book page 5

Punctuation

Have a quick punctuation quiz. Write the following punctuation marks on the whiteboard and invite learners to come up and write a sentence using each punctuation mark: . ? " " , ' Explain that the apostrophe shows possession.

Revise any of the punctuation marks that are not completely familiar. Recap on the uses of the comma that learners already know about, i.e. to separate items in lists, and at the end of speech before a speech mark.

Complete question 1 as a whole class or in groups, and check that learners record the sentences accurately in their books. Then discuss the questions in the 'Thinking deeper' box. Can any of learners explain how commas are used in these sentences?

If necessary, introduce the idea of clauses (parts of a sentence that contain a verb) and point out how the sentence 'What if Barnie told the police about them, and sent all the boys to the workhouse?' contains two clauses which are separated by a comma. Discuss how the comma helps us to identify the two clauses and see how they go together to make meaning in the sentence. Without the comma, it might not be so clear which words go together.

Workbook pages 4–5

Punctuation

Ask learners to complete questions 1, 2 and 3 as paired or group activities, or for homework. Try to have them complete at least one activity individually so you can assess their understanding more easily.

Answers
1
a What do you want for lunch? (with or without speech marks)
b I like playing football, cricket and tennis.
c Look, I can see a dragon! (or with an exclamation mark after 'Look')
d My sister loves going swimming. (or with an exclamation mark)
e Miguel, Tom, Sam and Kieran are playing tag on the beach.
f "Are we nearly there yet?" asked Molly.
g "Look out, or you'll crash!" (with or without speech marks)

2
a I ate a samosa, a packet of peanuts, an apple and a banana. **list**
b Tuesday is my favourite day, because we have swimming lessons. **clauses**
c My three best friends are Natalia, Grace and Tom. **list**
d I live next door to Natalia, but Grace and Tom live on the other side of town. **clauses**
e Whenever I go to see Grandma, she gives me a cookie. **clauses**

3
a My favourite month is March, mostly because that's when my birthday is.
b Ahmed's new top has stripes of red, green, white and blue.
c Ahmed wants to wear his top to play football, but his mum might be cross if he gets it dirty.
d If you want to see the new-born kittens, come home with me after school.
e The kittens' names are Mina, Jake, Harry and Snowball.

4
a Michael's
b children's
c girls'
d dragon's
e Grandad's
f women's
g brother's
h boys'

Student's Book page 6

Spelling and vocabulary

You could introduce this spelling work now, or cover it in weeks 2 and 3 if you prefer.

Ask learners to read the information about verbs with double consonants. Challenge them to close the book and then tell a partner what they remember about the spelling rules covered.

Write a list of verbs on the whiteboard (for example: 'pat', 'grin', 'trot', 'work', 'help', 'cover', 'follow', 'peel', 'cook') and ask volunteers to follow the rules as they add –*ed* and –*ing* to each verb. Go over the rules again if necessary so that all learners understand them.

Learners can then complete questions 1 and 2 independently or in pairs.

Answers
1 b hopping, sitting, swimming, pattering, waiting, digging, hooting
2
a   Ahmed is <u>putting</u> his socks on.
b   I love <u>eating</u> pizza.
c   Leena <u>waited</u> a long time for her brother.
d   Miguel's new top <u>fitted</u> him perfectly.

Workbook page 6

Spelling and vocabulary

Set Workbook page 6 as homework.

Answers
1 a putting **b** cleaned **c** sitting **d** sleeping **e** (correct) **f** (correct) **g** finding **h** (correct) **i** hopped **j** (correct)

Extension and support

Hand out copies of PCM 1, which tests learners' knowledge of punctuation. Ask learners to correct the text individually.

> More able learners should find the missing commas between clauses, and the commas before closing quote marks, as well as the more straightforward end-of-sentence punctuation. They should also be able to write a brief paragraph that continues the action appropriately, with mostly correct punctuation.

> Less able learners may need help to identify the correct placement of commas and speech marks. They may struggle to write a continuation paragraph, but they should be able to write at least a sentence or two, which may not be correctly spelt and punctuated.

Answers
The correctly punctuated text is:
It was a freezing night on the streets of London, and Jim and his little sister Martha were trying to get to sleep. They only had a thin blanket, two old coats and a few sheets of newspaper to keep out the cold. Their stomachs were rumbling loudly, because they hadn't eaten a scrap of food since that morning.
"Are you asleep, Jim?" asked Martha. "I'm hungry!"
"I'm hungry too," muttered Jim. "But we've got no food left, so we'll just have to hope we can find some tomorrow."
Just then, the children heard a very unwelcome noise. A policeman was coming round the corner towards them.
"Hey!" he shouted. "What are you two doing here?"
The children looked at each other. It was too late to run! What could they do?

Weekly review

Level	Reading	Writing	Listening and speaking
■	This group may need help and support to fully understand a story set in an unfamiliar time and place; they may struggle to decode and understand unfamiliar words.	This group needs support to think of powerful alternative verbs that can be used in place of weaker verbs; they may not always use verbs accurately in their writing.	At times this group needs support to collaborate with others in an oral/aural task. They may struggle to organise their thoughts when reporting the group's views back to the class.
●	This group usually reads accurately and fluently, and is beginning to use inference to help them understand stories set in other times and places. They may need support to read and understand some unknown and unfamiliar words.	This group can usually think of a more powerful alternative for a familiar verb when prompted. They normally use verbs accurately in their writing.	This group demonstrates attentive listening, and they often remember to collaborate with others when working orally. Their ideas may not always be clearly organised when reporting the group's views back to the class.
▲	This group reads with accuracy, fluency and appropriate expression, often using inference to help them understand stories set in other times and places. They use a range of strategies to help them read and understand unfamiliar words, including checking meanings in a dictionary.	This group can often think of more than one powerful alternative verb that could be used in place of a familiar verb. They almost always use verbs accurately in their writing.	This group demonstrates attentive listening and collaborates effectively on oral/aural tasks. Their ideas are usually clearly organised and easy to understand, when reporting the group's views back to the class.

Week 2

Student's Book pages 7–10

Workbook pages 5–7

Introduction

Bring in a range of newspapers for learners to look at – ideally including some simpler/more popular ones and some more complex/broadsheet ones. Divide learners into pairs and groups, and give the groups three newspapers each. Challenge learners to find an interesting article in each of their papers, and read and compare the articles. (You could pre-select the articles if you prefer, instead of letting learners choose from complete newspapers.) They should then make notes about the similarities and differences between the articles, and why each one is interesting.

Follow this up by looking, as a whole class, at some of the common features of newspaper reports, including headline, author's by-line, summary sentence or paragraph introducing the report, quotes from interested parties, etc.

How many of these features can learners find in their chosen articles?

Ask each group to choose the article they feel is most successful, and present it to the class. Their presentations should mention the reasons why they like the article, and draw attention to any common newspaper features.

Student's Book pages 7–8

Reading and comprehension

Once you are sure that learners are familiar with the features and purpose of newspaper reports, introduce the newspaper extract in the Student's Book. Explain that this is a made-up newspaper article, but it is based on real historical events. Circulate as learners read the article aloud in their pairs, and answer any questions they have about unfamiliar vocabulary or the meaning of the passage.

Learners can then answer the comprehension questions in their pairs.

Answers
1
a Thomas Barnardo lived in Ireland.
b cold and lack of food
c He opened a Ragged School.
d He realised that some poor children needed a safe home to live in, and proper food to eat, as well as education.
e 'Destitute' means extremely poor. (Accept any accurate definition in learners' own words.)
f headline, date, newspaper name, reporter's name, quote from interested party
g The important event was when Barnardo turned a boy away and the boy later died from cold and starvation.
h (Accept any reasonable answer.) Learners may feel that Barnardo probably felt guilty and upset that the boy had died because Barnardo hadn't been able to help him.
j The main points of each paragraph are: 1) life is hard for poor children on the streets of London; 2) Thomas Barnardo has opened a Ragged School to help these children; 3) He has also opened a home for the children which is now open to all destitute children. (Accept any sensible summary of these points in learners' own words.)

Workbook page 5

Punctuation

If learners have not yet completed question 4, they could do these for homework or in class.

Answers
a	Michael's	**e**	Grandad's
b	children's	**f**	women's
c	girls'	**g**	brother's
d	dragon's	**h**	boys'

Learners could complete PCM 2 either now or later in the week.

Student's Book pages 9–10

Grammar

Write some sentences containing adjectives on the whiteboard, for example: 'I ate a delicious ice cream', 'Jared saw an enormous ship at the harbour', 'Bella's bedroom is very untidy'. Invite learners to come up and underline the adjectives, and circle the noun that goes with each. Rehearse the role of adjectives in describing nouns, if necessary. Then ask learners to think of some more adjectives, and see how long a list you can make together.

Ask learners to read the information on adjectives and to complete questions 1 and 2 either individually or in pairs.

Answers
1 Accept any choice of sentences or phrases containing adjectives.
2
a cool, cold, freezing
b medium-sized, big, enormous
c grown-up, elderly, ancient
d unusual, odd, extraordinary

Encourage learners to read the information on connectives on page 10 of the Student's Book. Prepare some cards or sheets of paper with the following connectives: 'because', 'but', 'and', 'or', 'however', 'so', 'therefore'. Invite learners to choose a card at random, and in pairs think of a sentence that includes the given connective. They can write the sentences in their books or on the whiteboard. Shuffle the cards and have another go, so that each pair writes at least two or three sentences with different connectives.

Learners can then complete activities 3 and 4 on Student's Book page 10 in their pairs. The answers are open, but look for accurate identification of connectives, and well-constructed sentences.

Workbook page 7

Grammar and writing

Learners could complete question 1 for homework.

Answers
and, because, because, however, or, but

Learners could also attempt question 2 at this point if you wish, or you could reserve this for the start of week 3 if you prefer.

Extension and support

Ask learners to write a newspaper report about a recent activity they did at school, or something interesting that has happened locally. Remind them to use what they have learnt about newspaper features, and to include as many of these as possible in their work. The most able learners should be able to do this without much support or scaffolding.

For those learners who need more support, distribute copies of PCM 4, which is a historical story writing frame.

Encourage all learners to use connectives appropriately, and remember to use the full range of punctuation.

Weekly review

Level	Reading	Writing	Listening and speaking
■	This group may need help and prompting to identify common journalistic features when reading newspaper articles.	This group is just beginning to identify and use adjectives, not always completely accurately. They can sometimes place adjectives in a hierarchy of scale from weakest to strongest.	At times this group needs support to contribute ideas and articulate their thoughts when preparing a presentation.
●	This group can identify several journalistic features when reading newspaper articles and, when prompted, may comment on the reasons or effectiveness of the features.	This group can identify and use a range of adjectives in their own writing, normally accurately. They can usually place familiar adjectives in a hierarchy of scale from weakest to strongest.	This group can normally contribute appropriately (though sometimes briefly) to a presentation, fleshing out their ideas when prompted.
▲	This group understands and can identify a wide range of journalistic features when reading newspaper articles. They can explain why the features are used and how they are effective.	This group can identify and use adjectives confidently, including less familiar ones. They can place adjectives in a hierarchy of scale from weakest to strongest.	This group contributes independently and appropriately to presentations.

Week 3

Student's Book pages 11–12

Workbook page 8

Before learners tackle writing their own historical story, give them the opportunity to read or listen to another historical story (based on any historical period). You could give learners a choice from the historical stories you have available in class, or choose a book and read part of it to them. If any learners have historical stories at home, encourage them to bring those in to share with the class.

Workbook page 8

Grammar and writing

While this preliminary work is happening, if learners have not already completed Workbook questions 3 and 4, they could do these for homework.

Answers
3 Learner's own answers.
4 freezing, ancient, ravenous, terrifying, tiny

Student's Book page 11

Writing

This piece of writing can be tackled as an End of unit review.

Learners can work in groups or pairs to do the preliminary questions 1 and 2.

Allow plenty of time for learners to think about these activities and record their notes. They can choose whether to write a story about Barnardo, based on information from the newspaper report, or a different historical story.

You could work with any less able or less confident groups, to help them structure the note-taking and to encourage them to discuss their ideas. PCM 3 can be used to help scaffold the note-taking for any groups that struggle with this.

When all groups have prepared a basic outline of their story, look back together at the example story on Student's Book pages 2–3. Discuss how the writer has divided the story up into paragraphs that move the action on. Tell learners that they are going to use a paragraph plan to help them write their story.

Look at questions 3 and 4. Explain to learners they will need to think about how the paragraphs in their story will work. One idea is to have a first paragraph that sets the scene and introduces the characters; a second paragraph that introduces a problem or issue; a third paragraph that shows a setback on the way to solving the problem; a fourth paragraph that shows how the problem is resolved; and a final paragraph that rounds off the story. Obviously, if time allows, more able learners may choose to write a longer story, with more than one paragraph for each of the suggested stages.

Extension and support
More able learners may be able to produce their own paragraph plan without additional support, once you have demonstrated the structure of the plan as suggested above.

Learners who need more support could use the plan framework on PCM 4 or 5.

Then give learners time to write a full draft of their story, working independently. You may wish to read and mark the drafts before learners revise them, so you can get a sense of which areas of their work need most attention.

Student's Book page 12
Redrafting and revising
Encourage learners to use the checklist to help them revise their own writing, before sharing it with their partner or group. Remind learners of the rules for commenting on other people's work, and write them on the whiteboard so learners can easily refer to them:

- Always think of at least one good thing to say about a piece of work.
- When you are suggesting things that the writer could improve, be polite and give helpful examples.
- Take turns to speak, and respect each other's point of view.

Allow time for learners to redraft and revise their stories. Circulate amongst the groups and offer help as necessary. Encourage learners to use their best handwriting in their final drafts, as these will be displayed.

When all learners have had the opportunity to finish their stories, share them with the class. Choose some to read aloud (with the authors' permission) and display all the stories on a noticeboard for everyone to read. Encourage learners to illustrate their stories for display.

Weekly review

Use this rubric to assess learners' progress as they worked through the activities this week.

Level	Reading	Writing
■	This group may need support when reading other historical stories as a preliminary to planning their own. They may need help to identify how paragraphs are used to move the story along.	This group can write a short and simple historical text based on information they have read, with support if necessary.
●	This group can read independently with some confidence and accuracy, but they may need support to understand how paragraphs are used to structure a story.	This group can write a simple historical text based on information they have researched, mostly with accurate grammar and spelling.
▲	This group reads with accuracy and fluency, and with prompting can explain their understanding of how paragraphs are used to structure a story.	This group can write a more extended historical text with accuracy and fluency, researching to find useful ideas and following a clear paragraph plan. Their work is mostly accurate in grammar and spelling.

Unit 2 Mars: the trip of a lifetime!

Unit overview

In this unit, learners will look at two different types of persuasive text: advertisements and persuasive arguments. They will answer comprehension questions and learn about the features of persuasive texts, including orders/commands to the reader, the use of fact and opinion, and the use of persuasive vocabulary including adjectives. They will extend their knowledge of commas and connectives, and using what they have learnt in the unit, they will research, plan and write their own persuasive text.

Reading	Writing	Listening and speaking
4R01 Extend the range of reading;	4W05 Make short notes from a text and use these to aid writing;	4SL1 Organise ideas in a longer speaking turn to help the listener;
4R02 Explore the different processes of reading silently and reading aloud;	4W06 Collect and present information from non-fiction texts;	4SL2 Vary use of vocabulary and level of detail according to purpose;
4R04 Use knowledge of punctuation and grammar to read with fluency, understanding and expression;	4W07 Reread own writing aloud to check punctuation and grammatical sense;	4SL3 Understand the gist of an account or the significant points and respond to main ideas with relevant suggestions and comments;
4R05 Identify all the punctuation marks and respond to them when reading;	4Wa2 Adopt a viewpoint as a writer, expressing opinions about characters or places;	
4R06 Apply phonic/spelling, graphic, grammatical and contextual knowledge in reading unfamiliar words;	4Wa4 Use more powerful verbs, e.g. 'rushed' instead of 'went';	
4R08 Express a personal response to a text, and link characters and settings to personal experience;	4Wa5 Explore degrees of intensity in adjectives, e.g. 'cold', 'tepid', 'warm', 'hot';	4SL6 Adapt the pace and loudness of speaking appropriately when performing or reading aloud;
4Rx1 Retell or paraphrase events from the text in response to questions;	4Wa6 Elaborate on basic information with some detail;	4SL7 Adapt speech and gesture to create a character in drama.
4Rx2 Note key words and phrases to identify the main points in a passage;	4Wa8 Show awareness of the reader by adopting an appropriate style or viewpoint;	
4Rx3 Distinguish between fact and opinion in print and IT sources;	4Wa9 Present an explanation or a point of view in ordered points, e.g. in a letter;	
4Rx4 Explore explicit meanings within a text;	4Wa11 Summarise a sentence or a paragraph in a limited number of words;	
4Ri2 Explore implicit meanings within a text;	4Wt1 Explore different ways of planning stories, and write longer stories from plans;	
4Rw3 Understand how expressive and descriptive language creates mood;	4Wt2 Begin to use paragraphs more consistently to organise and sequence ideas;	
4Rw5 Understand the use of connectives to structure an argument, e.g. 'if', 'although';	4Wp1 Use a wider variety of connectives in an increasing range of sentences;	
4Rw6 Understand how points are ordered to make a coherent argument;		

4Rw11 Investigate the grammar of different sentences: statements, questions and orders. 4Rv1 Identify different types of non-fiction text and their known key features; 4Rv3 Understand how persuasive writing is used to convince a reader.	4Wp2 Practise using commas to mark out meaning within sentences; 4Wp6 Use a range of end-of-sentence punctuation with accuracy; 4Ws1 Extend knowledge and use of spelling patterns, e.g. vowel phonemes, double consonants, silent letters, common prefixes and suffixes; 4Ws2 Investigate spelling patterns; generate and test rules that govern them; 4Ws3 Check and correct spellings and identify words that need to be learnt; 4Ws6 Extend earlier work on prefixes and suffixes.	

Related resources

- Audio files: *Would you like to go to Mars?*; *Visit Mars – for the trip of a lifetime!*; *The Incredible Robo*; *Don't send humans to Mars*
- A recording of *The Planets Suite* by Gustav Holst (optional)
- PCM 6: Persuasive writing checklist
- PCM 7: Using commas

Resource books or websites about Mars, and about your local area

---

Week 1

Student's Book pages 13–18

Workbook pages 9–12

What do learners already know about the planet Mars? Share their ideas, and if possible show them some photographs of the planet, for example from the NASA website.

If the opportunity arises, you could also play them part of 'Mars' from *The Planets Suite* by Gustav Holst. Ask learners to listen to the music with their eyes shut, and then to create their own picture or description of the planet, based on the atmosphere and pictures suggested by the music, as well as their existing knowledge about Mars.

Student's Book page 13

Listening and speaking

1 Explain to the class that they will be listening to an information text that has lots of facts about Mars. Ask them to write two headings in their notebooks: 'Good things about going to Mars' and 'Bad things about going to Mars'. Explain that, as they listen, you want them to make quick notes, arranging the facts that they hear under these two headings. You may need to demonstrate briefly how to do this. Then play the recording, or read the text to the class. Repeat the reading a second time to help learners collect all the relevant facts.

2 Listening text

Would you like to go to Mars? Here are some Martian facts to help you make up your mind!

- Mars is Earth's next-door neighbour! Earth is the third planet from the Sun, and Mars is the fourth planet. But even though they're neighbours in the Solar System, Earth and Mars are still about 225 million kilometres apart. It would take roughly 260 days to get from Earth to Mars.
- Mars is smaller, colder and drier than Earth. The average temperature on Mars

is −62° C. That's 62 degrees below freezing, which is colder than Earth's Arctic circle in the middle of winter!

- Mars is often called the 'Red Planet' because of its red soil. The soil on Mars is red because it is rusty (it contains iron oxide).
- Mars's rusty, dusty soil is very dry indeed. Sometimes there are enormous dust storms on Mars – big enough to cover the whole planet!
- Even though the surface of Mars is so dry, scientists have discovered that there is lots of frozen water under the surface of the planet. This means that if people ever travelled to Mars, they might be able to get the water they need by extracting and melting the ice.
- The air on Mars is mostly carbon dioxide, which is poisonous to humans – so any visitors would definitely need a spacesuit to survive!
- There are lots of interesting things to see on Mars. The massive volcano called Olympus Mons is three times bigger than Everest – and it is probably the biggest volcano in the whole Solar System. There is also an enormous canyon on Mars that is nearly as long as the United States of America is wide! And at night, you would see not one but two moons rising in the sky.

3 Organise learners into pairs, and remind them about the rules for paired work:

> **Paired work rules**
> - Take turns to speak.
> - Do not interrupt when the other person is speaking.
> - Listen to the other person's point of view and respond politely.
> - Ask each other questions to find out more about what you both think.
> - Decide how you will report back to the class. Both of you need to contribute to this.

Remind the pairs to use the discussion prompt in the Student's Book. Give them about five minutes to decide whether they are going to persuade others that it's a good thing or a bad thing to go on a trip to Mars, and to find their three best reasons. Then give them a further five minutes to think about how they can put their ideas most persuasively. Encourage them to make brief notes to remind them what they are going to say. Then ask each pair to make a short presentation to the class. You could have a vote at the end.

You could use this opportunity to talk with the class about some of the features of persuasive language, based on examples from the presentations. For example, pick out good examples of emotive language and rhetorical questions, such as: 'Who wouldn't want to visit this fascinating and beautiful planet? Would *you* want to miss this opportunity of a lifetime?'

Workbook page 9

Reading

The listening text also appears in the Workbook, page 9. Learners could complete the Workbook questions as homework, or as a follow-up activity in class. The answers to the Workbook activity are open, but learners should be able to justify why they feel a particular fact is a good or bad reason to go to Mars. In their persuasive paragraphs, learners should be able to pick up on some of the examples of persuasive language which you reviewed in class.

Student's Book pages 14–16

Reading and comprehension

1 Learners work individually, reading the text silently. Tell them to put up their hands if they find a word they don't know, and write these words, with their meanings, on the board.

Move around the classroom while the reading is in progress, assisting where necessary and reminding learners to read silently if necessary.

Learners could discuss and write answers to the comprehension questions in pairs, or you may prefer to do this activity as a whole-class group, in order to share thoughts and opinions more widely.

Many of the questions are open, but even for more closed questions, always allow learners their own variations in the answers, as long as the sense of the answer is correct, and the language used is correct.

Answers
2
a Olympus Mons is a massive volcano on Mars.
b An open question; learners should give clear reasons for their views.
c You would need a spacesuit to keep you warm, and to supply breathable air/oxygen.
d An open question; learners should give clear reasons for their views.

e An open question, but one possible answer would be 'Feel the unimaginable power of a Martian dust storm!'
f 'Hurry – don't lose your place on this unmissable trip!'
g For example, 'Mars is very different from Earth, but don't worry – we've got everything you need to stay safe and happy during your visit!'
h An open question, but learners may feel that the question at the start helps the reader to feel that the piece involves them.
i An open question; look for complete sentences with correct punctuation.

Extension and support

Ask learners to collect some more examples of advertisements and persuasive writing.

More able learners could be invited to find two advertisements – one which they feel is effective and one which is less effective. Ask them to tell the class about the persuasive features of each advertisement and why they feel one works better than the other.

Less able learners could work in groups or pairs, and focus on finding at least two advertisements to compare. Encourage them to annotate the advertisements to show some of the persuasive features. Then go through the advertisements as a group and see if you can find any more. You could give learners copies of PCM 6 to help with this activity.

Working in groups, the whole class could write their own advertisements for a made-up product or service of their choice. They could use PCM 6 as a checklist to help with this.

Thinking deeper

Use the prompts in the Student's Book to help learners understand the difference between facts and opinions. As a whole class, think up some statements of fact and statements of opinion, and write them on the board in two separate lists. Then learners can tackle the questions in the Student's Book independently or in groups.

Workbook page 10

Learners could complete in class or for homework.

Answers

1
a Mars would be a really fun place to visit. (O)
b No human beings have ever yet gone to Mars. (F)
c Mars is the fourth planet from the Sun. (F)
d Mars is colder than Earth. (F)
e Life on Earth is a lot more interesting than life on Mars. (O)
f Mars has two moons. (F)
g Nights on Mars are more beautiful than nights on Earth. (O)
h It is too dangerous for humans to visit Mars. (O)
i Humans need spacesuits to protect them if they visit Mars. (F)
j The soil on Mars is a much nicer colour than the soil on Earth. (O)
2 This question is open.

Student's Book page 17

Grammar

Remind learners about orders by using the prompts in the Student's Book. Encourage them to work in small groups to come up with two or three orders of their own, and write them on the board. Use this as an opportunity to correct any misconceptions.

Learners can then complete the Student's Book activity individually or in their groups.

Answers
a **1** Come with us for the experience of a lifetime!
b **2** Take your feet off the table! (or with final full stop)
c **3** Go to sleep at once! (or with final full stop)
d **4** Shut all the doors and windows. (or with final exclamation mark)
e **5** Help me find my mobile phone! (or with final full stop)
f **6** Come and play football with Rajiv, Emma and me. (Not all children may realise that 'play' is also imperative).

Workbook page 11

Grammar

Learners could attempt the related Workbook questions for homework, either now or later in the unit.

Answers

1
a Drink your milk quickly – it's time to go to school.
b Look out for crocodiles!
c Put the flour in the mixing bowl.
d Open the window so we can get some fresh air.
e Jump over the fallen logs.

2
a Come swimming with us.
b Help Mum get dinner ready.
c Wash your hands.
d Look after your sister.
e Eat your rice.

3 Open question: accept any sensible and correctly-structured question and order.

Extension and support

Bring in some newspapers, magazines and advertising leaflets, and ask learners to collect examples of statements, questions and orders. Give them a few sheets each and ask them to use different-coloured pens to highlight the different types of sentence.

More able learners should be able to do this activity independently with a high level of accuracy. Ask them to choose one good example of each sentence type and use them to make a poster showing the features of each type, for example: command/imperative verb at the start of an order, question word or verb at the start of a sentence.

You may need to model this activity for less able learners, who could work in pairs or groups. If some of learners in the class make posters to show the relevant features of each sentence type, the less able groups could use these as a prompt for the activity.

Student's Book page 18

Spelling

Use the prompts in the Student's Book to introduce the spelling rules for the prefix *un–* and the suffix *–able*. Then ask learners to attempt the questions.

Answers

a unforgettable, unexciting, unimaginable, unbeatable, unmissable
b unforgettable, unimaginable, unbeatable, unmissable
c Open question: accept any words that meet the criteria stated.
d Open question: accept any sensible and correctly spelt sentences.

Workbook page 12

Spelling and vocabulary

Learners could attempt the Workbook questions for homework.

Answers

1 a unpleasant **b** unkind **c** unhappy **d** unseen **e** unused **f** uneaten
Sentences are learners' own.
2 a usable **b** acceptable **c** adorable **d** fashionable **e** believable **f** regrettable **g** doable **h** enjoyable
3 Answers are open.

Follow this by exploring some more prefixes (such as *mis–*, *in–*, *ex–*) and suffixes (such as *–ment*, *–ly*, *–ing*) with learners. For each prefix and suffix, start by finding some examples and write them on the board. Ask learners to arrange them according to spelling, for example, whether and how the root word changes when the prefix or suffix is added.

Can they work out the spelling rules in each instance? Make a class poster to remind them of the rules, and add to it as learners meet more prefixes and suffixes.

Weekly review

Level	Reading	Writing	Listening and speaking
■	This group sometimes struggles to decode unfamiliar words and may need support to understand how a persuasive text manipulates the reader's emotions.	With support and guidance where necessary, this group can write a simple advertisement text using some persuasive language.	This group needs support to organise ideas for a persuasive oral presentation; they may need help to present their ideas clearly and may struggle to remember to use persuasive language.
●	This group usually reads accurately and fluently, with some appropriate expression. They are beginning to understand how persuasive texts manipulate the reader's emotions.	This group can write a simple advertisement text using a few persuasive devices effectively.	This group can identify some appropriate ideas to use in a persuasive oral presentation; they may struggle to keep the presentation on task at times.
▲	This group reads with accuracy, fluency and appropriate expression, and they understand many of the ways in which persuasive texts manipulate the reader's emotions.	This group can write a more sophisticated and persuasive advertisement text, using language that manipulates the reader's response.	This group can organise their ideas effectively for a persuasive oral presentation, including good use of persuasive language. Their presentation is normally effective and clear.

Week 2

Student's Book pages 19–23

Workbook pages 13–16

Introduction

Ask learners to form pairs or small groups, and design a robot. Give each group a sheet of paper and ask them to sketch their robot design. They should annotate their design with labels and captions that show what their fantasy robot can do. When the groups have finished, share their work and ideas as a whole class. Which robot would be the most useful? Which would be the most fun? If the class could choose just one robot to make, which would they vote for?

Student's Book page 19

Reading and comprehension

1 Introduce the robot advertisement in the Student's Book. Circulate as learners read the advertisement aloud or silently in their groups, and answer any questions they have.

2 Learners can then answer the comprehension questions in their groups.

Answers

2

a The robot can learn the layout of a room so that it can move around it without bumping into things.
b amazing, super-intelligent, wonderful, brilliant
c He has rechargeable solar-powered batteries.
d Robo would quickly learn the new room layout.
e Open question: accept any correctly identified question and statement quoted from the advertisement.
f Open question: look for sensible questions and answers that are grammatically correct.

Extension and support

Encourage learners to work in their groups and write an advertisement for the robot they invented. Challenge them to make it as persuasive as possible!

More able learners can be given the further task of including at least two questions, statements and orders in their advertisement. Look for correctly spelt and punctuated sentences with accurate use of grammar.

Less able learners can follow the structure of the Robo advertisement for support. Give them copies of PCM 6 if they need reminding about the features of persuasive writing.

Workbook page 13

Grammar

Learners could complete the Workbook questions on orders, questions and statements either in class or as homework.

Answers
1
a I like chocolate biscuits best. (S)
b Have you seen my football? (Q)
c Come here at once, Kieran! (O)
d Why do you always eat the strawberry sweets first? (Q)
e We wanted to go to the beach with Sam and Mina because it was so hot. (S)
f Be careful, or you'll wake the baby! (O)
g Mum says it's bedtime now. (S) (or Mum says, "It's bedtime now.")
h Who is the fastest runner in the class? (Q)
i Shut the door! (O)
j The monster was taller than a block of flats. (S) (or end with !)

Student's Book page 20

Listening and speaking

You could introduce this activity by sharing learners' responses to the prompts as a whole class rather than in pairs, if you prefer. You may need to model the activity for some learners, or invite a more confident member of the class to demonstrate how to talk like a robot, to get the others started. Give the pairs time to rehearse their scenes before bringing the class back together to enjoy the performances. Encourage the audience to give some constructive feedback to each pair, based on:

- how audible the performance was
- how well the performers conveyed the situation and the characters
- whether the performance told a good story.

Remind learners that when commenting on someone else's work, it's important always to make some positive comments as well as highlighting what could be improved.

If you wish, you could ask learners to write up their scenes in the form of a short story or play script, either in class or as homework.

Student's Book page 21

Reading

Introduce the idea of persuasive argument texts using the prompt in the Student's Book. You could read the text and complete the comprehension questions as a whole class rather than in pairs or groups, if you prefer. Either way, allow time for learners to discuss the ideas in the text and decide whether they agree with the writer or not. Encourage them to give reasons for their views; you may need to model this for them by stating your own view on the issue, with reasons.

Student's Book pages 22–23

Comprehension

Answers
a because people love exploring – in space as well as on Earth; also because we can make scientific discoveries by going to Mars.
b Reasons include the distance between Mars and Earth, which means there is a delay in communication and therefore that it would be hard for people on Earth to help people on Mars in the event of an emergency; that whatever happened on the trip, the people on Mars would have to deal with it themselves; and that we don't know what the effect of prolonged space travel would be on the human body.
c setting up a colony on the Moon, or developing space-based solar power
d because robots don't need food or many of the other supplies that humans need, and they don't need to be rescued if something goes wrong
e Open question so accept learner's own wording: the main point of the first paragraph is that even though humans love to explore, the author thinks we should not send humans to Mars.
f Open question: look for headings that show the main point of each paragraph.

Student's Book pages 22–23

Grammar

Use the information in the Student's Book to introduce or remind learners about connectives. Ask each pair of learners to choose a book and give them five minutes to see how many connectives they can find (keeping a list in their notebooks). Then bring the whole group back together to see how many connectives they have found. Are any of the connectives more common than the others?

Ask learners to answer the Student's Book questions on connectives. They could do this in their pairs or individually.

Answers

1 a Open question, but for example, three sentences with connectives that show the order of ideas are:
'Firstly, think about the cost.'
'Secondly, think about the safety issues.'
'Finally, there are many more effective things we could spend our money on.'
b Open question, but for example, two sentences with connectives that show how ideas are connected are:
'However, although the study of space is important, I believe that we should not be sending people to Mars.'
'It is far more expensive to send people to Mars than it is to send robots, because robots don't need food and water, and if something goes wrong they don't have to be rescued.'
c Accept any sentence with the connective 'and'.
d Accept any grammatical sentence using the connective 'but'.

Workbook page 14

Grammar

Learners could complete the Workbook questions on connectives for homework.

Answers
1
a Marta's room was very untidy, <u>but</u> Lucas's room was spotless.
b I like to hum under my breath <u>because</u> it makes me feel happy, but it annoys my sister.
c <u>First</u> you turn left, and <u>then</u> you cross the road under the bridge.
d I like chocolate ice cream <u>and</u> Maria likes strawberry, <u>but</u> neither of us likes vanilla.
e You'll miss the bus to school, <u>if</u> you don't hurry up.
f Mr Osei told Jacob off <u>because</u> he was late to school <u>and</u> he had forgotten his homework.
g <u>If</u> you want to be a good footballer, <u>first</u> you need to practise hard, <u>because</u> there are lots of skills to learn.
2 Accept any correctly structured sentences using the connectives 'first', 'next', 'then', 'because', 'however', 'also', 'if'.

Student's Book page 23

Grammar

Ask learners to read the information on commas, and then discuss it as a whole class. If necessary, remind learners that a clause is a part of a sentence that contains a verb (so for example, 'I went to the shops' is a clause containing the verb 'went', but 'on Saturday' is not a clause, because it has no verb). Why do learners think the sentences with commas might be easier to read? (Because the commas help to show where one clause ends and the next begins – without commas, the reader might not always notice the join between clauses and this could be confusing.) Challenge learners to find some more sentences which have commas between the clauses, and share the examples they find. Then ask learners to answer the Student's Book questions.

Answers
2 a After I came home from school, I went straight upstairs, because I wanted to see Marvin, my pet gecko.
b It was getting late, although the sun was still shining brightly, and I didn't realise that it was past my bedtime.
c Running down the road, Maria wasn't looking where she was going, so she bumped into Mrs Martinez, who was chatting to her friend.

Workbook pages 15–16

Grammar

Learners could tackle the Workbook questions on commas, connectives, tenses and comprehension either in class or for homework. You could use this as an opportunity to revise the differences between sentences using past, present and future verbs, if necessary.

Answers
a Jamelia fumbled in her backpack, and a shower of objects fell out: an apple core, a torch, a small folding magic wand, a half-eaten chocolate bar and a hair band.
b Jamelia pointed to the sky behind her brother's head, and Josh spun round, his mouth open in amazement. Flapping slowly towards them, its leathery black wings stretched wide against the sky, was the most enormous dragon either of them had ever seen.
"What a beauty," whispered Josh, as he looked towards the clump of trees where the dragon was landing.
"We've got to get a picture of this, or no one will ever believe it!"
Jamelia fumbled in her backpack, and a shower of objects fell out.
However, there was no sign of Jamelia's phone, because she had left it behind on the bus!
Jamelia looked up hopelessly, but Josh was already running across the field, and heading straight for the dragon.
c Learners should circle the following connectives (in order from the start of the story): 'and', 'as', 'or', 'and', 'and', 'however', 'because', 'but', 'and'.

d We've got to get a picture of this, or no one will ever believe it!
e Accept any past tense sentence from the story.
f Accept any present tense sentence from the story.
g a Salamander Black
h In the countryside, because the text says that the dragon landed by a clump of trees, and Josh ran across a field.
i The children have probably seen a dragon before, because they are more surprised at the size and beauty of it than amazed to have seen it at all! Also, Josh immediately identifies it as a particular type of dragon.
j his sister
k Josh seems to know a lot about dragons; Jamelia has a folding magic wand in her bag.
l Open question: accept any answer in keeping with the text.

Extension and support

Ask learners to complete PCM 7 so that you can assess their ability to use commas correctly in lists, in direct speech and to separate clauses. The most able learners should be able to complete this activity independently with a high level of accuracy.

Less able learners may need additional practice in using and identifying commas in these three situations. You could ask them to collect examples from their reading, and make a classroom display of examples of each type of comma use. Encourage them to refer to the display if they are not sure whether or how to use commas in a particular sentence.

Answers

1
a Jack's bike has blue handlebars, red mudguards, a black seat and a purple frame.
b "I have four pets," said Noah, "and I like helping to look after them."
c "My pets are a rabbit, a goldfish, a stick insect and a gerbil," said Noah.
d Charlie zoomed down the stairs, ran out through the front door, and rushed to the playground, because he wanted to be there before anyone else.
e The monster's favourite foods were snail kebabs, wasp sandwiches, creepy crisps and jellyfish ice cream.
f Michaela could hardly wait for Saturday, because she was going to spend the day with her cousins, and although it was a long journey, it was always fun to see them.
g "Come and have your dinner at once," said Mum, "or it will get cold."

2 Accept any accurately constructed and punctuated sentences showing commas in a list, in direct speech and to separate clauses.

Weekly review

Level	Reading	Writing	Listening and speaking
■	This group may need support to follow the concepts in a persuasive argument text. They may need help to identify persuasive language and comment on its effectiveness.	This group is beginning to understand how to use commas and connectives, but needs support to remember when to use them.	This group may need support when improvising a short scene in role; they may benefit from discussing ideas in advance and being shown how to use their voices and word choices to convey character.
●	This group can read and understand a persuasive argument text and can often identify specific examples of persuasive language, commenting on effectiveness when prompted.	This group can normally use commas and connectives with some accuracy. They are beginning to understand that commas can be used in different ways for different purposes.	This group can usually improvise a short and simple scene in role, sometimes needing help and support with preparation.
▲	This group can read and understand a persuasive argument text, identifying a range of different uses of persuasive language, and commenting on their effectiveness.	This group has understood some different ways of using commas for different purposes, and can use both commas and connectives effectively in their writing.	This group can improvise a short scene in role, including using language and expression effectively to communicate character.

Week 3

Student's Book pages 24–25

Student's Book pages 24–25

Before learners begin to write their own persuasive text, reread the Mars advertisement on pages 14–15 of the Student's Book. Explain that they will be writing their own persuasive text, giving reasons why readers should visit their own local area (or another place they know and like). Ask the group to think about good places to visit locally, or other places they have enjoyed visiting. Share their ideas for different places they could focus on in their texts.

Writing (Planning)
This activity can be undertaken as an End of unit review.

Ask learners to follow the prompts in the Student's Book as they plan their piece of writing. They could work in groups, in pairs or individually. It may help to divide learners up into pairs or groups depending on the places they have chosen to focus on.

Allow time for research – for those learners who are concentrating on the local area, you could bring in some information leaflets about local attractions and places to visit. You may also be able to arrange some visits from people involved in these attractions. Learners who have chosen to focus on another area could use books or the internet to find out information. Remind them to focus on things that would make a reader want to visit their location, rather than just general facts about the area.

If necessary, once learners have done their preliminary research and thinking, model how to divide the ideas and information they have found into paragraph sections. Each paragraph section should focus on a particular theme, as suggested in the Student's Book. Show learners how to create a paragraph plan by giving each paragraph a heading, and recording relevant facts and information under each heading.

Writing (Redrafting and revising)
PCM 6 can be used as a checklist to remind learners of the key elements they need to include in their persuasive texts.

Give learners the opportunity to write a full draft of their piece. You could choose to review the pieces at draft stage so that you have the opportunity to give learners pointers for improving their work.

Extension and support
More able learners may be able to structure their work as a persuasive argument text, giving reasons for their views about why their chosen place is a good one to visit. These learners should be able to write their pieces independently, even if they worked in a pair or group during the research phase.

> As learners write their persuasive pieces, you could work with any less able or less confident groups, to help them structure their work. Less able groups or individuals could write a relatively brief advertisement rather than a persuasive argument text, if you prefer.

Encourage learners to use the checklist on page 12 of the Student's Book to help them revise their own writing, before sharing it with their partner or group. Remind learners of the rules for commenting on other people's work, and write them on the whiteboard so learners can easily refer to them:

- Always think of at least one good thing to say about a piece of work.
- When you are suggesting things that the writer could improve, be polite and give helpful examples.
- Take it in turns to speak, and respect each other's point of view.

Allow time for learners to redraft and revise their writing. Circulate among the groups and offer help as necessary. Remind learners to take care with the presentation of their pieces and to include headings, bold text and illustrations to help persuade the reader.

Share all the advertisements and persuasive arguments with the class, and display them on a noticeboard for everyone to read. If appropriate, you could take a vote on which place sounds the most interesting to visit, based on the persuasive texts.

Weekly review

Level	Reading	Writing	Listening and speaking
■	This group may need support to read and understand unfamiliar text and may sometimes struggle to explain their understanding.	This group can write a short and simple persuasive text based on straightforward research, with support if necessary.	At times this group needs support to articulate their thoughts when discussing writing ideas, or commenting on others' writing.
●	This group can read most texts with some confidence and accuracy. They may sometimes need support to put their understanding into words.	This group can write a simple persuasive text based on research, mostly with accurate grammar and spelling.	This group can normally contribute appropriately (though sometimes briefly) to a discussion of writing ideas. They normally listen to and comment on others' writing courteously.
▲	This group reads with accuracy and fluency, and can normally explain their understanding of the text with little help or prompting.	This group can write a more extended persuasive text with accuracy and fluency, adding their own ideas to information they have read.	This group contributes independently and appropriately to discussions of writing ideas, and can make helpful suggestions for improvement when reviewing others' writing.

Unit 3 The power of the sea

Unit overview

In this unit, learners will read a range of poetry on the theme of the sea, including haiku and tanka. They will read some explanation texts related to the sea, and answer comprehension questions. Learners will also consider how each type of text uses language effectively, and write their own poems and explanation texts based on models in the Student's Book. They will learn more about powerful verbs, adverbs and adjectives, and explore spellings in the context of word families.

Reading	Writing	Listening and speaking
4R01 Extend the range of reading;	4W01 Identify syllabic patterns in multisyllabic words;	4SL2 Vary use of vocabulary and level of detail according to purpose;
4R03 Read further stories or poems by a favourite writer, and compare them;	4W02 Explore the layout and presentation of writing, in the context of helping it to fit its purpose;	4SL5 Listen carefully in discussion, contributing relevant comments and questions;
4R04 Use knowledge of punctuation and grammar to read with fluency, understanding and expression;	4W07 Reread own writing aloud to check punctuation and grammatical sense;	4SL6 Adapt the pace and loudness of speaking appropriately when performing or reading aloud.
4R05 Identify all the punctuation marks and respond to them when reading;	4Wa3 Choose and compare words to strengthen the impact of writing, including some powerful verbs;	
4R06 Apply phonic/spelling, graphic, grammatical and contextual knowledge in reading unfamiliar words;	4Wa4 Use more powerful verbs, e.g. 'rushed' instead of 'went';	
4R08 Express a personal response to a text, and link characters and settings to personal experience;	4Wa5 Explore degrees of intensity in adjectives, e.g. 'cold', 'tepid', 'warm', 'hot';	
4Rx1 Retell or paraphrase events from the text in response to questions;	4Wa6 Elaborate on basic information with some detail;	
4Rx2 Note key words and phrases to identify the main points in a passage;	4Wa8 Show awareness of the reader by adopting an appropriate style or viewpoint;	
4Rx4 Explore explicit meanings within a text;	4Wa9 Present an explanation or a point of view in ordered points, e.g. in a letter;	
4Ri1 Investigate how settings and characters are built up from details and identify key words and phrases;	4Wa11 Summarise a sentence or a paragraph in a limited number of words;	
4Ri2 Explore implicit meanings within a text;	4Wt1 Explore different ways of planning stories, and write longer stories from plans;	
4Rw1 Recognise meaning in figurative language;	4Wt2 Begin to use paragraphs more consistently to organise and sequence ideas;	
4Rw3 Understand how expressive and descriptive language creates mood;	4Wp1 Use a wider variety of connectives in an increasing range of sentences;	
4Rw4 Identify adverbs and their impact on meaning;		
4Rw6 Understand how points are ordered to make a coherent argument;		

4Rw9 Understand how paragraphs and chapters are used to organise ideas; 4Rw10 Compare and contrast poems and investigate poetic features; 4Rv1 Identify different types of non-fiction text and their known key features.	4Wp2 Practise using commas to mark out meaning within sentences; 4Wp4 Investigate past and present tenses and future forms of verbs; 4Wp5 Confirm all parts of the verb 'to be' and know when to use each one; 4Wp6 Use a range of end-of-sentence punctuation with accuracy; 4Ws3 Check and correct spellings and identify words that need to be learnt; 4Ws9 Build words from other words with similar meanings, e.g. 'medical', 'medicine'; 4Ws10 Collect and classify words with common roots, e.g. 'invent', 'prevent'.	

Related resources

- Audio files: *Old Man Ocean*; *Sea Haiku*; *Tanka*; *Tsunami*
- Audio recording of *Hebrides Overture: Fingal's Cave* by Felix Mendelssohn
- PCM 8: Word families
- PCM 9: Descriptive words and phrases

Resource books or websites to help learners research the topic for their own explanation texts

Week 1

Student's Book pages 26–30

Workbook pages 17–18

Introducing the unit

Elicit learners' experiences of the sea. These are likely to vary depending on how close to the sea they live. Groups that are very familiar with the sea should be able to talk about what it's like in different weathers, different times of day or times of year, and how it makes them feel. Groups that have less experience of the sea can be asked to imagine what it might be like to live near the sea, and share their experiences of visiting it.

Write a quick list of the advantages and disadvantages of living near the sea, recording learners' ideas.

Student's Book page 26

Speaking and writing

Explain to learners that they are going to look at some photographs of the sea and listen to a piece of music composed with the sea in mind.

Tell learners that in 1829 a German composer called Felix Mendelssohn visited the Scottish island of Staffa. On this island is a very special cave by the sea, called Fingal's Cave, which is over sixty metres deep. When the sea is stormy, the waves roar and rumble inside the cave, creating some very loud, atmospheric sounds. Mendelssohn was so inspired by his visit to Staffa that he wrote this piece of music about the cave.

Explain that you would like learners to look at the photographs as they listen to the music, and think about what it would be like to be standing by the sea. Ask them to use the bullet-point prompts on page 26 of the Student's Book to help them make some quick notes as they listen (or give them copies of PCM 9 to fill in).

Play the music at least twice to allow learners to record their thoughts, and then ask them to form pairs to discuss and improve their words and phrases. When learners have had a chance to do this, bring the class back together and make a list of the most descriptive phrases that the pairs have come up with.

Student's Book pages 27–28

Reading

Learners work in pairs, taking turns to read the poems out loud to their partners. Allow the pairs a few minutes to discuss the poems, and circulate as they do this so that you can help if any of the pairs have difficulties.

Bring the whole class back together briefly to talk about the poems and their initial responses. Ask individuals to tell the group which poem they liked best, and why. If any learners are unsure of the meanings of any of the poems, or if they are puzzled by any of the words, help them to understand. Write any puzzling words on the board, with their definitions.

Working in small groups, learners can then choose one of the poems and practise reciting it with appropriate expression. You could share their readings in class or in an assembly or performance for parents.

Learners could discuss and write answers to the comprehension questions in pairs, or you may prefer to complete this activity as a whole-class group.

Many of the questions are open, but even for more closed questions, always allow learners their own variations in the answers, as long as the sense of the answer is correct, and the language used is appropriate.

Answers
2
a The sea.
b The lines in italic print represent Old Man Ocean's answers to the poet's questions.
c Glass (making smooth glass rough) and stones (making rough stones round).
d Through the action of the sea over time; learners may mention time, the tide, the waves, the wind.
e He is talking about sailors who have died at sea.
f The simile is 'like angry grey ghosts'. The rest of the answer is open; look for clear reasons why it is or isn't an effective simile.

g An open answer – look for responses that make it clear the learner has understood the meaning of the poem and the setting.
h A cat. An open answer; learners may feel that cats are often sleepy, like the poet, and also they like fish.
i An open answer; learners should pick up that 'tickles' is a stronger and more unusual verb than 'shines', and it also suggests a happy, playful atmosphere.
j An open answer; look for some reasons for the learner's choice.

Extension and support

Give learners access to some more poetry books, and ask them to find another poem that they like, about the sea or about another aspect of nature.

More able learners could write or present a short piece comparing their chosen poem to one or more of the poems in this unit, saying which poem they prefer and why, and noting any differences or similarities.

Less able learners could work in groups or pairs, and practise reading the poem they have found out loud. Their reading should demonstrate that they have understood the poem. If they struggle with this, help them with any parts of the poem that are difficult.

Workbook pages 17–18

Reading

Learners could attempt the Workbook activity on Russell Hoban's poem 'The Crow' either in class or for homework.

Answers
2
a Loose, easy (also accept swaggering).
b Open question, but learners should pick up that the crow is a free spirit; he moves easily through the air, he doesn't sing like 'normal' birds but instead he shouts or laughs, and he swaggers, which suggests he feels at home and no one can tell him what to do.
c A raucous cry; shouting, laughing.
d go, know, crow; sing, bring, wing
e An open question, but perhaps the 'loaves of blue heaven' are glimpses of the blue sky underneath the bird's wing. Accept other reasonable attempts to answer this as well.
f An open question.
g An open question; look for some rationale or reason for the choice.

h An open question; look for at least one reason, ideally with some quotation from the text.

Student's Book page 28
Grammar
Use the prompts in the Student's Book to help learners understand how similes work. As a whole class, think up some similes using 'like' and 'as', and write them on the board. Then learners can tackle the open questions in the Student's Book independently or in groups.

Workbook page 18
Grammar
Learners could complete the Workbook questions on similes and metaphors in class or for homework.

As an additional task, ask learners which of the metaphors and similes they preferred from page 18 of the Workbook. Ask learners to write a metaphor about themselves, reminding them not to use 'as' or 'like'. Then ask them to write a simile about a friend, this time reminding them to use 'like' or 'as'.

Answers
1
a The sea is as cold as a murderer's heart. (S)
b The sun was shining like a bright mirror. (S)
c The moon is a silver flower. (M)
d The moon rose through the sky as slowly as a butterfly. (S)
e The prisoner was a caged lion, pacing up and down in his cell. (M)
f The children were wriggling like tadpoles. (S)
g The breeze was as delicious as strawberry ice cream. (S)
h The trees are tall ships sailing across a green sea. (M)

Student's Book page 29
Reading and writing
Learners can read the information about haikus and tankas and complete the questions, either now or in preparation for the poetry writing activity below.

Answers
1
The trees' bare branches
swish like thick ropes of seaweed.
This ra*in*-lashed garden,
hundreds of miles from the sea,
is suddenly an ocean.
2 An open answer.

Student's Book page 30
Grammar
Remind learners about adjectives and adverbs by using the guidance in the Student's Book, page 33.

Learners can then complete the Student's Book activity individually or in their groups.

Answers
a Powerful verbs from 'Old Man Ocean': look for one of the following – *pound*, *rolling*, *tolling*. Verbs with similar meanings: *pound*: *hammer*, *press*, *squash*; *rolling*: *moving*, *running*, *turning*; *tolling*: *ringing*.
b The two adjectives are *angry*, *grey*. Accept any reasonable explanation for the choice of these words (for example that they help to describe the way the sea moves and its colour).
c An open question: accept any appropriate adjectives.
d The adverb is *gently*. Accept any reasonable choice of alternative adverb.

Student's Book page 30
Writing
Use the prompts in the Student's Book to introduce the task, and then ask learners to attempt the drafting and writing of their poem individually or in groups or pairs. Encourage learners to use the information about haiku and tanka on page 29 for support, if they choose to write poems in one of these forms. Offer help to any groups that are struggling, and allow time for refining and re-drafting the poems before learners prepare a final version.

Encourage each group to add a picture to their poem, and display the finished poems on the classroom wall.

Extension and support
Encourage learners to write a simple rhyming poem, haiku or tanka about their local area or the view they can see from their window.

More able learners should be able to do this activity independently and choose a different style of poem from the one they chose for the main writing activity.

Less able learners may choose to write the same type of poem that they wrote for the main writing activity. They can work in a group, and may choose to present their poem orally rather than in writing.

Weekly review

Level	Reading	Writing	Listening and speaking
■	This group sometimes struggles to decode unfamiliar words and may have difficulty understanding some of what they read on a first reading.	This group can write simple sentences, often, but not always, with an accurate use of tenses. They usually remember capital letters and final punctuation.	At times this group needs support to listen and requires prompting in order to respond appropriately.
●	This group usually reads accurately and fluently, with some appropriate expression. They may need support to read more unfamiliar or challenging texts.	This group can write in clear sentences using capital letters and full stops. They normally use tenses and other appropriate sentence grammar with some accuracy. They attempt to find and use powerful words when prompted.	This group demonstrates attentive listening. They listen carefully and respond appropriately.
▲	This group reads with accuracy, fluency and appropriate expression, and they may be able to comment in accurate detail on what they have read after a first reading.	This group can write in clear sentences using capital letters and full stops. They can use tenses accurately. Their writing often includes powerful words, sometimes unprompted.	This group demonstrates attentive listening and engages with another speaker. They listen carefully and respond appropriately.

Week 2

Student's Book pages 31–34

Workbook pages 19–23

Introduction

Bring in some explanation texts, or use the example in the Workbook, page 19. Discuss with the group what an explanation text is for, and how it differs from instructions. For example, explanation texts normally explain a process; unlike instructions, they don't tell readers exactly how to carry out the process for themselves. They normally consist of statements in the present tense, rather than imperative/order sentences like instructions.

With the group, look at the examples of explanation texts. Draw learners' attention to any diagrams or helpful illustrations that show the process. Ask learners why they think explanation texts often include pictures. How do the pictures help?

Student's Book pages 31–32

Reading

Introduce the explanation text on tsunamis in the Student's Book. Briefly elicit what learners already know about tsunamis, and then allow time for them to read the text independently or in pairs. Circulate as learners read the text silently, and answer any questions they have.

Learners can then answer the comprehension questions in their groups.

Answers
2
a Japan **b** an earthquake **c** low **d** slowly
e Because the water gets shallower.
f towering
g An open question, but learners should notice that the tsunami can damage houses, buildings and land.
h An open question; accept any reasonable headings. Example headings: 1) Starting with an earthquake; 2) Long waves form; 3) A wall of water; 4) Damage and devastation.

i An open question, but learners should realise that the diagrams help to explain the process – because the process is quite complicated, the pictures make it easier to understand than words alone.

Student's Book page 32

Listening and speaking

Give learners time to practise describing the process to their partners. Circulate and listen to some of the explanations. Invite some of learners to explain how tsunamis are formed to the whole class.

Extension and support

Ask learners to think of a process that they understand well, for example how a seed turns into a young plant, and explain it orally to a partner.

More able learners should be able to explain the process clearly and in some detail.

Less able learners may need extra rehearsal or support when they are preparing their presentation.

Workbook page 19

Reading and writing

Learners could complete this in class or for homework.

Answers
2
a Separate off the cream.
b Shaken or stirred together vigorously.
c The liquid that forms when butter is made.
d After the butter is solid.

Workbook page 20

Grammar

Learners could complete the Workbook activity on tenses and the verb to be, in class or for homework.

Answers
1 Present.
2 Butter is made from milk. First, the cream is separated from the milk. The cream is put into a container and shaken, or churned, until it gets thick.
3 Butter was made from milk. First, the cream was separated from the milk. The cream was put into a container and shaken, or churned, until it got thick.
4
a The boys were playing cricket on the beach.
b Last Wednesday the weather was very hot.
c We are going to the playground after school.

d In the future. we will be able to live on the Moon.
e I am bringing my little sister with me, because Mum and Dad are out shopping.

Student's Book page 33

Grammar

If you haven't already used it, use the information on adverbs and adjectives on page 33 to remind learners of the difference between these types of words. Then ask learners to complete the activity independently or in pairs.

Answers
1 Adjectives: grey, happy, sparkling, dark, fabulous, shallow, big. Adverbs: sadly, gently, dangerously, hungrily, quickly.
2
a big, huge, gigantic
b tired, exhausted
c peckish, hungry, ravenous
3 An open question; accept any reasonable adverb or adjective to fill each gap.

Workbook page 21

Grammar

Learners could attempt this either in class or as homework.

Answers
1
a Jake (bravely) dived into the deep, green pool.
b Sasha's sister Kia was small, but noisy.
c I looked both ways (carefully) before crossing the busy road.
d "You're acting like silly little monkeys!" said Mrs Kelly, (crossly).
e The trees were waving about (furiously) in the strong wind.
2 An open question; accept any sentences using the given adjectives and adverbs appropriately.

Student's Book page 34

Spelling

Use the prompts in the Student's Book to introduce the topic of word families. Write up another word family on the board and invite learners to come and add words (for example, the *please* word family includes *pleasure, pleasant, unpleasant, displease, pleasing*).

Then learners can complete the Student's Book activities either independently or as a whole group.

Answers
1 Possible answers include:

- medic: medical, medicine, medicate, medicinal
- happy: unhappy, happier, happiest, happily
- invent: inventor, invention, inventive, invented
- ease: easy, easily, uneasy, disease

2 Open question, so accept any reasonable sentences using the target words.

Workbook pages 22–23

Spelling

Learners could attempt this either in class or as homework.

Answers

1
- real: really, reality, realistic, unreal, surreal;
- appear: reappear, apparently, appearance, disappear, appearing;
- dark: darkest, darker, darkening, darkness, darkly.

2 An open question so accept any accurate sentences using the target words appropriately.

3 Possible words in the *able* family include *unable, disabled, ability, disability, ably*.

Extension and support

Encourage learners to build up word families for as many different root words as possible. Give them copies of PCM 8 to support this. When all learners have created at least one word family, make a wall display and look as a whole group for spelling patterns and rules that show how the spelling of the root word varies with different suffixes and prefixes.

More able learners should be able to include words which share a root and meaning but which have a different spelling from the root word (for example understanding that pleasure comes from the same root as please).

Less able learners may stick to word family is varied only by adding suffixes and prefixes.

Weekly review

Use this rubric to assess learners' progress as they worked through the activities this week.

Level	Reading	Writing	Listening and speaking
■	This group may need support to follow the concepts in an unfamiliar explanation text. They may need to be reminded to use the pictures as well as the words to gain information.	This group can identify and use adverbs and adjectives with support, not always completely accurately. They are beginning to understand the concept of word families.	At times this group needs support to contribute ideas and articulate their thoughts in discussion, or when preparing a presentation.
●	This group can tackle most unfamiliar texts, reading silently and usually with concentration. They may need support to put their understanding into words.	This group can normally use adverbs and adjectives with some accuracy, and can self-correct when prompted. They can contribute ideas and words when putting together word families.	This group can normally contribute appropriately (though sometimes briefly) to a discussion or presentation, fleshing out their ideas when prompted.
▲	This group reads with accuracy and fluency, and can normally explain their understanding of the text with little help or prompting.	This group has understood the difference between adverbs and adjectives, and can accurately arrange adjectives in order of strength. They can think of some less-obvious words to add to word families.	This group contributes independently and appropriately to discussions and presentations.

Week 3

Student's Book pages 35–38

Student's Book pages 35–36

Reading

Ask learners to read the explanatory diagrams about how sand is made, either independently or in small groups or pairs. Listen and support learners as necessary, while they explain the process to their groups/partners.

Before learners turn their explanations into writing, use the board to model how to lay this out, with four clear sections, each with a heading. Encourage learners to work independently as far as possible; some learners may benefit from working in a pair or small group.

Student's Book pages 37–38

Writing

Ask learners to follow the prompts in the Student's Book as they plan their explanation text. Depending on the support and research materials you have available in school, you may want to guide them towards particular topics on this list; however, if learners are enthusiastic and knowledgeable about particular subjects, encourage them to follow these up.

Learners could work in groups, in pairs or individually. It may help to divide learners up into pairs or groups depending on the topics they have chosen to focus on.

Allow time for research, and support learners as they gather information. You may need to remind them to focus on information that helps to explain the process, rather than general information about their chosen topic. Encourage them to use their explanations about sand as a model for this.

Remind learners that they need a clear structure, with a heading for each step in the process.

Give learners the opportunity to write a full draft of their piece, including diagrams. You could choose to review the pieces at draft stage so that you have the opportunity to give learners pointers for improving their work.

Extension and support

More able learners may be able to write a longer and more complex explanation, possibly including some extra background information about the topic, as well as a range of helpful diagrams or illustrations.

Work with any less able or less confident groups, to help them structure their work. These learners could write a briefer text, possibly with most of the information conveyed via labelled diagrams. They could use their diagrams as the basis of an oral presentation rather than a long piece of writing.

Encourage learners to use the checklist on page 12 of the Student's Book to help them revise their own writing, before sharing it with their partner or group. Remind learners of the rules for commenting on other people's work (see Teacher's Guide page 25).

Allow time for learners to redraft and revise their writing. Circulate among the groups and offer help as necessary. Remind learners to take care with the presentation of their pieces and to make sure their diagrams are clear and easy to follow.

Share all the explanation texts with the class, and display them on a noticeboard for everyone to read.

Weekly review

Level	Reading	Writing	Listening and speaking
■	This group may need support to read and understand unfamiliar text and may sometimes struggle to explain their understanding.	This group can write a short and simple explanation text based on information they have read, with support if necessary.	At times this group needs support to contribute ideas and articulate their thoughts in discussion, or when preparing a presentation.
●	This group can read most texts with some confidence and accuracy. They may sometimes need support to put their understanding into words.	This group can write a simple explanation text based on information they have read, mostly with accurate grammar and spelling.	This group can normally contribute appropriately (though sometimes briefly) to a discussion or presentation, fleshing out their ideas when prompted.
▲	This group reads with accuracy and fluency, and can normally explain their understanding of the text with little help or prompting.	This group can write a more extended explanation text with accuracy and fluency, adding their own ideas to information they have read.	This group contributes independently and appropriately to discussions and presentations.

Formal assessment 1

Use this test to assess how well learners have managed to cover the objectives from the last three units. Hand out the sheets and let learners complete them under test conditions. Collect and mark their tests, recording the results in your class record book. Use the mark scheme below.

Assessment 1 Mark Scheme **Total 26**

Question 1

Reading

A handlebars (1)

B dancing (1)

C Any two from: 'just a touch of stiffness', 'as though neither of you were sure of the steps', 'you wobble', 'hanging on for dear life', 'all that kept you from falling'. (2)

D A description in the learner's own words that shows they have understood the scene shows someone riding a bike in the street. (2 – one mark for describing the scene accurately, and one for using their own words rather than quoting from the text)

E Accept any reasonable summary of how the poem makes the learner feel, provided reasons are given. (2 – one mark for saying how it makes them feel, and one for giving comprehensible reasons related to the text).

Question 2

Spelling, grammar and punctuation

A leading, hanging, dancing, falling (2 – allow half a mark for each correct word)

B

grip – gripping

extend – extending

wobble – wobbling

keep – keeping (2 – allow half a mark for each correct spelling)

C Any two from: 'as though', 'with', 'then', 'as if' (1 – allow half a mark for each correct connective)

D "You must grip them carefully,

both at the same time

as though you were leading

a partner onto the dance floor." (2 – allow one mark if both opening and closing speech marks are present and correctly placed, and one mark for a full stop at the end)

E cautious nervous frightened terrified

adequate good excellent world-beating

(2 – allow one mark per set of adjectives in the correct order)

Question 3

Writing

A (4 – allow half a mark for each correctly identified fact/opinion)

- This is the world's most amazing bicycle. (opinion)
- It's ideal for nervous cyclists and people who are just learning to ride. (opinion)
- It has a lightweight titanium frame and chunky puncture-proof tyres. (fact)
- It comes in a range of colours including black, silver, turquoise, orange and flame-red. (fact)
- It can be used on every type of surface – including roads, fields, mountains and even sandy beaches. (fact)
- It is every cyclist's dream. (opinion)
- It stops automatically if the rider is in danger. (fact)
- If you fall off or crash, the bike's built-in crash pads activate automatically and catch you. (fact)

B

Accept any persuasive advertisement that fulfils the brief in the question. Allow one mark for each of five sentences. Each sentence should contain a fact, an opinion and/or an example of persuasive language. (5)

Unit 4 Other people, other places

Unit overview

This unit introduces learners to a range of stories from different cultures: Eritrean, Kenyan and Native American. Learners will listen to and read stories and answer comprehension questions. They will learn about the five-stage structure that many stories follow, and analyse stories using this structure. They will review the use of apostrophes for possession, speech punctuation, adverbs and adjectives, and they will revise the correct formation of present, past and future tenses. They will learn how breaking longer words into syllables can help with spelling. They will finish the unit by planning and writing their own story based on the five-stage structure.

Reading	Writing	Listening and speaking
4R01 Extend the range of reading;	4W01 Identify syllabic patterns in multisyllabic words;	4SL1 Organise ideas in a longer speaking turn to help the listener;
4R02 Explore the different processes of reading silently and reading aloud;	4W05 Make short notes from a text and use these to aid writing;	4SL2 Vary use of vocabulary and level of detail according to purpose;
4R03 Read further stories or poems by a favourite writer, and compare them;	4W07 Re-read own writing aloud to check punctuation and grammatical sense;	4SL3 Understand the gist of an account or the significant points and respond to main ideas with relevant suggestions and comments;
4R04 Use knowledge of punctuation and grammar to read with fluency, understanding and expression;	4Wa1 Write character profiles, using detail to capture the reader's imagination; 4Wa2 Adopt a viewpoint as a writer, expressing opinions about characters or places;	
4R05 Identify all the punctuation marks and respond to them when reading;		
4R06 Apply phonic/spelling, graphic, grammatical and contextual knowledge in reading unfamiliar words;	4Wa3 Choose and compare words to strengthen the impact of writing, including some powerful verbs;	4SL5 Listen carefully in discussion, contributing relevant comments and questions;
4R07 Read and perform playscripts, exploring how scenes are built up;	4Wa4 Use more powerful verbs, e.g. rushed instead of went;	4SL6 Adapt the pace and loudness of speaking appropriately when performing or reading aloud;
4R08 Express a personal response to a text, and link characters and settings to personal experience;	4Wa5 Explore degrees of intensity in adjectives, e.g. cold, tepid, warm, hot;	
4Rx1 Retell or paraphrase events from the text in response to questions;	4Wa6 Elaborate on basic information with some detail;	4SL7 Adapt speech and gesture to create a character in drama;
4Rx4 Explore explicit meanings within a text;	4Wa10 Explore alternative openings and endings for stories;	4SL8 Comment on different ways that meaning can be expressed in own and others' talk.
4Ri1 Investigate how settings and characters are built up from details and identify key words and phrases;	4Wa11 Summarise a sentence or a paragraph in a limited number of words;	
4Ri2 Explore implicit meanings within a text;	4Wt1 Explore different ways of planning stories, and write longer stories from plans;	
4Rw1 Recognise meaning in figurative language; Recognise meaning in figurative language; 4Rw2 Understand the impact of imagery and figurative language in poetry, including alliteration and simile, e.g. as … as a … ;	4Wp3 Experiment with varying tenses within texts, e.g. in dialogue;	
	4Wp4 Investigate past and present tenses and future forms of verbs;	

4Rw3 Understand how expressive and descriptive language creates mood; 4Rw7 Understand the main stages in a story from introduction to resolution; 4Rw8 Explore narrative order and the focus on significant events.	4Wp5 Confirm all parts of the verb to be and know when to use each one; 4Wp7 Use speech marks and begin to use other associated punctuation; 4Wp8 Learn the use of the apostrophe to show possession, e.g. girl's, girls'; 4Ws1 Extend knowledge and use of spelling patterns, e.g. vowel phonemes, double consonants, silent letters, common prefixes and suffixes; 4Ws2 Investigate spelling patterns; generate and test rules that govern them; 4Ws3 Check and correct spellings and identify words that need to be learned; 4Ws5 Revise rules for spelling words with common inflections, e.g. -ing, -ed, -s; 4Ws6 Extend earlier work on prefixes and suffixes; 4Ws7 Match spelling to meaning when words sound the same (homophones), e.g. to/two/too, right/write.	

Related resources

- Audio files: *The Clever Farmer*, *Abunuwasi's House*; *The Brave Baby*
- PCM 10: The Clever Farmer
- PCM 11: The structure of a story
- PCM 12: The Selkie Wife

Books or Websites containing stories from around the world

Week 1

Student's Book pages 39–43

Workbook pages 24–27

Introducing the unit

Talk with learners about how people all over the world have always loved to tell stories. Every country and area has its own traditional stories, and the old stories change over time as they are retold; meanwhile, new stories are always being created.

Explain that stories often tell us something about the place they came from. They may give us information about what the place is like, and what it is like to live there. Often, stories tell us something about the people who invented them, too – for example, the things they enjoy, and the difficulties and dilemmas they have faced.

Student's Book page 39

Listening and speaking

Tell learners that they are going to hear a story from Eritrea in Eastern Africa. The first time they hear the story, they can just listen and enjoy it; but on the second listening, they should make some notes about what the story tells us about the setting and characters. Ask learners to write these headings to help them structure their notes:

- Where the story is set
- What the place is like
- Who the main characters are
- What the characters are like.

Play the audio recording or read the story aloud to the class twice. The text of the story is on PCM 10. If you wish, you can give learners copies of the text so they can follow it as you read.

Allow time during and after the second reading, so that learners can discuss and make notes on the characters and setting in pairs. Encourage them to use vivid descriptive phrases to bring the characters and setting to life. Share the pairs' ideas with the whole class, and record the best words and phrases on the board for later.

Workbook pages 24–25
Learners could complete this in class in their pairs, or independently for homework.

Ask learners to practise retelling the story briefly in their pairs. They don't have to remember all the details, but they should try to make their retelling interesting for the listener by using some of the descriptive words and phrases they thought of, and by adding emphasis through their voices and gestures. Share some of the retellings with the whole class.

Student's Book pages 40–41

Reading
Learners work in pairs, reading the story silently at first and then taking turns to read it out loud to their partners. Circulate as they do this, so that you can help with any unfamiliar words. Then ask learners to discuss the comprehension questions in their pairs, and write the answers.

Many of the questions are open, but even for more closed questions always allow learners their own variations in the answers, as long as the sense of the answer is correct, and the language used is appropriate.

Answers
2
a In a town in Kenya.
b Abunuwasi

c He wanted to leave town, and he needed the money so he could build or buy a new house somewhere else.
d He thought that if he didn't buy it, Abunuwasi might get fed up and leave town anyway, so that the merchant could get the whole house for free.
e In learners' own words: Abunuwasi wanted his friends to pretend that they were going to destroy the bottom half of the house, so that the merchant would think that his own half of the house was bound to be destroyed too, and so the merchant would buy the bottom part of the house in order to keep his own part safe.
f Open question, so accept any reasonable answer – learners should pick up that perhaps it was a good idea for Abunuwasi to move a long way away from the merchant, as well as anyone else he might have annoyed in the area.
g Open question; learners should give a reason for their opinion.
h Open question; accept any appropriate simile.
i Open question; the two most obvious sentences are 'If you don't believe me, just listen to this story ...' and 'Well, of course, if Abunuwasi knocked down the bottom half of the house, there was no hope for the top half!'

Extension and support
Talk about how traditional stories often use 'storytelling language' – they are written to sound like spoken stories. Share any examples of this that learners can think of, from stories they know.

More able learners could complete the 'Thinking Deeper' activity on storytelling language. They should understand that the author wanted the reader to enjoy the story in the same sort of way that a storyteller's audience would; this kind of language makes the story more vivid. Look for at least one example of spoken-style language in their opening sentence.

Less able learners could look for examples of storytelling language in another traditional story.

Student's Book page 42

Punctuation, speaking and reading
Use the prompts in the Student's Book to remind learners how direct speech is punctuated. As a whole class, share some examples of correctly punctuated direct speech from books learners have been reading, and write them on the board. Then

learners can tackle the first question in the Student's Book independently.

Answers
1
- "You've broken my best pen," said Abbie crossly.
- "No I haven't," said Li. "It was broken when I found it."
- "Never mind, Abbie. You can borrow my pen," said Nadine.

Allow time for learners to re-read *Abunuwasi's House* and role-play the conversation. Share some of the role plays with the whole class, and draw learners' attention to some of the different ways of using words, tone of voice, facial expression and gesture to show how the merchant and Abunuwasi are feeling. Which role plays do learners think are the most effective, and why?

Then ask the pairs to write out their conversations as correctly punctuated direct speech.

Workbook pages 25–26

Punctuation, speaking and reading

Learners can attempt this independently, either in class or as homework.

Answers
1
"Come on," said Mum. "We've got to go shopping."
"Oh!" moaned Ali. "Do we have to?"
"Yes," said Mum. "We've got no food left in the house."
"All right then," said Ali. "I'll go and get my coat."
"Good," said Mum. "If you help with the shopping, I'll take you swimming later."
2 "Come back," said the cat. "I only want to play with you."
"No thank you!" said the bird. "I know what your games are like!" (Accept correctly-punctuated variants on this.)

Student's Book page 43

Comprehension

Introduce the five-stage story structure using the prompts in the Student's Book. Make sure that learners understand the terminology before they move on to the comprehension exercise.

Give learners copies of PCMs 10 and 11, and ask them to work in groups to analyse *The Clever Farmer* using this structure – alternatively, you could do this as a whole class. Learners could use different coloured pens to show which parts of the story on PCM 10 belong in each stage of the story structure. Review this so that you can see whether learners have understood the concepts; if they haven't, you could work as a whole class and use PCM 11 to analyse another story that is already familiar to learners.

When they have understood the concepts, give each pair a clean copy of PCM 11 to help them analyse *Abunuwasi's House* using the five-stage structure, and ask them to sum up the relevant part of the story in each row of the chart.

Follow this up with an opportunity for learners to retell either *The Clever Farmer* or *Abunuwasi's House* in pairs or small groups. Give learners time to practise their retellings and work on making them really powerful and interesting. They can use their notes on PCM 11 to remind them of the story; encourage them to add their own details to interest the listener, and to choose their words carefully to help convey the emotions in the story. Remind them too to use their voices, facial expressions and gestures to convey the story. Share some of the retellings with the whole class, and pick out some good aspects of each one to compare.

Student's Book page 43

Punctuation

Remind learners about apostrophes by using the guidance in the Student's Book on page 43. Learners can then complete the activity individually.

Answers
a Anna's eyes are blue, and Ella's are brown.
b The girls' shoes are under their beds.
c Dad forgot to make the children's sandwiches.
d It's Michael's birthday, but he isn't very happy.
e I haven't seen Maria's sister today.

Workbook pages 26–27

Punctuation

Learners can tackle this independently, either in class or as homework.

Answers
1 a Jake's toys were all over the floor.
b The children's faces were covered in chocolate.

c The dragon's cave was dark and damp.
d Mara's job was to fill up her pet hamsters' water bowl.
e The girls' bicycles had flat tyres.
f Rahel looked everywhere for Sam's lost bear.
g The men's changing room was very crowded.
h We scattered the chickens' food all over the yard.
i The rabbit's leg was broken.
j My mobile phone's battery is dead.
2 Accept any correctly punctuated sentences about the target objects.

Weekly review

Level	Reading	Writing	Listening and speaking
■	This group sometimes struggles to decode unfamiliar words and may have difficulty understanding some of what they read on a first reading.	This group can write simple sentences, and attempt some punctuation of direct speech (not always accurately). They are beginning to understand how to use apostrophes of possession.	At times this group needs support to organize ideas and use language appropriately when storytelling.
●	This group usually reads accurately and fluently, with some appropriate expression. They may need support to read more unfamiliar or challenging texts.	This group can write in clear sentences, normally using basic sentence punctuation accurately. They know how direct speech should be punctuated but do not always apply this accurately in their writing. They can use apostrophes of possession accurately in simple contexts.	This group uses some appropriate language, tone and gesture when storytelling, but sometimes needs reminding to keep the tone consistent.
▲	This group reads with accuracy, fluency and appropriate expression, and they may be able to comment in accurate detail on what they have read after a first reading.	This group can write in clear sentences and have a good understanding of basic punctuation, including punctuation of simple direct speech. They almost always use apostrophes of possession accurately.	This group demonstrates good simple storytelling ability, often with appropriate use of language, tone and gesture.

Week 2

Student's Book pages 44–48

Workbook pages 27–29

Introduction
Explain that learners are going to read another story – this time a Native American one. The story has been told very simply, and they are going to use it as the basis for a retelling with some extra detail.

Student's Book pages 44–45

Reading
When learners have read *The Brave Baby*, they can tackle the comprehension questions independently or in pairs.

Answers
2
a Because the chief was fierce and brave.
b Open question, but he probably assumed that anyone who wasn't afraid of him would have to be a man.

c She was calm; she played with her stick and smiled.
d Because the chief shouted at her.
e He wanted to make Wasso do as he said. No – Wasso did not do as the chief said.
f Less angry, and tired.
g The two best adjectives are *proud* and *courageous*. Accept any sensible sentence that describes the chief and uses these correctly.
h Open question. Accept any sentence that describes the old woman and uses an appropriate adjective other than 'old' and 'wise'.
i Open question; accept any sensible division of the story into these stages.

Workbook pages 27–28

Writing

Encourage learners to complete the activities independently. The questions are open, so accept any appropriate and accurate use of adverbs and adjectives that fulfils the question criteria.

Extension and support

Encourage learners to use their notes dividing *The Brave Baby* into stages, to help them retell the story.

More able learners should be able to retell the story fluently, and they may add extra dialogue or details, either remembered from the original story or invented.

Less able learners may simply convey the main points of the story in order, with little elaboration. Prompt them, if necessary, to use appropriate storytelling language.

Student's Book page 46

Speaking, listening and writing

Introduce the activity using the prompts in the Student's Book. Allow plenty of time for learners to act out the story in their groups of three before they plan how to add extra detail to the story; acting it out will help them to understand the kinds of details it would be helpful to add.

Give learners copies of PCM 10 to help them make their notes on each section of the story. Review their notes and ideas before they go on to write their stories. This will enable you to see if they have understood what kinds of details to add. It may also be helpful to get learners to act out the story in their groups again, with the extra bits, before they write.

Depending on how much time you have, you may want to ask learners to complete the writing activity quite quickly, as a preparation for the longer writing activity in Week 3. If time allows, however, they could spend longer on this, writing and reviewing a first draft before they work on a final draft which they can share with the rest of the class.

Extension and support

More able learners can work on their stories independently. Challenge them to add extra dialogue to help draw the reader into the story. They should be able to sum up the message of the story briefly at the end.

Some groups may struggle to rewrite the story, especially if this writing task has to be done quite quickly. In that case, allow them to work up a group retelling of their new version of the story, and present it orally to the class instead of in writing.

Encourage all learners to tackle the 'Thinking Deeper' questions. These are open questions, so accept any answers that use adjectives and adverbs appropriately and accurately. Less able learners can do this exercise through group discussion; more able learners should be able to work independently and in writing.

Student's Book pages 47–48

Spelling

Use the prompts in the Student's Book to introduce the idea of splitting longer words into syllables to help with spelling them. If necessary, remind learners about syllables by clapping the syllables in their names and in some other familiar words. Use the suggested spelling tips to analyse the spellings of some multi-syllable words from books learners have recently read, or work together on the list of words from *The Brave Baby* in the Student's Book. Encourage learners to apply these strategies when they encounter new multi-syllable words. You could make a shared list of longer words split into syllables, and put it on the wall for reference.

Use the text of Abunuwasi's House (Student's Book, pages 40–41) to introduce or remind learners about homophones. The text contains the homophones too/two/to, new/knew, their/there and know/no. Ask learners to find these homophones in the text, and discuss the differences in meaning. Make a list of the homophones on the board and ask learners to help you write a sentence using each of them. Explain that when we are trying to work out which spelling of a homophone word to use, it helps to think about the meaning of the word and remember which spelling goes with which meaning.

Workbook pages 28–29
Spelling

Learners can complete the activities independently, in class or as homework.

Answers
1
a happily (3)
b correct (2)
c kicking (2)
d somebody (3)
e underneath (3)
f beautiful (4)
2
a somebody
b whenever
c favourite
d everyone
e beautiful
3
a I saw where Mum put the cakes.
b I've got too much homework to do.
c Ben is good at reading and writing.
d I would love to go swimming.
e It's a long way to London.
f Dad is not here this evening.
4 Open questions: accept any sentences using the homophone words correctly.

Student's Book page 48
Grammar

When learners have read *The Brave Baby*, they can tackle the activity independently or in pairs, refreshing their knowledge of the past, present and future tenses as well as direct speech.

Workbook pages 29–30
Grammar

Learners can complete the activities independently, in class or as homework.

Answers
1
a I was excited because it was my turn to go down the water slide.
b Priti wore her best blue sari.
c We walked into town.
d Michael and Ruben argued again.
2
a Dad will be in New York
b I was nine on Saturday.
c Sabah and Emily were the winners.
d We will be happy to see Grandma.
3
a Mum became very cross when we got mud on the carpet.
b I wrote my name carefully.
c The dragon flew over the rooftops.
d Ruth and Jacob came swimming with us.
e A large parcel stood in the corner of the room.

Weekly review
Use this rubric to assess learners' progress as they worked through the activities this week.

Level	Reading	Writing	Listening and speaking
■	This group may need support to explain their understanding of a story when discussing it with others. They can retell a story in simple terms, sometimes with prompting.	This group often needs support to write a new version of a known story; their written retellings are simple and may miss some details.	At times this group needs support to tell stories effectively. When prompted they can use some simple storytelling language effectively.
●	This group can contribute to a discussion about a story, and can attempt a retelling with little support. They may sometimes need support to put their understanding into words.	This group can tackle a simple retelling of a known story and may be able to add some extra details of their own, with some support if necessary.	This group can orally retell a simple story effectively, with some good use of voice and gesture and some appropriate storytelling language.
▲	This group can contribute fluently to a discussion about a story, and can retell a story with minimal prompting and support.	This group can retell a familiar story confidently, usually getting the sequence correct and adding appropriate details in places.	This group can orally retell a known story effectively, using their voices and choice of vocabulary effectively to engage the listener.

Week 3

Student's Book pages 49–50

Introduction

For the main writing activity, learners will write their own version of a story that follows the five stages outlined earlier in this unit. There are several ways of tackling this, depending on the amount of support your class needs.

One option is to give learners access to a range of traditional tales from your own country or area, or from elsewhere around the world. You could let learners read a selection of stories and choose one to use as the basis of their own retelling – or you could select one or two appropriate stories yourself and ask the group to choose one of these.

Alternatively, learners could write their own new versions of *The Clever Farmer* or *Abunuwasi's House* (if they haven't already retold these in detail earlier in the unit). This option might be appropriate for less confident learners.

A further option is to allow learners to make up their own new story which follows the five-stage story structure.

Student's Book pages 49–50

Writing

Ask learners to follow the prompts in the Student's Book as they plan their explanation text. They could work in groups, in pairs or individually. It may help to divide learners up into pairs or groups depending on the story they have chosen to focus on, so that those working on the same story can support each other. Encourage plenty of discussion, and prompt learners to practise telling their story out loud – or even acting it out – before they begin their first written draft.

Support learners as they work on structuring their stories. They could use PCM 11 as a format for collecting their notes on what happens at each stage of the story. If necessary, model this note-taking process for them.

Because, ideally, learners should be trying to write a story that includes expressive language, interesting details and dialogue, it may take them more than one session to write a complete draft; so allow plenty of time for the planning and drafting stages.

The prompts in the Student's Book can be used as a checklist to remind learners of the key elements they should be checking at draft stage. After an initial read-through of their own stories, encourage learners to swap stories with a partner and comment on each other's work. Remind them of the need to be constructive, and to find things to comment on positively as well as making suggestions for improvement.

It is worth reading learners' stories yourself at draft stage too, if possible, so that you can also make suggestions.

After the redrafting stage, give learners the opportunity to write a full draft of their piece, including pictures if they wish. You could make a class book containing all the finished stories.

Extension and support

More able learners should be able to write a longer and more complex story, adding believable dialogue and some interesting details they have thought of for themselves.

Less able or less confident learners may write a shorter story, and it is likely to be quite close to the original model story in terms of language, dialogue and structure. They may need extra support at all stages of the project. Some groups may not be able to create a full written version of their story, in which case they could be invited to present the story orally to the class instead.

Give learners PCM 12, which is a very short outline of a Scottish story called *The Selkie Wife*. Ask learners to use PCM 11 to help them analyse the story, so they can identify which parts of the story correspond to the five stages. They could present this either in chart form using PCM 11, or by highlighting or underlining the different sections in different colours.

The Selkie Wife fits the five-part structure like this:

- Introduction – paragraphs 1 and 2
- Problem/build-up – paragraphs 3 and 4
- Climax – paragraph 5
- Resolution – paragraph 6
- Conclusion – paragraph 7

If time allows, you could also ask learners to retell the story, adding details and dialogue to make it more interesting. They could either write their own new version of the story, or retell it orally for an audience.

Weekly review

Level	Reading	Writing	Listening and speaking
■	This group may need support to read and understand an unfamiliar story, and may need support to analyse its structure and retell it.	This group can summarise and retell a simple story with support.	At times this group needs support to structure their retelling; they may need to be reminded to include important details.
●	This group can read most texts with some confidence and accuracy, and can retell a straightforward story once they have read it several times. They may sometimes need support to put their understanding of structure into words.	This group can write a retelling of a story, including some dialogue and other telling details, with occasional support.	This group can normally retell a story orally with minimal support, remembering to add some interesting details.
▲	This group reads with accuracy and fluency, and can retell a story with little support. They understand how the story fits the five-stage structure, and can explain their understanding.	This group can write a more extended retelling with accuracy and fluency, adding their own ideas to improve the story.	This group retells stories fluently and interestingly, with little additional support.

Unit 5 The only problem is ...

Unit overview

In this unit, learners will read stories and poems that deal with issues and dilemmas. They will read, perform and compare two poems by Michael Rosen, and will write their own poem in a similar style using these as models. They will read and answer comprehension questions on two stories that focus on children in difficult situations, and attempt a similar piece of writing of their own, dividing their story into clear paragraphs. They will practise spelling words with common letter strings but different pronunciations, and revise the grammar of statements, orders and questions. They will also explore powerful verbs and adjectives, and look at what a well-chosen adverb can add to a sentence.

Reading	Writing	Listening and speaking
4R01 Extend the range of reading;	4W01 Identify syllabic patterns in multisyllabic words;	4SL1 Organise ideas in a longer speaking turn to help the listener;
4R02 Explore the different processes of reading silently and reading aloud;	4W05 Make short notes from a text and use these to aid writing;	4SL2 Vary use of vocabulary and level of detail according to purpose;
4R03 Read further stories or poems by a favourite writer, and compare them;	4W07 Re-read own writing aloud to check punctuation and grammatical sense;	4SL3 Understand the gist of an account or the significant points and respond to main ideas with relevant suggestions and comments;
4R04 Use knowledge of punctuation and grammar to read with fluency, understanding and expression;	4Wa1 Write character profiles, using detail to capture the reader's imagination; 4Wa2 Adopt a viewpoint as a writer, expressing opinions about characters or places; ;	4SL5 Listen carefully in discussion, contributing relevant comments and questions;
4R05 Identify all the punctuation marks and respond to them when reading;	4Wa3 Choose and compare words to strengthen the impact of writing, including some powerful verbs;	
4R06 Apply phonic/spelling, graphic, grammatical and contextual knowledge in reading unfamiliar words;	4Wa4 Use more powerful verbs, e.g.s rushed instead of went;	4SL6 Adapt the pace and loudness of speaking appropriately when performing or reading aloud;
4R07 Read and perform playscripts, exploring how scenes are built up;	4Wa5 Explore degrees of intensity in adjectives, e.g. cold, tepid, warm, hot;	4SL7 Adapt speech and gesture to create a character in drama;
4R08 Express a personal response to a text, and link characters and settings to personal experience;	4Wa6 Elaborate on basic information with some detail;	
4Rx1 Retell or paraphrase events from the text in response to questions;	4Wa10 Explore alternative openings and endings for stories;	4SL8 Comment on different ways that meaning can be expressed in own and others' talk.
4Rx4 Explore explicit meanings within a text;	4Wa11 Summarise a sentence or a paragraph in a limited number of words;	
4Ri1 Investigate how settings and characters are built up from details and identify key words and phrases;	4Wt1 Explore different ways of planning stories, and write longer stories from plans;	
4Ri2 Explore implicit meanings within a text;	4Wp3 Experiment with varying tenses within texts, e;g; in dialogue;	
4Rw1 Recognise meaning in figurative language; Recognise meaning in figurative language;		

4Rw2 Understand the impact of imagery and figurative language in poetry, including alliteration and simile, e.g. as ;;; as a ;;; 4Rw3 Understand how expressive and descriptive language creates mood; 4Rw7 Understand the main stages in a story from introduction to resolution; 4Rw8 Explore narrative order and the focus on significant events.	4Wp4 Investigate past and present tenses and future forms of verbs; 4Wp5 Confirm all parts of the verb to be and know when to use each one; 4Wp7 Use speech marks and begin to use other associated punctuation; 4Wp8 Learn the use of the apostrophe to show possession, e.g. girl's, girls'; 4Ws1 Extend knowledge and use of spelling patterns, e.g. vowel phonemes, double consonants, silent letters, common prefixes and suffixes; 4Ws2 Investigate spelling patterns; generate and test rules that govern them; 4Ws3 Check and correct spellings and identify words that need to be learned; 4Ws5 Revise rules for spelling words with common inflections, e.g. -ing, -ed, -s; 4Ws6 Extend earlier work on prefixes and suffixes; 4Ws7 Match spelling to meaning when words sound the same (homophones), e.g. to/two/too, right/write.	

Related resources
- Audio files: *The Youngest*; *Meeting Mr Faulkner*; *The Longest Journey in the World*; *The New Boy*
- PCM 13: Reading aloud
- PCM 14: Write your own poem

Week 1

Student's Book pages 51–56

Workbook pages 31–33

Introducing the unit

Explain to learners that stories, plays and poems can often help us to think about difficult issues. If we are going through a difficult time, or have a problem, it can be very helpful to read about someone who has had a similar experience. Sometimes stories and poems about problems and dilemmas can also help us to think about how we would react if we ever found ourselves in difficult circumstances.

Encourage learners to contribute to a list of stories, films etc. that they have read or seen, which dealt with a problem or issue. You may be surprised how many stories fit this category! Sometimes, even fantasy stories (like Cressida Cowell's *How to Train Your Dragon* series) touch on real-life problems and dilemmas in a way that can be very interesting and helpful.

Student's Book pages 51–52

Reading, listening and speaking

Tell learners that they are going to listen to a poem by Michael Rosen. Read it aloud to the class with lots of expression, or play them the audio recording.

Ask learners what the narrator's main problem is in this poem, and clarify that it's about what it's like to be the youngest in the family, with a bossy big brother.

Then give learners time to read the poem aloud in their pairs, and discuss it using the prompts in the Student's Book. Walk around the class while they do this, so that you can check their understanding and make sure they are listening and responding appropriately to each other. Clarify any aspects of the poem that may be puzzling them.

The answers to the prompt questions are open, and largely a matter of personal opinion and interpretation, so accept any sensible responses. Encourage learners to back up their opinions with reasons, and quotations from the poem.

You may want to pause before they get to point 8 (choosing one of their stories to tell to the class). Encourage learners to make some notes to help them organize their story before they tell it. If they jot down the main points of the story in sequence, in about three to four sentences, this will help them to stick to the point and tell their story effectively.

When the pairs have had time to tell their stories, ask learners to practise reading the poem in groups of four. Give them time to read the poem through several times before they perform it, and listen to their practice readings so that you can give guidance if necessary.

Extension and support
More able learners should be able to produce a lively group performance of the poem, with all members of the group contributing appropriately.

Less able learners may need support in dividing the reading up between them, and help with working out how to read some of the lines expressively. PCM 13 contains a checklist to help learners with expressive reading; this may be a useful prompt for some groups.

Student's Book pages 53–54
Reading
Before learners work independently to read *Meeting Mr Faulkner* and answer the questions on it, you could read the text aloud to the whole group (or play the audio recording). This may help learners to understand the text, if some of the idiom used is unfamiliar to them. Circulate as they go on to read independently, so that you can check that they understand and help with any unfamiliar words. Then ask learners write the answers to the questions.

Many of the questions are open, but even for more closed questions, always allow learners their own variations in the answers, as long as the sense of the answer is correct, and the language used is appropriate.

Answers
2
a Judith
b 'I saw Jude's eyes widen to saucers' or 'Jude rushed upstairs, clutching her booty to her chest'.
c Open question; learners may feel that Kitty isn't quite sure whether she likes Gerald yet, and maybe she is worried or unhappy at the idea of her mum having a new friend like him.
d He doesn't show any sign of being worried about it – he cleverly speaks in such a way that Kitty doesn't have to answer if she doesn't want to.
e Open question; accept any reasonable response.
f 'Just then Floss padded in through the front door, and started rubbing up against his trouser legs as if she'd known and loved him all her life' or 'I was still trying to work it out (and Floss was still purring shamelessly) when Jude came thundering downstairs.'
g He doesn't know Floss's real name, but he doesn't want to ask Kitty what it is, so he uses 'Buster' as a nickname.
h Accept any reasonable synonyms for 'enraptured' and 'ambled'.
i Accept any three sentences from the text that use powerful verbs.
j An open question; accept any description that reflects the picture of Kitty built up in the text.
k Gerald knows which door leads to the kitchen, so Kitty thinks he must have been into the kitchen before.
l An open question; accept any reasonable answer that accords with the text.

Workbook page 31
Reading
Learners could complete this activity as a follow-up to reading *Meeting Mr Faulkner*. More able learners will be able to complete this activity independently for homework; less able learners may benefit from completing it in groups, with some assistance as necessary.

Answers
1
a He (wasn't) a posh banker, though he (did) (have) the most enormous box of chocolates (tucked) under one arm.

b I sidled out of the shadow.
c They were those rich, dark, expensive, chocolate-coated cream mints.
d Jude rushed upstairs, clutching her booty to her chest.
e Jude came thundering downstairs.
f He tipped the enraptured Floss into Jude's arms, and ambled past me with a nod.

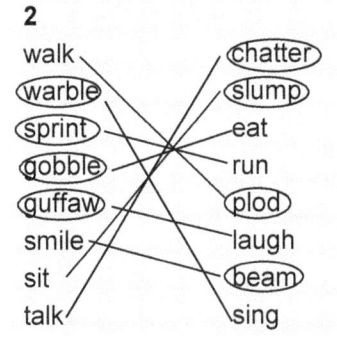

2

walk — chatter
warble — slump
sprint — eat
gobble — run
guffaw — plod
smile — laugh
sit — beam
talk — sing

Student's Book pages 55

Grammar
Use the prompts in the Student's Book to remind learners how adverbs are used. Encourage learners to think of an adverb each, and write their adverbs on the board. Then, as a whole group, think of a sentence using each adverb.

Learners can complete the questions in the Grammar section and the 'Thinking Deeper' box independently or in pairs. Some learners may need support with the 'Thinking Deeper' activity.

Answers
1
a   As he spoke, he was looking at Jude, but he did glance at me briefly.
b   He peered closely at a photo of me as a toddler.
c   "What a face!" he said admiringly.
2
Open question; accept any reasonable choice of more interesting/expressive adverbs.

Thinking deeper
1 The adverb describes how the person opened their mouth – i.e. as if they didn't believe it.

2 Open question – accept any grammatical reworking of the sentences including an appropriate adverb.

Workbook page 32

Grammar
Learners could attempt these activities independently, either in class or as homework. Review their work to make sure that they have understood how to use adverbs correctly.

Answers
1
a I stupidly put the ice cream in the oven instead of in the freezer.
b Jonathan jumped around excitedly.
c Samira looked sadly out of the window.
d "Yippee! We've got my favourite food for dinner!" yelped Mica delightedly.
e Rafiq clumsily dropped his glass on the floor.
f Miserably, Santi plodded home.
g "Never mind, Michael," Ella whispered softly.
h Mr Wong loudly shouted, "Go back to your seats at once!"

2 Open question; accept any accurately rewritten sentences with appropriate use of adverbs.
3 Learners' own answers.

Student's Book page 56

Grammar
Use the prompts in the Student's Book to remind learners about the structure of questions and statements. You could link this also to previous work on the structure of orders, and ask learners to give you examples of each sentence type. Write their suggested examples on the board, correcting any inaccuracies, as a preparation for the activities in the Student's Book.

Answers
3
a We saw the Eiffel Tower.
b I ate the cake.
c The boys were wearing sports gear.
d Miss Beckson was angry with Class 2.
e I was worried about the maths test.
4
a Have you done your homework?
b What is your favourite colour?
c Is Maya at home?
d What time do you go to bed?
e Do you have any pets?

Workbook page 33

Reading and writing
Ask learners to complete this activity either as homework or in class.

Answers
1
a Don't let me see you do that ever again! (O)
b How many sweets have you got left? (Q)
c Daniel's favourite red top had holes in it. (S)
d When did you first come to this school? (Q)
e Be careful when you are using knives! (O)
f I have always wanted to visit Barcelona. (S)
2 Open question; accept any accurately written and punctuated questions, statements and orders.

Weekly review

Level	Reading	Writing	Listening and speaking
■	This group may find it difficult to read a poem out loud with appropriate expression and fluency. They may need support to pay attention to sentence grammar and punctuation in order to read aloud fluently.	This group may need further practice to understand the structure of simple sentence types, and they may need support to remember all the relevant aspects of grammar, spelling and punctuation when writing their sentences.	At times this group needs support to organize ideas and use language appropriately when conveying their ideas in a whole-class or large group setting.
●	This group usually reads aloud accurately and fluently, with some appropriate expression. They may need support to read and fully understand more unfamiliar or challenging texts.	This group can normally identify different types of simple sentence, and write their own simple sentences conforming to most of the relevant grammar, spelling and punctuation rules.	This group can tell a simple story in a whole-class or large group setting, mostly sticking to the point and using appropriate language.
▲	This group reads aloud with accuracy, fluency and appropriate expression, creating an interesting experience for the listener and showing good understanding of what they have read.	This group can identify the three basic sentence types and write their own examples, showing a good understanding of basic punctuation, grammar and spelling.	This group demonstrates good simple storytelling ability, using their voices, facial expressions and vocabulary choices effectively.

Week 2

Student's Book pages 57–59

Introduction

Explain that learners are going to read another poem by Michael Rosen. You may choose to read or play this poem to the whole class before learners re-read the poem independently or in pairs. Allow time for learners to read the poem a couple of times before they answer the comprehension questions.

Student's Book pages 57–58

Reading
When learners have read the poem, they can tackle the comprehension questions independently or in pairs.

Answers
2a They are brothers, getting ready to go to bed.
b Neither of them wants to be the last into bed because they are scared of the dark.
c Open question, but learners should pick up that the journey into bed probably feels very long because the narrator is scared of the dark.
d Open question, but learners should understand that he probably feels relieved or happy; they may think he might feel a bit boastful or teasing as well.
e Water in a pipe.
f Open question. Learners may feel that there could be dangers in the room (it would be possible to trip over something in the dark, for instance) – but most of the dangers are in the narrator's head, caused by his fear of the dark.
g "I'm not scared!" or 'it takes so long', or 'It's the Longest Journey in the World'.
h Open question – accept any sensible answer that reflects the line chosen by the learner.
i Open question – accept any sensible opinion with clear reasons.

j Possible answers include: both poems tell us about a conversation; both poems are written in very natural, speech-like language; both poems tell us a lot about how the narrator feels; both poems have repeating lines; both poems are about family relationships.

Extension and support

More able learners should be able to answer the comprehension questions independently with minimal support.

Less able learners may benefit from discussing the questions with a partner before they write.

Student's Book page 58

Listening and speaking

Introduce the activity using the prompts in the Student's Book. Allow plenty of time for learners to practise reading and performing their chosen poem in their pairs before they perform it. Encourage learners to make some notes about their reasons for choosing their poem, and to practise explaining their reasons as well as practising the poem performance. You could give copies of PCM 13 to the pairs as a prompt to help them prepare for performance.

Student's Book page 59

Writing

The writing activity on PCM 14 offers a more scaffolded approach to writing a poem. There are various ways of organising this work, depending on the needs of learners:

- You could ask learners to complete the PCM before they tackle the Student's Book writing activity.
- You could use the PCM as the basis for a whole-class or large group poem, which would give you the opportunity to model the process for any learners or groups who might otherwise struggle with this.
- You could ask less able learners to complete the PCM instead of the Student's Book activity.
- You could ask learners to complete the PCM after doing the Student's Book activity, as reinforcement.

The answers to the PCM are open. The final poem should be written in learners' notebooks or on paper.

The Student's Book prompts take learners through the more open-ended writing activity in some detail. Allow plenty of time for them to complete all the stages, including the revision stage.

Extension and support

More able learners may be able to use the Student's Book prompts to structure their writing with little extra support.

It may be necessary to work with less able groups to make sure they understand all the steps and know what they need to do.

Celebrate learners' completed poems by creating a class display of their illustrated final work, and/or organising a performance session where everyone who wishes to can read their finished poem to the class.

Weekly review

Level	Reading	Writing	Listening and speaking
■	This group may find it difficult to read a poem out loud with appropriate expression and fluency. They may need support to pay attention to sentence grammar and punctuation in order to read aloud fluently.	This group is likely to need plenty of support when writing a less familiar type of text such as a poem. They will need plenty of opportunities to rehearse their work orally before writing, and they may benefit from a more structured/scaffolded approach to the activity.	This group needs plenty of practice and support when working up a poem for performance.
●	This group usually reads aloud accurately and fluently, with some appropriate expression. They may need support to read and fully understand more unfamiliar or challenging texts.	This group can work mostly independently to write a poem based on a clear model, though they may need some support to include poetic features such as repeating lines, interesting and vivid vocabulary choices, etc.	This group can work on a good straightforward performance of a poem with minimal support.
▲	This group reads aloud with accuracy, fluency and appropriate expression, creating an interesting experience for the listener and showing good understanding of what they have read.	This group can write an effective short poem based on a clear model, and will often include poetic features such as repeating lines, well-chosen vocabulary, etc.	This group can work mostly independently to produce an effective performance of a simple poem.

Week 3

Student's Book pages 60–62

Workbook pages 34–36

Student's Book pages 60–61

Reading, Comprehension

Before learners read *The New Boy* independently or in pairs, briefly discuss how they think it might feel to have just arrived in a new country, as well as a new school, not being able to speak the same language as everyone else. If any of learners have experienced this situation themselves, invite them to talk about it if they wish to (but don't pressurise them to share their experiences if they would rather not).

Then read *The New Boy* to the class, or play the audio, before learners tackle the text and questions for themselves. You may want to explain that the author of this story, Jamila Gavin, moved from India to the UK as a child, so her own experiences colour her writing. If learners are interested, you can do some research to find out more about this award-winning author

Answers

1

a Hindi

b Open question; learners may say that he is used to sitting on the ground, not at a table, or that he might be feeling awkward because he is new to the school.

c Because he is used to living somewhere with far fewer big buildings, cars etc., where you can see the sky and the ground and where food is grown locally.

d Open question; accept any three differences that are supported by the text.

e Open question; learners may feel that it is because the other children are pleased that Amrik is trying to speak English, and they find what he has said/the way that he said it amusing. If learners feel that it is because they are teasing Amrik, point out that the text doesn't really show much evidence of that – though of course some learners might well want to tease a new boy in this situation.

f Open question; accept any two reasonable ideas for ways of helping Amrik settle in.

g Open question; learners may say that the author's personal experience of moving to Britain from India give her writing more emotion, and make it more true-to-life.

Student's Book page 61
Reading and writing

Remind learners about how paragraphs are used in fiction, using the prompts in the Student's Book if you wish. Look at some books in the classroom to find examples of new paragraphs being used for a new speaker, and new paragraphs being used when something new happens in the story.

You can use this as an opportunity to draw learners' attention to the similarities between paragraphs and chapters – both are used to organize ideas in a book, as generally authors start a new chapter when something exciting or important happens in a story.

Remind learners if necessary that when using paragraph breaks for direct speech, we only need a new paragraph when a new speaker starts – we don't need a paragraph break if the same speaker continues, even if there's a sentence or two with no speech, between their speeches. So in the last paragraph of the Workbook text, there is no new paragraph before '"We won't get far without these!"', because the speaker is still Charlie.

Review learners' work on paragraphs to make sure they have understood the rules for paragraph breaks when writing their own continuation to the story.

Workbook page 34
Reading and writing

Invite learners to complete this activity either in class or as homework.

Answers
Paragraph breaks are shown with a double oblique line below.
"Come on, Charlie," said Maya. "We're going to miss the bus!" // "Hang on!" snapped Charlie. "Give me a moment – I'm nearly ready." // "Well," said Maya, "I'm going to the bus stop. I'll see you there – if the bus doesn't get there before you do!" // Maya skipped off down the road to the bus stop. Her friend Patsy was already waiting there. // "Hi, Patsy!" yelled Maya. "Are you going to the match too?" // "Of course!" said Patsy. "I wouldn't miss it – it's not every day that your team gets to the final!" // Just then, Charlie came running up, panting and puffing. "I think you forgot something, Maya," he gasped. He was waving a pair of tickets for the match. "We won't get far without these!"

Extension and support
If learners need more practice at using paragraphs appropriately, you could tackle the 'Thinking Deeper' activity on page 61 of the Student's Book as a whole-class or group activity, with teacher support as necessary.

More able learners may be able to complete this activity independently.

Answers
1 Paragraph 1: new event; paragraph 2: new event; paragraph 3: new speaker; paragraph 4: new speaker; paragraph 5: new event; paragraph 6: new speaker; paragraph 7: new speaker; paragraph 8: new speaker.
2. An open question. Review learners' work so that you can check they have understood the rules for creating new paragraphs.

Student's Book page 61
Spelling

Tackle this activity together as a whole-class activity.

Ask learners to come up to the board and write down any *ou* words they find in the extract, so that you have a complete list. Then model how to group the words according to how the *ou* is pronounced.

Finish by spending five minutes looking through other written materials in the classroom for extra *ou* words. You could make the sorted lists of *ou* words into a permanent classroom display, so that learners can add more words to the appropriate list as they come across them in their reading.

Answers
1 and **2**
ou as in 'round':
ground; our; out; playground; around; plough
ou as in 'soup':
you;
ou as in 'would':
could;
ou as in 'country':
countryside
ou as in 'flavour':
colour
3 Learners' own answers.

Invite learners to tackle the second activity, on words with the letter string *ough*, in groups or independently.

Answers
1 plough

2
cough
bought, ought, thought
rough, enough
borough, thorough
bough, drought
through
dough
enough

3 Encourage learners to add as many more *ough* words as possible to their lists.

Workbook page 35

Spelling

Learners can complete the Workbook spelling activity either in class or as homework.

Answers

1
ea as in 'head': dead, bread, breakfast, healthy, meadow, stealth, feather, thread, tread, spread,
ea as in 'teach': beach, seat, deal, heal, steal, leaves, feast, steam, reach, team, bead, treat, peak, leather
ea as in 'steak': great, break

2 Open questions; accept any accurately spelled sentences that use the target words appropriately.

Student's Book page 62

Writing

Ask learners to undertake this activity as an end of unit review activity. Before they start, remind them how to use a paragraph plan: by thinking about the main point they wish to get across in each paragraph and writing this as a heading on the plan, and then making notes about what they will say in each paragraph under each heading.

You may prefer learners who are struggling with writing to work collaboratively in groups on the planning and revision aspects of this activity; encourage them to write their final piece independently, however, so you can use it to assess their skills and understanding.

Tell learners that they can write as themselves, saying how they think they would feel if they were in a similar situation to Amrik; or they can write in character as someone else.

Workbook page 36

Writing

Learners could do this activity either in class or as homework, in preparation for the writing activity. Answers are open, but use this as an opportunity to check that learners understand what constitutes a 'more interesting' word, and encourage them to use more adventurous word choices if necessary.

Extension and support

Less able learners may need support to write their paragraph plans. You could talk them through the process as a group, modelling how you would go about planning this piece of work in paragraphs yourself, before they attempt to write their own plan.

Remind all learners, especially the more able, that you are expecting them to choose their words carefully for this piece, and use interesting and vivid words wherever possible, so the reader can imagine what is happening very clearly.

Page 62 of the Student's Book gives a checklist of things to look out for when revising learners' pieces. Remind them also of the need to use their best joined handwriting in their final work, so that it is easy to read and looks good on display.

Weekly review

Level	Reading	Writing
■	This group may need support to understand how stories are divided into paragraphs.	With support, especially at the planning stage, this group can write a simple recount using a paragraph plan.
●	This group should be able to grasp the concept of paragraphing with limited support.	This group can write and plan a short imaginative recount with little support.
▲	This understands clearly the concept of paragraphing and can explain with minimal support how a text is divided into paragraphs.	This group quickly grasps the concept of a paragraph plan and can independently apply this to their own short recount.

Unit 6 Making the headlines

Unit overview

This unit explores a range of journalistic writing, giving learners the opportunity to read and write different types of newspaper and magazine articles, including news reports, non-chronological reports and instructions. Learners will discuss the texts in groups and answer comprehension questions before writing their own texts based on the models provided. They will learn about the key features of journalistic writing, and practise summing up the key point of a text in few words. They will practise techniques for spelling words with more than one syllable, find out how to use commas around phrases in parenthesis, and continue to explore the use of connectives.

Reading	Writing	Listening and speaking
4R01 Extend the range of reading;	4W02 Explore the layout and presentation of writing, in the context of helping it to fit its purpose;	4SL4 Deal politely with opposing points of view;
4R02 Explore the different processes of reading silently and reading aloud;	4W05 Make short notes from a text and use these to aid writing;	4SL5 Listen carefully in discussion, contributing relevant comments and questions.
4R04 Use knowledge of punctuation and grammar to read with fluency, understanding and expression;	4W06 Collect and present information from non-fiction texts;	
4R05 Identify all the punctuation marks and respond to them when reading;	4W07 Re-read own writing aloud to check punctuation and grammatical sense;	
4R06 Apply phonic/spelling, graphic, grammatical and contextual knowledge in reading unfamiliar words;	4Wa2 Adopt a viewpoint as a writer, expressing opinions about characters or places;	
4R08 Express a personal response to a text, and link characters and settings to personal experience;	4Wa7 Write newspaper-style reports, instructions and non-chronological reports;	
4Rx1 Retell or paraphrase events from the text in response to questions;	4Wa8 Show awareness of the reader by adopting an appropriate style or viewpoint;	
4Rx2 Note key words and phrases to identify the main points in a passage;	4Wt2 Begin to use paragraphs more consistently to organise and sequence ideas;	
4Rx3 Distinguish between fact and opinion in print and IT sources;	4Wp1 Use a wider variety of connectives in an increasing range of sentences;	
4Rx4 Explore explicit meanings within a text;	4Wp2 Practise using commas to mark out meaning within sentences;	
4Ri2 Explore implicit meanings within a text;	4Wp6 Use a range of end-of-sentence punctuation with accuracy;	
4Rw5 Understand the use of connectives to structure an argument, e.g. if, although;	4Ws1 Extend knowledge and use of spelling patterns, e.g. vowel phonemes, double consonants, silent letters, common prefixes and suffixes; 4Ws2 Investigate spelling patterns; generate and test rules that govern them;	
4Rv1 Identify different types of non-fiction text and their known key features;	4Ws3 Check and correct spellings and identify words that need to be learned; :	
4Rv2 Read newspaper reports and consider how they engage the reader.	4Ws5 Revise rules for spelling words with common inflections, e;g; -ing, -ed, -s.	

Related resources

- Audio files: *Malala's award*; *Mini Mars mission*; *Fossil hunt*; *Make your own fossil!*
- PCM 2: Reading newspaper reports
- PCM 15: Who, what, when, where, why?
- PCM 16: Non-chronological reports
- PCM 17: Instructions

Documentary film about Malala's life: 'He called me Malala'

Week 1

Student's Book pages 63–66

Workbook pages 37–40

Introducing the unit

Bring in examples of several different types of newspaper to share with learners. (Check through in advance to make sure there are no articles that would be inappropriate to share with learners; if necessary you can just choose the most appropriate parts of the paper to show them.)

Invite each group or pair to choose an article that interests them. Give them five or ten minutes to read the article and then ask them to tell the class broadly what it is about. Make a list of the topics on the board so that learners can see that newspapers include a variety of different topics, from national and international news to sport, fashion, music and TV reviews.

Use learners' chosen articles to introduce or review the key features of a newspaper report:

- headline
- journalist's byline
- first summary sentence or paragraph (often in bold type)
- puns or jokes (if appropriate to the subject matter)
- emphatic or engaging language to grab the reader's attention
- quotations from witnesses or people involved in the story
- photographs of a key moment or person in the story.

Invite learners to find as many of these features as possible in their chosen article.

Then introduce learners to the idea that journalists often try to answer the following questions in the first few paragraphs of an article:

- **Who** is the article about?
- **What** happened to them, or what did they do?
- **When** did it happen?
- **Where** did it happen?
- **Why** or **how** did it happen?

Choose a couple of the newspaper articles and, as a whole class, try to identify the answers to these questions.

Ask learners to complete PCM 15 to give them further individual practice in answering these '5W' questions. This also gives you the opportunity to assess whether they have understood the principle.

Student's Book pages 63–64

Reading, listening and speaking

Tell learners that they are going to read and think about a newspaper article about a famous person, Malala Yousafzai. Ask them to share anything they already know about Malala. Then read the newspaper article aloud to the class, or play the audio recording.

Give learners an opportunity to read the text for themselves, and then discuss it in pairs. Circulate as they discuss, so that you can check how well they are listening and responding to each other, and contributing their own ideas. Praise any learners whom you hear dealing politely with an opposing viewpoint (for example, if one partner feels that Malala deserved her Nobel prize and the other does not).

If all of the pairs agree that Malala deserved her prize, you could play 'devil's advocate' and take the opposing view yourself, inviting learners to explain their reasons for thinking she deserved it. Use this as an opportunity to model courteous ways of dealing with opposing views.

Learners can work independently or in pairs to answer the comprehension questions. Many of the questions are open, but even for more closed questions, always allow learners their own variations in the answers, as long as the sense of the answer is correct, and the language used is appropriate.

Answers
3
a Who: Malala Yousafzai. What: received the Nobel Peace Prize. When: she heard about it during a chemistry lesson at school. Where: Malala originally lived in Pakistan; now she

lives in Britain. Why: she received the prize because of her bravery and work campaigning for the right to education.
b about 57 million
c She was calm – she decided to go to all her lessons and finish her day at school as usual.
d She is the youngest person/the first young woman ever to receive it
e Open question, but something like 'The Nobel Peace Prize is highly respected, and Malala received it together with another campaigner for children's rights.'
f It is a summary sentence that gives the reader the gist of the whole article.
g Open question: accept any sensible headline that sums up the story in five words or fewer.

Extension and support
You could ask a more able group or pair to discuss the questions in the Student's Book in front of the class. Ask the rest of the class to look out for good examples of the way the pair listen and respond to each other, and respect each other's views.

Less able learners may need further opportunities to practise responding appropriately to opposing viewpoints. You could choose a topic on which you know opinion is divided (such as which is the best football team/rock group etc.) and ask them to discuss it, modelling polite ways of disagreeing. ('I understand why you might think that, but my opinion is …' etc.)

Thinking deeper
Tackle these questions as a whole class, as it's important for all learners to understand how newspaper articles engage the reader.

Answers
1 The first paragraph tells us why Malala's work is important and why she was given the prize.
2 It's an open question as to whether learners feel this is an effective opening. On the plus side, it gives very important information about Malala and her award. It also stresses that Malala has worked hard to achieve what she has achieved.
3 Two sentences about Malala's feelings are I'm proud I'm the first Pakistani and the first young woman or the first young person who is getting this award. It's a great honour for me.' The writer probably wanted to include these because it makes Malala easier for the reader to identify with, if we know how she felt – we might imagine we would feel a bit like that ourselves, in her position.

Workbook page 37
Reading, listening and speaking
Ask learners to complete the activity for homework, using the article on page 63 of the Student's Book. The answers to this activity are open; accept any description that fits with the picture of Malala given in the article.

Workbook page 38
Reading, listening and speaking
If there is time, you could ask learners also to undertake this activity either at home or in

class. This activity also links well with later work in this unit, so it can be covered later on if that is preferable.

Student's Book page 65
Workbook page 39
Spelling
Use the prompts in the Student's Book to review the strategies for spelling multi-syllabic words with the whole class. They could work on the activity as a whole class, individually or in pairs. The words in the passage with more than two syllables (excluding names) are: chemistry, another, recognized, promoting, especially, million, recovered, continues, campaigning, decided, considered, organisations, outstanding, achievements, respected, slavery.

The rest of the questions are open, depending on the strategies learners choose to use, so it is worth circulating while they work on this activity so that you can check their understanding.

The Workbook spelling activity links with this work. It looks at the spelling of words with common inflections such as -ing and -ed. These are often multi-syllabic words, but the rules are mostly common to words of any length.

Answers
1
a	park	Spelling: parked, parking
b	dance	Spelling: danced, dancing
c	try	Spelling: tried, trying
d	jog	Spelling: jogged, jogging
e	step	Spelling: stepped, stepping
f	stamp	Spelling: stamped, stamping
g	carry	Spelling: carried, carrying
h	slope	Spelling: sloped, sloping
i	glide	Spelling: glided, gliding
j	bury	Spelling: buried, burying
k	drift	Spelling: drifted, drifting
l	change	Spelling: changed, changing
m	jump	Spelling: jumped, jumping
n	pin	Spelling: pinned, pinning

2
a walked b hurrying, tripped c placed d lifting
e married f voted g knitted h sliding

Student's Book page 66

Punctuation

Use the prompts in the Student's Book to show learners how commas can be used to separate out part of a sentence that is not essential to the meaning of the whole sentence. (You could introduce the term 'in parenthesis' for these phrases and clauses if you wish, but it isn't essential.) If this is new to learners, it may work well to tackle these questions as a whole class; otherwise, they can complete the questions independently or in pairs.

Answers

1 Malala shares this year's award with Kailash Satyarthi, **from India**, who has worked for children's rights and against child slavery.
2 a Kim's cat, whose name was Fluffy, was extremely fierce.
b My favourite to surfood, which I only have on my birthday, is pancakes.
c Kamal's little sister, who is only three, won a singing competition.
d My next-door neighbour, whose name is Mr Fanelli, grows delicious strawberries.
e I did the washing up, even though it wasn't my turn, because I wanted to surprise my mother.

Workbook page 40

Punctuation

Ask learners to complete this activity either as homework or in class.

Answers

1 a My dad, who goes out for a run every morning, is training for a 10-kilometre race.
b The sky, which had been so sunny in the morning, was now covered in thick clouds.
c I just nibbled one of the cookies, although Mum had told me not to, because they looked so delicious.
d Ali's hair, which hadn't been cut for a long time, was dangling in his eyes.
e I felt very cold, even though it was August, so I put on my thick coat.
2 Open question; accept any clauses or phrases that make sense in the context.

Weekly review

Level	Reading	Writing	Listening and speaking
■	This group may need support to read and understand a straightforward newspaper text, especially if it contains unfamiliar language or concepts.	This group may need further practice to understand the rules and tricks for spelling multi-syllable words and words with common inflections. They may need support to understand how commas can be used to separate out part of a sentence that gives extra information.	At times this group needs prompting to listen and respond appropriately in discussion, especially when there are opposing viewpoints.
●	This group can understand the gist of a straightforward newspaper article but may need help with aspects that are outside their experience.	This group can apply several rules and tricks for spelling multi-syllable words with little support; they may need reminding of other rules. They are often able to identify where commas should be used to separate out part of a sentence that gives extra information.	This group is learning to listen more effectively and respond more appropriately in discussion, and can sometimes think of polite ways of dealing with opposing viewpoints.
▲	This group is able to read and understand a straightforward newspaper article independently and accurately.	This group can apply several rules and tricks for spelling multi-syllable words, and may be able to derive their own spelling rules with support. They are able to identify where commas should be used to separate out part of a sentence that gives extra information.	This group normally listens effectively and responds appropriately in discussion, and can often think of polite ways of dealing with opposing viewpoints.

Week 2

Student's Book pages 67–70

Introduction
Explain that learners are going to read, talk about and answer questions on another newspaper article, before they go on to write one of their own. Read the article 'Mini Mars mission' to learners, or play the audio recording.

Student's Book pages 67–68
Reading, Listening and speaking
Give learners a chance to read the article independently, and then discuss the questions in the Student's Book in groups or pairs. It may be worthwhile recapping the difference between fact and opinion, before learners start (see Unit 2, page 16). Ask learners why they think a journalist might include opinions as well as facts in a newspaper article. (For example, people interviewed and quoted in the article might express an opinion; or the journalist might state or imply their own opinion. The use of opinions might help to engage the reader and make them think about their own opinion on the subject, and whether they agree with the stated opinions.)

You could ask learners to write the answers to the questions independently after they discuss them, or you could bring the whole class together to answer the questions orally once the groups or pairs have discussed them.

Answers
1
a Open question, so accept any accurate summary – for example 'A thirteen-year-old girl called Alyssa Carson wants to go to Mars when she grows up, and she is already training to be an astronaut with support from NASA.'
b and c Open question; accept any mind map with words and phrases that describe Alyssa.
d Open question; look for a reasoned explanation of the learner's views.
e The puns include 'high hopes', 'out of this world', 'watch this space'.
f Open question; learners may feel the puns help to engage the reader's attention and make them smile.
g Open question; look for a reasoned explanation of the learner's views.
h Accept any sentences that convey a fact/opinion; example of a sentence with a fact: 'She began training when she was only three years old!' A sentence with an opinion: 'I have made it this far and I don't think I'll be changing my mind.'
i The first planned Mars flight is due in 2033. Alyssa must have been born in about 2001, so she would be about 32 by the time she reaches Mars.

Student's Book pages 69–70
Writing
Planning and writing their own newspaper report should take learners at least two sessions. You may want to guide their choice of person to focus on; for example, you might choose to arrange a visit from an interesting person who lives locally, and ask the whole class to write about them. If some learners do choose to focus on a famous person, it's worth reviewing their choices before they start, to check that appropriate research material is available on websites and/or in books. If their first choice causes problems because of a lack of appropriate material, you can then guide them towards an alternative choice.

Learners can use the prompts in the Student's Book to help them structure the planning, drafting and final writing phase of their article. Circulate among the groups as they work, to check that they understand what to do and to help keep them on track if necessary.

Extension and support
More able learners should be able to research their subject in reasonable depth (asking polite but probing questions if they are interviewing someone, or collecting and noting down useful information from books and websites). They may write an extended article running to several paragraphs. Remind them to make sure that their paragraphs are well organized, so that all the facts about a particular topic are grouped together.

Less able learners may benefit from using PCM 2 to help them structure a much briefer article. They could write collaboratively in a group, rehearsing their sentences orally before writing.

Weekly review

Level	Reading	Writing	Listening and speaking
■	This group may need prompting to apply what they learned in the first part of this unit to reading a further newspaper account. However, they should be starting to find it easier to identify the key elements of a newspaper report and understand the structure.	This group is likely to need plenty of support when researching writing a newspaper report. They are likely to benefit from a structured/scaffolded approach to the activity.	This group may need support to stay on track when discussing what they have read
●	This group is getting to know the key features and structure of a newspaper report and can often identify these in reading.	This group can work mostly independently to write a newspaper report based on a clear model, though they may need some support to include all of the key features of the genre.	This group can normally discuss their reading sensibly, taking turns and listening to each other..
▲	This group reads and understands a range of simple newspaper reports and can talk about the key features and structure.	This group can use the key features of a newspaper report effectively to write a simple article, drawing on models they have read and on their own research.	This group can work mostly independently to discuss their reading, listening and responding to each other's points courteously.

Week 3

Student's Book pages 71–74

Workbook page 41

Student's Book pages 71–73

Reading

To introduce this part of the unit on magazine texts, bring in a range of magazines for learners to look at. Magazines about animals, sports and history are often a good choice, as are the weekend magazine supplements included with some newspapers. Distribute the sample magazines and ask learners to note down all the different types of text they can find. Then share their findings as a whole class. Make the point that magazines often contain a very wide range of different types of text, including non-chronological reports, explanations, quizzes, interviews and instructions.

Give learners time to read 'Fossil Hunt' and 'Make your own fossil' (or play the audio recording). They can then tackle the comprehension questions individually or in pairs.

Answers

2

a 'Make your own fossil' is an instruction text, and 'Fossil Hunt' is a non-chronological report. Learners may mention various clues, including a bulleted equipment list, numbered instructions and order-style sentences beginning with command verbs for the instructions; and clear headings that pose questions that are answered in the text, with paragraphs grouping similar information together, for the non-chronological report.

b Open question, but learners may feel that a variety of different kinds of text helps to make the magazine more interesting to read, and also make it more likely that every reader will find something they want to read.

c Somewhere where there is sedimentary rock, such as a beach, field or farmland.

d Your eyes.

e Fossil hunting can be dangerous, for example if there are rockfalls or a risk of getting cut off by the tide.

f Open question, but for example, three attention-grabbing sentences are: 'Here's what you need to know if you want to be a fossil hunter!', 'If you are very lucky and live in the right place, you might even find a fossil in your garden!' and 'The best bit of kit is your eyes!'

g Open question; learners may mention that the headings help the reader to see what the report is about, and to find the information they need.
h You use it to make the shape of the fossil, by pouring it over modelling clay that has the impression of a toy or shell in it.
i You take the plastic toys out, because you need to pour the plaster into the impression left behind by the toys.
j Most of the questions are orders; you can tell because there is a command verb at or near the start of the sentence and the sentences address the reader directly.
k Open question; probably because the numbers help the reader to see the order in which things have to be done.
l Open question; learners may mention that the instruction text starts with an attention-grabbing opening aimed at making the reader feel it would be good to make a fossil.
m Open question. Learners may feel that the instructions could be easier to follow if precise instructions were given for using the plaster of Paris, or if there were photos showing each stage of the process.

Briefly recap learners' earlier work on connectives if necessary, and then use the prompts in the Student's Book to introduce the idea that connectives are used differently in different types of text. You could go through the questions in the Student's Book as a whole class, or ask learners to answer them independently.

Answers
3
a I went down to the beach (and) jumped straight into the waves.
b (Unfortunately/however/next), I trod on a crab.
c My toe went bright red, (because/as/after/when) the crab nipped it.
d I showed my sister, (but/and) she just laughed at me.
e (However/meanwhile/despite this), when I got home, Mum gave me a plaster for my sore toe.

Extension and support
Ask more able learners to write a list of connectives that are particularly useful when presenting a point of view or an argument – for example, *therefore, however, moreover, because, on the other hand, despite this, so, in conclusion*. Challenge them to write a couple of paragraphs giving their point of view on an issue of their choice, and to use as many appropriate connectives as possible.

Give less able learners some examples of texts that state an argument or point of view, and ask them to find as many connectives as they can in the texts.

Workbook page 41
Reading
Learners could complete this activity in class or as homework. Ask them to work independently on this, so that you have an opportunity to assess their understanding.

Answers
1
a First, take a paper plate and put the mug or glass down in the middle of it. Draw round the mug or glass so there is a circle in the middle of the plate.
b Next/then cut the circle out of the middle of the plate so you are left with a ring.
c Next/then do the same with three of the other plates.
d Colour or paint the rings using bright colours.
e Finally/next/then, take the cardboard tube and stick it to the last plate with sticky tape, so it will stand upright.
f Now/finally/then throw your rings and see how many you can get to land over the tube!

2
a First, (take) a paper plate and (put) the mug or glass down in the middle of it. (Draw) round the mug or glass so there is a circle in the middle of the plate.
b Next/then (cut) the circle out of the middle of the plate so you are left with a ring.
c Next/then (do) the same with three of the other plates.
d (Colour) or (paint) the rings using bright colours.
e Finally/next/then, (take) the cardboard tube and (stick) it to the last plate with sticky tape, so it will stand upright.
f Now/finally/then (throw) your rings and (see) how many you can get to land over the tube!

Student's Book page 74
Writing
Ask learners to undertake this as an end of unit review activity. Before they start, remind them about the structure of non-chronological reports and instructions. You can use PCMs 16 and 17 as a focus for this, or ask learners in more able groups to look at the examples in the Student's Book and write their own list of common features in instructions and reports.

Before learners start planning their pieces, check that they have chosen a sensible topic (probably connected to a favourite hobby or sport) and that they have the necessary resources to research it if they need to. It may simplify things if you can organize the class into a few groups who are writing on similar topics, so that they can share research and support each other.

Sample learners' work and discussions as they begin the drafting and writing process, and remind them to use the stylistic features of reports and instructions in their own writing (using PCMs 16 and 17 to jog their memories if necessary). Encourage them to use the checklists in the Student's Book to make sure that they include all the necessary elements in their writing.

You could make a class magazine using the learner's finished pieces, and leave it in the library or book corner for other classes to browse through.

Extension and support

You can simplify this task further for learners who are struggling with writing. For example, you may ask them to choose just one piece of writing (for example the instructions) rather than two. You could ask them to use PCM 16 or PCM 17 to structure their writing (and if you wish they could actually complete the writing on a copy of the relevant PCM).

More able learners could write a more extended non-chronological report on their chosen topic, perhaps including a mock interview or quotes from a famous person, or a quiz for the reader.

Weekly review

Level	Reading	Writing
■	This group may need support to understand the structure and features of different types of non-fiction writing. It may help them to discuss what they have read in a group or pair, before answering comprehension questions.	This group may need support and scaffolding to write a straightforward instruction text and/or non-chronological report.
●	This group can identify some key differences between instructions and non-chronological reports, and can work mostly independently to answer straightforward comprehension questions.	This group can write and plan a short instruction text and non-chronological report with little support.
▲	This group understands the key features and structure of instructions and non-chronological reports, and can work independently to answer comprehension questions on them.	This group can accurately use the key features of instruction texts and non-chronological reports in their own writing.

Formal assessment 2

Use this test to assess how well learners have managed to cover the objectives from the last three units. Hand out the sheets and let learners complete them under test conditions. Collect and mark their tests, recording the results in your class record book. Use the mark scheme below.

Assessment 2 Mark Scheme **Total 27**

Question 1

Reading

A Accept any clear and accurate sentence that sums up the main point of the report in the learner's own words, e.g. 'Felix Baumgartner broke the world record for the highest skydive when he jumped from 39 kilometres above Earth.' (1)

B Joe Kittinger was the holder of the previous skydiving world record, having jumped from 31 kilometres above Earth, so he had useful experience which would allow him to help Felix. (Or similar sentence in the learner's own words.) (1)

C It was lifted up by a huge helium balloon. (1)

D Accept any two accurate sentences that describe Felix Baumgartner drawing on information from the text, in the learner's own words. (2 – one mark for each sentence)

E Nine minutes. (1)

F Highest BASE jump from a building. (1)

G Learner's own words, but they should make the point that it is an attention-grabbing opening and/or that the question makes the reader think about what they are reading. (1)

Question 2
Grammar, vocabulary and punctuation
A Statement: accept any sentence from the report that is a statement. Question: 'Have you ever wondered what it would be like to jump from 39 kilometres above the surface of the Earth?' Order: 'Ask Felix Baumgartner – the only human being who has ever tried it.' (3 – one mark for each correct sentence)

B Find out about the champion skydiver Felix Baumgartner.

Tell your friends about Felix's amazing adventure. (2 – one mark for each correctly rewritten sentence)

C But for Felix, the ultimate challenge was to <u>annihilate</u> Colonel Joe Kittinger's record for the highest ever skydive. (beat, smash or a similar verb of the learner's choice)

Less than a minute after <u>evacuating</u> the pod, he had reached his maximum speed of 1,358 kilometres per hour. (leaving, or a similar verb of the learner's choice)

(2 – half a mark for each correct underlining, and half a mark for each alternative verb)

D Felix Baumgartner, the record-breaking skydiver, is the only person who has ever jumped from 39 kilometres above Earth.

Felix made his amazing jump, having spent many months preparing for it, in October 2012.

(2 – one mark for each correctly punctuated sentence.)

Question 3
Writing
A 10 marks – allow one mark for each of five sentences, and one mark for fulfilling each of these criteria:
- a headline
- a punchy opening
- the key facts
- the learner's own opinion of what Felix did
- at least two sentences with powerful verbs.

Unit 7 Inventions

Unit overview

This unit looks at two different types of reference text: alphabetically organized encyclopaedias and explanations. Learners will read extracts from an encyclopaedia about inventions, and explanations about how some of the inventions work. They will answer comprehension questions and practise writing their own encyclopaedia entries and explanations, based on the model texts they have read. They will also write a letter to a newspaper putting forward their own point of view and giving reasons. The unit also includes a poem on the subject of inventions, and offers opportunities to explore alphabetical order, revise end-of-sentence punctuation and look at past, present and future tenses in a range of different types of sentence.

Reading	Writing	Listening and speaking
4R01 Extend the range of reading;	4W02 Explore the layout and presentation of writing, in the context of helping it to fit its purpose;	4SL1 Organise ideas in a longer speaking turn to help the listener;
4R04 Use knowledge of punctuation and grammar to read with fluency, understanding and expression;	4W05 Make short notes from a text and use these to aid writing;	4SL2 Vary use of vocabulary and level of detail according to purpose;
4R05 Identify all the punctuation marks and respond to them when reading;	4W06 Collect and present information from non-fiction texts;	4SL4 Deal politely with opposing points of view;
4R06 Apply phonic/spelling, graphic, grammatical and contextual knowledge in reading unfamiliar words;	4W07 Re-read own writing aloud to check punctuation and grammatical sense;	4SL5 Listen carefully in discussion, contributing relevant comments and questions;
4R08 Express a personal response to a text, and link characters and settings to personal experience;	4Wa2 Adopt a viewpoint as a writer, expressing opinions about characters or places;	4SL6 Adapt the pace and loudness of speaking appropriately when performing or reading aloud.
4Rx1 Retell or paraphrase events from the text in response to questions;	4Wa6 Elaborate on basic information with some detail;	
4Rx2 Note key words and phrases to identify the main points in a passage;	4Wa8 Show awareness of the reader by adopting an appropriate style or viewpoint;	
4Rx4 Explore explicit meanings within a text;	4Wa9 Present an explanation or a point of view in ordered points, e.g. in a letter;	
4Ri2 Explore implicit meanings within a text;	4Wa11 Summarise a sentence or a paragraph in a limited number of words;	
4Rw5 Understand the use of connectives to structure an argument, e.g. if, although;	4Wt2 Begin to use paragraphs more consistently to organise and sequence ideas;	
4Rw6 Understand how points are ordered to make a coherent argument;	4Wp1 Use a wider variety of connectives in an increasing range of sentences;	
4Rv1 Identify different types of non-fiction text and their known key features;	4Wp3 Experiment with varying tenses within texts, e.g. in dialogue;	
	4Wp4 Investigate past and present tenses and future forms of verbs;	

4Rv3 Understand how persuasive writing is used to convince a reader.	4Wp5 Confirm all parts of the verb to be and know when to use each one;	
	4Wp6 Use a range of end-of-sentence punctuation with accuracy;	
	4Ws3 Check and correct spellings and identify words that need to be learned;	
	4Ws8 Use all the letters in sequence for alphabetical ordering;	
	4Ws9 Build words from other words with similar meanings, e.g. medical, medicine;	
	4Ws10 Collect and classify words with common roots, e.g. invent, prevent.	

Related resources

- Audio files: *Encyclopaedia of Inventions*; *A Good Idea*; *How do zips work?*
- PCM 18: Writing a letter
- PCM 19: Letter to a newspaper

Week 1

Student's Book pages 75–79

Workbook pages 42–43

Introducing the unit

Bring in a range of reference texts for learners to look at – including dictionaries, encyclopedias and other clearly-organized reference books. You could also give access to searchable reference websites such as the Natural History Museum website (nhm.ac.uk).

Give each group or pair different types of reference texts, and tell them that they have ten minutes to look at how their texts are organized, and what a reader might use them for. Ask them to make brief notes about this so that they can feed back to the rest of the class.

Share learners' thoughts about their reference texts. Look in particular at how these texts are organized. For example, many reference texts use alphabetical ordering; others use clear headings that are grouped thematically so that the reader can easily find particular information. Historical texts are often organized chronologically. Talk about how it's particularly important for a reference text to be clearly organized, since this helps the reader to find specific information.

Spend some time looking at how illustrations are used in the reference texts, and identifying what extra information they add to the text.

Ask each group or pair to think of at least one question that can be answered using one of their reference texts. Then swap texts and questions with another group, and find out the answer to the other group's question.

Student's Book pages 75–78

Reading

Learners can read the extract from *An Encyclopaedia of Inventions* either silently to themselves, or out loud in a group or pair. You may wish to play the audio recording through once before learners do this. Circulate while they are reading so that you can answer any questions or explain words they do not know.

Learners can then answer the comprehension questions individually or in pairs. Many of the questions are open, but even for more closed questions, always allow learners their own variations in the answers, as long as the sense of the answer is correct, and the language used is appropriate.

Answers
2 a John Montagu, Earl of Sandwich, because he created the first sandwich.
b Cardigan and Wellington boot
c It was made of wood, and it had no pedals.
d 1938
e 1913
f They keep the windscreen clear of rainwater, so the driver can see properly.

g It was cleaner because there was less risk of spilling ink; it was also quicker and more convenient.
h leather
i Open question, but key words and phrases include: 'said to have been invented by John Montagu', 'didn't want to stop for a proper meal', 'meat between two slices of bread'.
j Open question; answer should be along the lines of 'John Montagu invented the sandwich because he didn't want to stop playing cards and eat a proper meal'.
k Alphabetically by name of invention.
l aeroplane
ballpoint pen
   battery
bicycle
cardigan
   central heating
   computer
fridge
   light bulb
   microwave
sandwich
   scooter
   telephone
   washing machine
wellington boot
   wheelchair
windscreen wiper
3 badminton, baseball, basketball, cricket, football, rounders, rugby, squash, table tennis, tennis, volleyball

Alphabetical order
If learners are not familiar with the idea of using more than one letter in a word to work out alphabetical order, use the 'Alphabetical order' box to introduce this idea. It can help to write the words on separate slips of paper, so that learners can experiment with putting them in order, and only write the words as a list once they are sure.

Extension and support
More able groups can complete the 'Alphabetical order' activity independently, and they may also be able to create their own alphabetic list (perhaps related to a favourite hobby) using up to the first four or five letters of some words to determine the correct order.

Less able learners may need further opportunities to practise ordering words alphabetically. If they are struggling, give them a list of words that can be ordered using the first letter of each word alone, and make sure they have access to a chart or list showing alphabetical order. Once they are confident in ordering words alphabetically using the first letter, introduce some words where they need to look at the second letter, and so on.

Workbook pages 42–43
Spelling
The Workbook activity on alphabetical order provides extra practice, and can be completed in class or as homework.

Answers
1 anteater; antelope; elephant; elk; hare; hippopotamus; kangaroo; koala; lion; lizard; mouse; rabbit
2 Bains; Burroughs; Howard; Hussain; Khan; Latimer; Lau; Patel; Persaud; Peters; Smithson; Wang
3 Open question; check that learners have put their chosen names in the correct alphabetical order from left to right.

Student's Book pages 78–79
Listening and speaking
Circulate while learners discuss the prompts in the Student's Book in their pairs or groups. Some groups may need help to remember to listen to each other's views and respond courteously to others who don't agree with them. You could model this for them if necessary, by suggesting an alternative, politer way of responding. Remind learners to make notes so they can remember their key reasons for deciding on the most and least important inventions. Encourage them to practise explaining their reasons so that they are able to do so concisely when presenting their group's views to the rest of the class.

If you wish, you could have a vote to find the most popular and least popular invention.

Workbook page 44
Reading
Before learners turn their notes from the speaking and listening activity into a letter explaining their views, you may wish to give them PCM 19 and ask them to complete the Workbook activity, which includes a helpful model of a letter to a newspaper. Alternatively, this activity can be done later, either in class or as homework.

Answers
1. The internet helps people to stay connected, even if they live far apart; it contains useful information; it is a source of entertainment; it is convenient for shopping.
2. It helps people who live far apart to stay in touch.

3 6 January
4 Open question; look for at least open reason to explain the learner's opinion.
5 Open question; look for a clear explanation and at least two supporting reasons.
6 Any three connectives from: first of all; so; but; also; secondly; if; in addition; when; and; in conclusion/
7 Accept any correctly identified and written sentence in the present tense.
8 Accept any correctly written version of the sentence that changes it to the past tense.
9 Key words and phrases: connect people; far apart; video calls; speak; see; email; stay in touch. Accept any sentence that sums up the main point of the paragraph, for example: *The internet connect people who live far apart, as they can use video calls and email to stay in touch.*
10 Accept any sentence that sums up the main point of the letter, for example: *The internet is the best invention of the last hundred years because it helps people stay in touch, it is a source of information and enjoyment and it can make life easier.*

Student's Book page 79

Writing
Learners can use the prompts in the Student's Book, along with their notes, to help them structure their own letter. Encourage them to use the bulleted lists at first draft stage, so they can check they have included all the necessary information and features.

Extension and support
More able learners should be able to write a letter that presents their argument in an ordered way, working mostly independently. However, it may be useful to review their work at draft stage so that you can prompt them to make any necessary changes.

Less able learners may benefit from using the letter writing frame on PCM 18 to help them structure their letter. They may also work in pairs or groups, discussing the letter as they write. You can support them by checking their work at each stage, and discussing what they need to do so that they understand. Their final draft could be a collaborative effort or written individually, as you prefer.

Weekly review

Level	Reading	Writing	Listening and speaking
■	This group may need support to read and use an alphabetically organized reference text. They may benefit from answering the comprehension questions orally or as a group.	This group may need support when writing a letter that explains their views. They will benefit from rehearsing their views orally and from using a writing frame to help structure their letter.	At times this group needs prompting to listen and respond appropriately in discussion, especially when there are opposing viewpoints.
●	This group can understand a simple alphabetically organized reference text and should be able to work mostly independently, with some support from the teacher as necessary.	This group may need some support initially when writing a letter that explains their views, but they should be able to finish the task fairly independently.	This group is learning to listen more effectively and respond more appropriately in discussion, and can sometimes think of polite ways of dealing with opposing viewpoints.
▲	This group is able to read and understand an alphabetically organized reference text independently and accurately.	This group can work independently to write a letter that explains their views, using an existing letter as a model if necessary.	This group normally listens effectively and responds appropriately in discussion, and can often think of polite ways of dealing with opposing viewpoints.

Week 2

Student's Book pages 80–83

Workbook page 45–46

Introduction
Explain to learners that this week they are going to read and think about a poem about an invention, and then they will design and write about a new invention of their own.

Student's Book pages 80–81
Reading
Play the audio recording of the poem to learners, or read it aloud to them. Then ask them to read it through out loud in their pairs, taking one role (inventor or questioner) each. If possible, give the pairs time to practise and perfect their reading, adding suitable expression and emphasis, and maybe also developing some actions to go with the poem. The pairs could then take turns to perform the poem for the class.

You could ask learners to write the answers to the questions independently, or to discuss them first in their pairs or groups.

Answers
2
a Open question; look for a good description of the invention in the learner's own words. The description should cover the key facts: the invention is to help Mum get the dinner ready, and it has different arms that do different things including stirring gravy, peeling and chopping potatoes, and going to the shop to buy potatoes.
b Open question, but learners should spot that the start of the poem says 'I might just make one of my inventions' – this suggests that the inventor has made inventions before.
c Open question – look for good clear reasons for the learner's view.
d The greengrocer's.
e There is money in the basket, so the greengrocer can take out the money and put in the potatoes.
f In case someone tries to steal the money.
g To help Mum/so that Mum can have time off.
h Because the invention won't be ready in time for dinner (if ever!).
i Open question; accept any question and answer from the poem.
j Open question; the speakers are the inventor and someone else, who could be a friend or a family member (though not Mum).

Student's Book page 81
Grammar
Learners could complete these questions independently, or you may prefer to discuss the questions as a whole class and complete them orally.

Answers
1 Accept any sentences from the poem that are in the present and the future.

2
a I will go into town with Mara and Jake.
b Dad is cross with us.
c Uncle Ike will make lamb curry for dinner.
d My favourite TV show was *Dinosaur Wars*.
e It will be bedtime when we get to Gran's house.
f Jamie is running home because it is raining.

Workbook page 45
Grammar
Learners can complete this activity independently, in class or for homework.

Answers
1
a Orla won the running race.
b I was glad to see Ella.
2
a We will go to the beach on Saturday.
b They will paint Grace's bedroom pink.
3
a Janine sees the three kittens.
b Mum is going to the shops. (or 'Mum goes').
4
It was Saturday afternoon, and I was bored. Well, can you blame me? Nothing interesting will ever happen in our house. I had played all my games and read all my books, and I had nothing to do.
Suddenly, there was a knock on my bedroom door. I got a shock!
"Who is that? What do you want?"
I crept to the door and opened it. You will never guess what I saw!

Extension and support
More able learners should be able to identify the tenses used, and change tenses as required, working mostly independently.

Less able learners may benefit from working together as a group to answer these questions, with teacher support as needed.

Student's Book page 82
Grammar
Encourage learners to read through the poem in their pairs before they add the missing punctuation – this will help them work out which sentences are questions or exclamations, and which are simple statements.

Answers
I'm bored with walking to school.
Today I'm going to fly there!
But where are your wings?

Here they are, in my bag.
They're a bit crumpled,
but they're not broken.
How do they work?
I just pull this string
and jump up into the air
as high as I can.
Then I make a wish and –
look – I can fly!

Workbook page 46
Grammar

Learners can then complete independently.

Answers
1 a I'm so glad you're coming round to our house to play!
b Do you like chocolate?
c It's my dad's birthday on Wednesday.
d My teacher's name is Mrs Ismael.
e There's a wasp on your arm!
f I've never felt so happy!
g There's a dragon in the playground!
h How many sisters do you have?
i Dad's favourite colour is green.
j On Saturday we went to the shops.
Question 2 is open, so accept any accurately punctuated sentences that fit the brief.

Student's Book page 83
Listening and speaking

Ask learners to use the prompts in the Student's Book to help structure their discussion about their inventions. If any learners struggle to think of an idea for an invention, prompt them to think about their favourite hobby or activity – what could they invent that would help them with this?

Circulate among the groups so that you can make sure they are discussing the inventions constructively. Remind them to make notes of their ideas, so that they can use these in the writing activity that follows.

Extension and Support

The notes in the Student's Book, page 83, can be used to structure the writing activity. Encourage learners to re-read the *Encyclopaedia of Inventions* to help them structure their pieces in a similar way.

Support less able learners as they work and check that they go through all the suggested stages as they write.

When learners have written their pieces, review them as a whole class. Make a list of the inventions and ask learners to order the list alphabetically. Then you can make an alphabetically organized class Encyclopaedia of Inventions!

Weekly review
Use this rubric to assess learners' progress as they worked through the activities this week.

Level	Reading	Writing	Listening and speaking
■	This group may need extra practice and support to read a poem out loud with appropriate expression and actions.	This group needs support to write a short encyclopedia entry based on a clear model text.	This group may need support to stay on track when discussing their ideas.
●	After practising, this group should be able to understand how to read a poem aloud with some appropriate expression, intonation and actions.	This group can work mostly independently to write a short encyclopedia entry based on a model text.	This group can normally discuss their ideas sensibly, taking turns and listening to each other.
▲	This group is able to develop a performance of a poem with appropriate expression, intonation and actions, working mostly independently.	This group can confidently use most of the features of a short encyclopedia entry in their own writing, with minimal support.	This group can work mostly independently to discuss their ideas, listening and responding to each other's points courteously.

Week 3

Student's Book pages 84–86

Workbook pages 47–48

Student's Book page 84
Reading
Give learners time to read *How do zips work?* (or play the audio recording). They can then tackle the comprehension questions individually or in pairs.

Answers
3
a Open question; answers along the lines of 'The teeth of a zip are the metal bits that stick out on either side of the zip and lock together when the slider is pulled.'
b Ingenious.
c It forces the teeth on either side of the zip together (to close the zip) or apart (to open the zip).
d Open question; perhaps in order to separate out the information clearly and make it easier to read and follow.
e The present tense. Open question; perhaps because the text is describing something that is happening (or could be happening) in the present, not just in the past or future.
f Open question; perhaps because diagrams can help to convey a complex process more clearly than words alone.

Student's Book page 85
Writing
This short writing activity provides useful practice for the longer writing activity that concludes this unit.

Use the prompts in the Student's Book to structure this activity, and circulate as learners work on their explanations, in pairs or individually. You could introduce the task by discussing what learners have to do as a whole class, and talking about the information that the diagram gives us. You could model how to turn this information from the diagram into a few sentences of continuous text.

Extension and support
More able groups should be able to write a brief explanation text modelled on the one about zips, using just the information from the Student's Book.

Less able groups may benefit from working collaboratively on this task, and you may want to work with the group so that you can make sure they understand what they need to do.

Student's Book page 85
Spelling
Introduce this activity by reminding learners about their previous work on word families and words based on a common root. Explain that when we make a noun from a verb, the noun normally ends in 'ion' or 'ment'. You could do Spelling activity 1 as a whole class, and then ask learners to complete the 'Thinking Deeper' activity independently.

Answers
1 invent
move
judge
act
imagine
2 open question

Thinking deeper

Answers
1 Noun.
2 Words from the 'enjoy' family, including enjoy, enjoying, enjoyable, unenjoyable.
3 Words from the 'agree' family, including agreement, agreeing, agreeable, disagreeable, disagreement.

Workbook pages 47–48
Spelling
Learners can complete this activity either in class or as homework.

Answers
1
excitement — excite
celebration — celebrate
management — manage
connection — connect
agreement — agree
decision — decide
definition — define
argument — argue
diversion — divert
measurement — measure
education — educate
operation — operate
2
a announce
b contradict
c punish
d demonstrate
e entertain
f co-operate
g encourage

3
a decoration
b possession
c assessment
d navigation
e payment
f irritation
g announcement

Use this work as an opportunity to revise spelling patterns for adding other common suffixes and inflections, as well as *-ment* and *-ion*; for example *-ing*, *-ed* and *-s*.

Student's Book page 86

Writing

Ask learners to undertake this activity as an end of unit review activity. Encourage them to use the short explanation text that they wrote about ballpoint pens as a model for this piece of work. (It may be worth displaying one or two good examples from the class on the wall, so that learners who may not have produced a clear model themselves can use these to help them structure their work.)

Encourage learners to rehearse their explanations orally before they start to write; explaining things orally is a good preparation for writing. Listen in to the pairs' verbal explanations as they do this, and prompt them to include any aspects of the explanation that they may have forgotten.

Check that learners make clear notes under the headings suggested, and that they use these notes to help them structure their final text. Encourage learners to use the prompts in the Student's Book when they check their work.

Extension and support

More able groups could write an additional explanation text based on the invention that they made up, earlier in the unit. Can they explain clearly how their invention would work, and draw a diagram to go with this?

Less able groups may benefit from a sheet to help them structure their explanation, with the headings suggested in the Student's Book notes presented for them, with space to write under each heading.

Weekly review

Level	Reading	Writing	Listening and speaking
■	This group may need support to understand the structure and features of explanation texts and other reference texts. It may help them to discuss their understanding out loud before writing.	This group may need support and scaffolding to write a straightforward explanation text.	This group may need help to stay on track when discussing texts they are reading and writing.
●	This group can identify some key features of explanation texts and other reference texts, and is beginning to understand how these texts work.	This group can write and plan a short explanation text with little support.	This group can work mostly independently to rehearse what they are going to write orally before writing.
▲	This group understands the key features and structure of explanation texts and other reference texts, and can replicate many of these in their own writing.	This group can accurately use the key features of explanation texts to help them write an interesting and comprehensible explanation.	This group uses discussion to refine their ideas for writing, helping them to make improvements to their final text.

Unit 8 Putting on a show

Unit overview

In this unit, learners will read a playscript version of the musical story *Peter and the Wolf*, and also read and compare a story and a playscript about a real-life dilemma. They will explore the common features of playscripts, answer comprehension questions and have a go at writing their own mini-plays. They will act out their plays and explore various drama activities in role. They will look at powerful verbs and adverbs, and will practise spelling words with the common prefixes *im-*, *in-*, *ir-* and *il-*, and the suffixes *-able* and *-ible*. They will also revise alphabetical order, and apply it when using dictionaries.

Reading	Writing	Listening and speaking
4R01 Extend the range of reading;	4W02 Explore the layout and presentation of writing, in the context of helping it to fit its purpose;	4SL1 Organise ideas in a longer speaking turn to help the listener;
4R02 Explore the different processes of reading silently and reading aloud;	4W04 Look for alternatives for overused words and expressions;	4SL2 Vary use of vocabulary and level of detail according to purpose;
4R04 Use knowledge of punctuation and grammar to read with fluency, understanding and expression;	4W07 Re-read own writing aloud to check punctuation and grammatical sense;	4SL3 Understand the gist of an account or the significant points and respond to main ideas with relevant suggestions and comments;
4R05 Identify all the punctuation marks and respond to them when reading;	4W08 Write sentences, dictated by the teacher, from memory;	
4R06 Apply phonic/spelling, graphic, grammatical and contextual knowledge in reading unfamiliar words;	4Wa1 Write character profiles, using detail to capture the reader's imagination;	4SL5 Listen carefully in discussion, contributing relevant comments and questions;
4R07 Read and perform playscripts, exploring how scenes are built up;	4Wa2 Adopt a viewpoint as a writer, expressing opinions about characters or places;	4SL6 Adapt the pace and loudness of speaking appropriately when performing or reading aloud;
4R08 Express a personal response to a text, and link characters and settings to personal experience;	4Wa3 Choose and compare words to strengthen the impact of writing, including some powerful verbs;	
4Rx1 Retell or paraphrase events from the text in response to questions;	4Wa4 Use more powerful verbs, e.g. rushed instead of went;	4SL7 Adapt speech and gesture to create a character in drama;
4Rx4 Explore explicit meanings within a text;	4Wa8 Show awareness of the reader by adopting an appropriate style or viewpoint;	4SL8 Comment on different ways that meaning can be expressed in own and others' talk.
4Ri1 Investigate how settings and characters are built up from details and identify key words and phrases;		
4Ri2 Explore implicit meanings within a text;	4Wt1 Explore different ways of planning stories, and write longer stories from plans;	
4Rw1 Recognise meaning in figurative language; Recognise meaning in figurative language;	4Wp3 Experiment with varying tenses within texts, e.g. in dialogue;	
4Rw2 Understand the impact of imagery and figurative language in poetry, including alliteration and simile, e.g. as ... as a ... ;	4Wp4 Investigate past and present tenses and future forms of verbs;	
4Rw3 Understand how expressive and descriptive language creates mood;		

4Rw4 Identify adverbs and their impact on meaning.	4Ws1 Extend knowledge and use of spelling patterns, e.g. vowel phonemes, double consonants, silent letters, common prefixes and suffixes;	
	4Ws2 Investigate spelling patterns; generate and test rules that govern them;	
	4Ws3 Check and correct spellings and identify words that need to be learned;	
	4Ws6 Extend earlier work on prefixes and suffixes;	
	4Ws8 Use all the letters in sequence for alphabetical ordering.	

Related resources

- Audio files: *Peter and the Wolf* (summary); *Peter and the Wolf*;
- *A Difficult Decision*; *A Difficult Decision* (script)
- PCM 20: Peter and the Wolf: story summary
- PCM 21: A Difficult Decision: character cards

Week 1
Student's Book pages 87–90

Workbook page 49

Introducing the unit
Explain to learners that they will be reading and acting out some playscripts. Share any experience of plays learners may have seen or performed in themselves. Talk about some of the differences between playscripts and stories:

- Stories often describe things in detail; playscripts tend to concentrate on the words the characters say
- Stories use direct speech, punctuated with speech marks etc.; playscripts have the characters' names in the margin followed by the words they say, without speech marks
- Instead of long descriptive passages or details of how characters think and feel, playscripts have stage directions to tell the actors how to move and speak their lines
- In stories, the author can describe what is happening and give the reader information about things that might be happening in different times and places; in playscripts, the plot is driven by the words the characters say, almost as if the audience were there with them in real time.

Student's Book page 87
Listening and speaking

Tell learners that the first playscript they will look at is based on the story of *Peter and the Wolf* by Prokofiev. If possible, play a recording of *Peter and the Wolf* to the class so that they can enjoy the music and begin to get a sense of the story.

Then read the short summary of the plot of Peter and the Wolf aloud to learners, or play the audio. The text of the summary is on PCM 20. Explain to learners that while they listen to the summary, they should make some quick notes to help them remember the main points of the story.

When learners have listened to the summary at least once, ask them to take turns to retell the story to their partners. Circulate and listen to the retellings so that you can assess how well learners are able to summarise and retell the story.

Extension and support

Encourage learners who are able to retell the story accurately to think of ways of making their retelling more interesting. For example, the story summary doesn't include any dialogue. Can they make up some words for the characters to say in their retelling?

If any learners are struggling, give them copies of PCM 16 and ask them to use this to help structure their retelling. Tell them that they shouldn't just read the summary out – you want them to annotate it and find the key words and phrases that will help them retell each part of the story. Then they can use these key words in their retelling.

If you would like to give learners more practice at retelling a story concisely, give them some picture books and ask them to read the story and then retell it. They can note down the main things that happen and some key words to help them retell each incident.

If necessary, model for learners how to role-play the interview between the wolf and the TV reporter. Encourage learners playing the wolf to think about how the wolf might feel about the end of the story, and what he might do in the future.

You could use this as an opportunity to explore different ways of saying similar things. For instance, maybe in one pair's interview, the wolf feels very bitter towards Peter and is planning to escape from the zoo and get his revenge. This wolf might express himself very angrily. The wolf in another pair's interview might be more relaxed about it; perhaps still cross with Peter, but feeling that life in the zoo won't be so bad. Learners could look at different ways of expressing these thoughts, and compare the sort of language used in each.

Student's Book pages 88–90

Reading
Ask learners to read the playscript carefully before they answer the questions. It would be very helpful if learners have the opportunity to read the playscript aloud in a group of eight (or a group of four, doubling up parts). If time allows, encourage them to add movement to their reading, and to use their voices as expressively as possible. If necessary, remind them not to read the stage directions (in brackets) out loud, but silently. They can use the information in the stage directions to help them act out their role expressively.

Answers
2
a Because Grandfather knew that a wolf lived in the forest, and he thought Peter would be in danger if he played in the meadow.
b He is sent to his room.
c Duck.
d To make a lasso to trap the wolf by his tail.
e Flies round and round the wolf's head until he is dizzy.
f Because he knows that Peter has been very brave.
g Open question; learners should realise that these are stage directions, and they help the actor understand how to move and how to say the lines.
h The words in capitals need to be spoken loudly and with lots of emphasis.
i Open question; look for responses that describe Peter accurately, including information about what he looks like, what he does and what kind of person he is.
j Open question; accept any sensible answer that fits with the text.

Thinking deeper
Use the 'Thinking Deeper' prompts to have a class discussion about the differences between playscripts and stories. Learners' answers to question 1 should include:

- Playscripts are laid out differently from stories, with the speaker's name in the margin and no speech marks.
- Playscripts use stage directions to describe what is going on, to help the actors act out the scene. Stories often use narration to describe what is going on, and sometimes stories tell us about things that can't be seen or heard (which is less common in plays).

In answer to question 2, the ways in which playscripts make it easier for actors to see what they have to do include:

- setting out the speeches clearly on separate lines
- putting the name of the speaker in the margin so actors can just glance down the margin to find their character's next speech
- putting stage directions in italics so they look different from the words the actors speak
- describing how the actor should move and speak in the stage directions.

Student's Book page 90

Grammar

Learners could complete the Student's Book grammar activity in pairs, or you may prefer to tackle it as a whole class.

Answers
1 creeping, prowls, jumping, ran, waddled, tried to run, runs, catches up, climbed, ran, scrambles, fly, flying, plodded, skipped.
2 Open question; look for actions that show the learner has understood the meaning of the word, and clarify if necessary.
3 creeping (present), prowls (present), jumping (present), ran (past), waddled (past), tried to run (past), runs (present), catches up (present), climbed (past), ran (past), scrambles (present), fly (present), flying (present), plodded (past), skipped (past).
4 The present tense; learners should realise that this is because the characters are talking about the action as it happens, and therefore they are using the present tense.
5 Open question, but learners should notice that the Narrator is telling the story as if it were something that had already happened, so the past tense is appropriate.

Workbook page 49

Grammar

Learners could tackle this activity either in class or as homework. This activity can also be done later in the unit, if you prefer.

Answers
1
1 Charles stomped crossly out of the room.
2 Maxine grabbed the plate and hurled it out of the window.
3 "How dare you do that?" Mum thundered.
4 Romy's cat, Alexia, slunk in through the door.
5 "It wasn't my fault," muttered Sam.
6 The hippopotamus wallowed in the soft river mud.
7 Eight pigeons strutted towards us, looking for food.
8 I yelled at my brother because he used my pens without asking.
2 open; accept any answers that use the correct adverbs.

Weekly review

Level	Reading	Writing	Listening and speaking
■	This group may struggle to read a playscript fluently out loud; they may need several readings to become confident enough with the text to start adding expression and actions.	This group may need to be prompted and/or supported to write short notes to remind them of the key events in a story.	This group may need support and help to improvise a simple scene that draws on their understanding of a scene they have read.
●	This group should be able to read a playscript with some accuracy, and some use of appropriate expression, after one or two readings.	This group can listen to a story with some attention, and take notes to help them remember at least some parts of the story.	This group can improvise and act out a short scene that links in some ways to a scene they have read.
▲	This group can read a playscript with accuracy and fluency and appropriate expression, often on the first reading.	This group can write appropriate summary notes as they listen to a story, noting only the most important parts of the story.	This group demonstrates good understanding of a scene they have read and can use ideas from this to improvise their own scene.

Week 2

Student's Book pages 91–95

Workbook pages 50–51

Introduction

Explain that learners are going to read and compare a story and a playscript version. Ask them to read the pieces silently to themselves; they can then discuss the comprehension questions in pairs before they go on to write the answers.

Student's Book pages 91–92
Reading

Answers
2
a The simile is 'like a whirlwind'. It's an open question whether learners find this effective or not, but they should give the reasons for their opinion.
b wearily; excitedly; despondently; calmly; thoughtfully (learners' definitions may vary)
c Sample definitions: 'tighten our belts' means spending less money, 'make it up to you' means doing something nice to make up for something bad, 'miss out on' means having to go without something.
d Because they can't afford to go on holiday this year.
e Get a kitten for the children.
f Aditya quite likes the idea. You can tell because Mum says both the children have wanted a kitten for a long time, and also because he and Anjali smile at each other when they are thinking about the kitten.
g Open question; accept any reasoned response that fits with the story.
h Some differences include:
- The story tells us about Anjali's mood, which is a feeling inside her and not necessarily visible. The playscript tells us about Anjali's body language and voice, and how she actually shows what she is feeling.
- The playscript adds a detail ('serious faces') that would help the actors playing Anjali's family. This isn't included in the story.
- The story is in the past tense, but the playscript stage direction is in the present tense.

i Open question about how the playscript version could help the actor playing Anjali; learners might mention that the playscript makes it very clear what she has to do in order to show how she is feeling.

Student's Book page 93
Writing

Use the Student's Book activity to check that learners have understood how to convert a story into a playscript. The activity is quite straightforward – learners only have to put the characters' speeches into playscript format, and where the narrative gives a clue about how a character speaks or moves, they can convert this into a stage direction.

Learners who find this activity difficult could work in groups, and go through the lines orally before writing them down.

Give all the groups time to act out their playscript before moving on to the Listening and speaking activity. This will help them get into role as the story characters when they attempt the role play.

Student's Book pages 93–94
Listening and speaking

Use the Student's Book prompts to structure this role play activity. Allow plenty of time for learners to think about 'their' character's likely response before they start acting it out. It could be helpful if you can circulate at this point and make sure that all learners have at least three points to make on behalf of their character. If they don't, ask the groups to pause and discuss the ideas they have, and see if they can add further ideas for each character.

When the groups have finished their role play, you could ask them to describe to the whole class how their conversations went. Did any of the groups reach agreement? Did any end up having an argument? Share some ideas about why this might have happened, if so. Ask the actors to recap the conversation and, as a group, look at alternative ways of putting the characters' ideas forward, which would be less likely to end in an argument.

Across the whole class, share the groups' final decisions about whether to get the kitten or send Anjali on the trip. Is there a general consensus across the class?

Extension and support

Less confident groups may benefit from having several goes at the conversation, especially if they find it hard to stay in role as their given character.

Groups that struggle to understand their characters' motivation could be given PCM 21, which contains prompt cards for each character to get the conversation started. (You could give these cards to all groups if you wish.)

More able groups can be encouraged to record their conversation in playscript format.

Student's Book pages 94–95
Spelling

The story and playscript contain several words with the prefixes *in-* and *im-*, and the suffixes *-able* and *-ible* (*incredible, impossible, affordable*). Ask learners to spot these words in the story, and point out that although they are spelled differently, the prefixes *in-* and *im-* mean the same (they make a root word mean its opposite). The same is true of the suffixes -*able* and -*ible*, which mean 'able to do or be something' (so *possible* means *able to be done*, and *credible* means *able to be believed*).

Use the prompts in the Student's Book to teach the rules for spelling words with the prefixes *in-*, *im-*, *il-* and *ir-*, and the suffixes -*ible* and -*able*.

Answers
1
inhuman
illogical
immortal
insane
impolite
inconvenient
irrational
inaudible
2
reasonable
intelligible
terrible
allowable
reliable
incredible
edible
acceptable
3 This is an open question; look for sentences that are correctly spelled and show an understanding of the meaning of the target words.

Reinforce this and any other current spelling work by dictating some sentences for learners to write down. This will enable you to assess whether they can identify the correct spelling pattern for a particular word aurally. Here are some example sentences using the prefixes and suffixes above:

1. The rocket went on an incredible journey through space.
2. It is impossible to find anything in my messy bedroom.
3. My dad's writing is so bad, it is illegible.
4. The road is bumpy and irregular.
5. My bed is nice and comfortable.
6. My little brother is quite immature.

Read these aloud to learners twice, speaking slowly and clearly, and give learners time to write each sentence down before moving on to the next one. When they have finished, collect their sentences in so that you can assess how accurately they were able to spell the target words. If they struggle to remember the whole sentence for long enough to write it, do some more practice, beginning with shorter sentences and working up to longer ones.

Workbook page 50

Spelling

Learners can also complete this activity either in class or as homework.

Answers
1 invisible
illogical
incredible
impossible
irrelevant
immature
incorrect
2
Down
1 invisible
2 impossible
3 incorrect
4 incredible
Across
4 irrelevant
5 illogical
6 immature

Workbook page 51

Spelling

Learners can also complete this activity either in class or as homework.

Answers
1
a After working hard all day in the garden, Grandad was asleep in a comfortable chair.
b The tiny kittens looked adorable.
c I'll never get all my homework done tonight – it's impossible!
d James ate his dry, stale sandwich, but it wasn't very enjoyable.
e My little brother's handwriting is absolutely terrible.
f The sunset was an incredible shade of purple, with pink clouds.
g If possible, I'd like to go to the park after school.
h The painting on the museum wall was very valuable.
i The weather today is really horrible.
j Emma's family have an old car that keeps breaking down – it's not very reliable.
k I bought a big bag of sweets at the market for a very reasonable price.
l I'm feeling much better now – my spots are nearly invisible.

Weekly review

Level	Reading	Writing	Listening and speaking
■	This group may need support to understand and identify the differences between the way a story is written and the way a playscript is written.	This group may need extra structure and support when changing a story into a playscript; they will benefit from lots of practice.	This group may need support to work on a simple, structured role-play as a group.
●	This group has a good understanding of some of the differences between stories and playscripts.	This group can convert a simple story into a playscript mostly accurately, and may include some stage directions derived from the story text.	This group can work mostly independently on a group role-play. They may sometimes lapse out of character.
▲	This group understands the main differences between stories and playscripts and can also identify some more subtle differences related to the way playscripts are used.	This group can convert a simple story into a playscript, making appropriate changes and sometimes adding details to make the playscript easier for actors to use.	This group works together effectively and independently on a role-play, using what they know about characters from the text and also adding their own ideas.

Week 3

Student's Book pages 95–96

Workbook page 52

This week, learners will write their own playscript about an issue or dilemma, using what they have learned about playscript structure.

The Student's Book contains some prompts and ideas for possible topics, though if you prefer you could substitute ideas that are more appropriate for your particular class. Depending on the needs of your learners, you may decide to give them a topic to write about yourself rather than giving them a free choice. Alternatively, you could ask them to create a playscript version of part of a novel they have recently read.

Less able or confident groups could be asked to write a playscript version of the role-play they undertook in Week 2, based on the story *A Difficult Decision*. The role-play work will give them a head-start in understanding the characters and they will already have ideas about how the different characters would react.

Whatever approach you take, it is important to give learners the opportunity to rehearse their scenes out loud in a group before they write them down.

This writing exercise can be used as an end of unit review opportunity.

Student's Book pages 95–96

Writing

Ask learners to follow the prompts in the Student's Book as they plan their dialogues. They could work in groups, in pairs or individually. (Group working is helpful, especially for less able groups, since the whole group can role-play and support each other in writing the same story.) Encourage plenty of discussion, and prompt learners to practise telling their story to a partner before they begin writing.

Learners will need to think carefully about their dialogues and plan how to include descriptions as well as interesting speeches, so it may take them more than one session to write a complete draft. It's therefore helpful to allow plenty of time for the planning and drafting stages.

Workbook page 52

Spelling

Some learners may benefit from completing the Workbook activity on alphabetical order during this writing exercise. This activity is helpful in reminding learners how to look up unknown words in a dictionary – which is something they may well need to do as part of checking their work. The definitions below are examples, so accept other accurate definitions.

Answers

2

Word	Definition
alligator	a large reptile a bit like a crocodile
anger	an unpleasant feeling of rage and unfairness
angrily	in an angry way
balance	put something in a steady position so it doesn't fall
bath	a tub you can fill with water and lie down in to wash
beetle	an insect with hard wing cases
brim	the very top edge of something
fairground	a place where fairs take place
flying	travelling through the air
seahorse	a small fish that lives in the sea and looks a bit like a horse
seaside	the land next to the sea
submarine	a vehicle that can travel underwater
subtle	not very obvious or showy
trainers	sports shoes
triangle	a shape with three sides
triple	three times, or having three parts
valiant	brave
valuable	worth a lot of money

The prompts in the Student's Book can be used as a checklist to remind learners of the key elements they should be checking at draft stage. If time allows, the groups could perform their plays to the rest of the class at draft stage in order to get additional feedback before making a final version.

It is helpful to either watch or read the plays yourself at draft stage too, so that you can comment and steer the groups to write a successful final draft.

When all the plays are complete, give the groups an opportunity to act them out – perhaps to parents, or to other classes in an assembly.

Extension and support

More able learners should be able to write a longer and more complex playscript, perhaps with parts for four or more characters. Encourage them to try to find a resolution to the dilemma they are writing about, within the playscript.

Less able or less confident groups may write a shorter and simpler playscript, perhaps based on the story A Difficult Decision or on another structured idea which you have given them. They may not be able to resolve the dilemma they were writing about within their playscript – however, their playscript should give a sense of the issues involved.

Weekly review

Level	Writing	Listening and speaking
■	This group can write a simple playscript when working within a clear structure. They can include some simple stage directions as well as speech.	At times this group needs support to listen and respond appropriately to others when role-playing and when acting from a playscript.
●	This group can work more independently, and may be able to come up with their own scenario for their playscript. They can include stage directions where necessary. Their playscript may or may not resolve the dilemma they are writing about.	This group can normally listen and respond to each other in their group when role-playing or acting from a playscript. They listen to each other's work and ideas and sometimes give helpful advice.
▲	This group can write a longer and more complex playscript, including powerful verbs and adverbs (especially in the stage directions). They can work independently and are able to come up with ideas for improving and extending their playscript.	This group can work independently, listening and responding to each others' ideas appropriately and giving advice. They listen and respond to each other appropriately when role-playing or acting from a playscript.

Unit 9 Imaginary worlds

Unit overview

This unit gives learners the opportunity to read a fantasy story set in space, and to write their own fantasy story using the five-stage structure. They will also compare and contrast two poems about imaginary creatures, and write a detailed description of a setting, as well as writing their own non-rhyming poem about a mythical creature. They will answer comprehension questions, practise their Listening and speaking skills by making a presentation and acting out an alternative ending to a story, revise how to write and punctuate direct speech, and explore a range of spelling patterns. They also identify homonym pairs and learn to use meaning to help them decide which word of a pair to use.

Reading	Writing	Listening and speaking
4R01 Extend the range of reading;	4W04 Look for alternatives for overused words and expressions;	4SL1 Organise ideas in a longer speaking turn to help the listener;
4R02 Explore the different processes of reading silently and reading aloud;	4W05 Make short notes from a text and use these to aid writing;	4SL3 Understand the gist of an account or the significant points and respond to main ideas with relevant suggestions and comments;
4R04 Use knowledge of punctuation and grammar to read with fluency, understanding and expression;	4W07 Re-read own writing aloud to check punctuation and grammatical sense;	
4R05 Identify all the punctuation marks and respond to them when reading;	4W08 Write sentences, dictated by the teacher, from memory;	4SL4 Deal politely with opposing points of view;
4R06 Apply phonic/spelling, graphic, grammatical and contextual knowledge in reading unfamiliar words;	4Wa2 Adopt a viewpoint as a writer, expressing opinions about characters or places;	4SL5 Listen carefully in discussion, contributing relevant comments and questions;
4R08 Express a personal response to a text, and link characters and settings to personal experience;	4Wa3 Choose and compare words to strengthen the impact of writing, including some powerful verbs;	4SL7 Adapt speech and gesture to create a character in drama.
4Rx1 Retell or paraphrase events from the text in response to questions;	4Wa4 Use more powerful verbs, e.g. rushed instead of went;	
4Rx2 Note key words and phrases to identify the main points in a passage;	4Wa5 Explore degrees of intensity in adjectives, e.g. cold, tepid, warm, hot;	
4Rx4 Explore explicit meanings within a text;	4Wa8 Show awareness of the reader by adopting an appropriate style or viewpoint;	
4Ri1 Investigate how settings and characters are built up from details and identify key words and phrases;	4Wa10 Explore alternative openings and endings for stories;	
4Ri2 Explore implicit meanings within a text;	4Wa11 Summarise a sentence or a paragraph in a limited number of words;	
4Rw1 Recognise meaning in figurative language; Recognise meaning in figurative language;	4Wt1 Explore different ways of planning stories, and write longer stories from plans;	
4Rw3 Understand how expressive and descriptive language creates mood; 4Rw4 Identify adverbs and their impact on meaning;	4Wp3 Experiment with varying tenses within texts, e.g. in dialogue;	

4Rw7 Understand the main stages in a story from introduction to resolution;	4Wp4 Investigate past and present tenses and future forms of verbs;	
4Rw8 Explore narrative order and the focus on significant events;	4Wp6 Use a range of end-of-sentence punctuation with accuracy;	
4Rw10 Compare and contrast poems and investigate poetic features.	4Wp7 Use speech marks and begin to use other associated punctuation;	
	4Ws1 Extend knowledge and use of spelling patterns, e.g. vowel phonemes, double consonants, silent letters, common prefixes and suffixes;	
	4Ws2 Investigate spelling patterns; generate and test rules that govern them;	
	4Ws3 Check and correct spellings and identify words that need to be learned;	
	4Ws4 Spell words with common letter strings but different pronunciations, e.g. tough, through, trough, plough;	
	4Ws7 Match spelling to meaning when words sound the same (homophones), e.g. to/two/too, right/write.	

Related resources

- Audio files: *Sheetal's First Landing*: introduction; *Sheetal's First Landing*; *The Last Dragon*; *Lost Magic*
- PCM 11: The structure of a story
- PCM 22: Sheetal's First Landing: introduction
- PCM 23: Story mountain

Week 1

Student's Book pages 97–102

Workbook pages 53–55

Introducing the unit

Begin by playing the audio recording of the introductory part of *Sheetal's First Landing* (or reading it aloud to the class) twice. The text of the story is on PCM 22. If you wish, you can give learners copies of the text so they can follow it as you read.

Student's Book page 97

Listening and speaking

Tell learners that the first time they hear the story you just want them to listen carefully and enjoy it. The second time, they should make some notes using the prompts in the Student's Book. Encourage them to use the bullet point prompts to make headings they can write under, to speed up the note-taking process.

Ask learners where this story is set (on a planet far from our world). How do they know this? Spend a few minutes looking for clues about the setting in the story. Establish that this is a fantasy story set in an imaginary world. Make links with any similar stories or films that learners may be familiar with.

After the second reading, allow plenty of time for learners to discuss their prediction ideas in pairs and prepare to present these to the rest of the class. Agreeing on a shared prediction may be challenging for some pairs, so support them as they discuss this and if necessary model how to listen politely to each other and arrive at a compromise. Then give each pair a limited amount of time (perhaps two minutes) to explain what they think will happen next in the story.

You can use PCM 22 for a follow-up spelling activity. Give each pair of learners a copy of the PCM and a highlighter pen. Ask them to highlight all the words that have a long *ee* vowel sound (regardless of spelling). They can then classify the words they find into groups according to spelling pattern, and think of some other words with each spelling pattern to add to their list. You could use the lists as the basis of a classroom wall display, and learners could continue to add words that they find in their reading to the appropriate lists. The lists can then be used for spelling practice and revision.

The relevant words from the extract are:
- *ee* spelled *i*: alien, mysterious
- *ee* spelled *ee*: Sheetal, been, needed
- *ee* spelled *y*: galaxy, party, safety, very, busy, really, everything, happy, everybody, quickly, everyone, possibly
- *ee* spelled *e*: enormous, me, be, we
- *ee* spelled *ea*: leap, leader

The text also includes the word 'people', but don't focus on 'eo' as a spelling pattern because it is really unique to this word!

You can use PCM 22 to revise other spelling patterns too – for instance, learners could use it to identify and group words with other long and short vowel phonemes, words with common inflections such as -*ing* and -*ed*, words with prefixes and suffixes, homophones, etc.

Workbook page 53

Listening and speaking

Answers

Silent c	Silent b	Silent g	Silent k	Silent n
science	doubt	sign	knight	autumn
scene	bomb	gnome	knee	column
ascend	lamb	gnat	knew	hymn
scientist	debt	foreign	knife	solemn
scenic	crumb	resign	kneel	
scent	comb	campaign	know	
scenery			knot	

Silent w	Silent t	Silent u	Silent l
wreck	bristle	guitar	calm
wrong	castle	guilty	balm
wriggle	listen	guess	walk
wrinkle	jostle	disguise	chalk
wrap	rustle	guest	talk
wreckage	thistle		half
			calf

Student's Book pages 98–100

Reading, Comprehension

Learners can tackle the reading and comprehension individually or in pairs. Circulate as learners read the story, and answer any questions they may have. If there are words that they don't know, discuss the meanings and write the words and definitions on the board for future reference.

Many of the comprehension questions are open, but even for more closed questions, always allow learners their own variations in the answers, as long as the sense of the answer is correct, and the language used is appropriate.

Answers
1
a She is winched down.
b Open question. The most obvious detail is the 'desert of blue-white sand', but learners may also feel that the weather is not like that on Earth (depending on how different it is from their local weather!) and the alien tomb is unlike anything we find on Earth.
c The most obvious similes are 'The sun's shining through the roof hatch like a spotlight', 'big things like cocoons,' 'the distant rain sounded like someone raking gravel.' Learners may also spot 'frog-like creatures' and 'Then it was as if giants were hurling buckets of water everywhere.' Learner's explanation of what their chosen simile is describing should link accurately to the text.
d So that her mum, and the others in the landing party, know that she is safe.
e Open question. Learners should pick up that this represents Sheetal's initials and her age. They may feel that she writes this because she is proud of being 9, and/or because it's her first landing and she wants to make her mark.
f Open question: accept any correctly punctuated sentence of dialogue in the present/past tenses as appropriate.
g Open question: look for a concise summary sentence such as 'Sheetal walked across to the tomb and was winched up on to the roof.'

h Open question; accept any three clear summary sentences, for example 'Sheetal went over to the tomb and was winched up to the top. Then she was winched inside the tomb, where she saw the alien mummies and placed the sensors. When she got back to the spaceship she saw on the cameras that the tomb had flooded and the aliens were coming alive.'

Extension and support

Check that learners understand that dialogue often uses different tenses from those in the main narrative.

- More able learners could complete the 'Thinking Deeper' activity on tenses in narrative. They should understand that dialogue often refers to the past or future as well as the present, because the characters might be talking about things they have done in the past or are going to do in the future.
- Less able learners could work in pairs or groups to find more sentences from the story that are in the past, present and future. They could use PCM 22 for this too, annotating the PCM to show which tense each sentence uses.

Workbook page 54

Grammar

Follow this up by asking learners to complete the Workbook activity on tenses in speech, either in class or for homework.

Answers

1
a "I am going to count up to ten, and then I will come and find you!" (future)
b "How many biscuits did you eat?" (past)
c "It is Dad's turn to cook dinner today." (present)
d "Gran said I could take Fluffy for a walk." (past)
e "My favourite colour is red." (present)
f "We are going to go to America on holiday next year." (future)
2
a "Molly is going to come round to my house today." (future)
b "We will go/are going down to the park after school." (future)
c "I hope there will be pasta for tea." (future – 'is' is also acceptable here)
d "David was the winner of the running race." (past)
e "When I was little, my favourite toy was a bear." (past)
f "We had/ate a big chocolate cake on my birthday." (past)
g "Are you ready to go out?" (present)
h "Mum is calling you!" (present)
i "My favourite team is Real Madrid." (present)

Student's Book page 101

Listening and speaking

Circulate while learners discuss what might happen after the end of the story, and prepare to act it out in their groups. Help them to negotiate together so that everyone gets a chance to put their ideas forward. Give them time to rehearse their scene; the groups could then take turns to perform it for the whole class. Encourage them to use their voices and gestures to help make the scene vivid for the audience.

After all the groups have performed, talk about the different ideas. Did all the groups have different ideas, or were some of them similar?

Use the prompts in the Student's Book to introduce learners to the idea of a story mountain. Point out how it is similar to the five-stage story structure they learned about in Unit 4 (and spend a few minutes recapping this if necessary).

You could use the story mountain on PCM 23 to analyse *Sheetal's First Landing*. This is an interesting story to analyse because of the open ending. Point out to learners that even though the story doesn't tie up all the loose ends at the end, it still ends at a satisfying point. One way of mapping the story to the five-stage structure is:

- Introduction: Sheetal leaves the spaceship and goes down on to the planet surface.
- Build-up: she walks across to the tomb and is winched up to the roof.
- Climax: she winches down into the tomb and sees the alien mummies.
- Resolution: she attaches the sensors and returns to the ship.
- Climax: the sensors show the aliens coming alive ...

While the groups discuss how well their story idea fits the structure, circulate among them so that you can help to resolve any problems. Learners could use PCM 23 to record their ideas.

Student's Book page 102

Grammar

Use the Student's Book prompts to remind learners about expressive and descriptive language. You could undertake questions 1 and 2 as a whole class, and learners could then tackle question 3 in pairs or independently.

Answers
All three questions are open; the choice of sentences for questions 1 and 2 is partly a matter of opinion, but if you tackle these questions as a whole class there will be an opportunity to discuss the options and share reasons for a particular choice of sentence. For question 3, accept any appropriate and grammatically structured sentences that fulfil the question requirements.

Extension and support
- More able groups should be able to revise their story to make it reflect the five stage structure with little help or support. Encourage them to discuss the options and make sure that everyone in the group has a chance to put forward ideas.
- Less able groups may benefit from your assistance to think of ways in which their story can be made to fit the structure. Prompt them to take notes to remind them of their new story structure.

Workbook page 55
Grammar
Learners can attempt this activity independently, either in class or as homework. Answers to all questions are open; accept interesting and powerful verbs, adverbs and adjectives of the learner's choice, as long as they fit with the target sentences.

Weekly review
Use this rubric to assess learners' progress as they worked through the activities this week.

Level	Reading	Writing	Listening and speaking
■	This group sometimes struggles to decode unfamiliar words and may have difficulty understanding some of what they read on a first reading.	This group can write simple sentences, understanding and applying some spelling rules. They usually remember to add final punctuation to sentences.	At times this group needs support to organize ideas and use language appropriately when discussing and agreeing ideas and acting out a story.
●	This group usually reads accurately and fluently, taking into account sentence punctuation. They generally show good basic understanding, but may need support to read more unfamiliar or challenging texts.	This group can write in clear sentences, normally using basic sentence punctuation accurately. They know some spelling rules and can apply them when prompted, and sometimes independently.	This group uses some appropriate language, tone and gesture when acting out a story, but sometimes needs reminding to keep the tone consistent.
▲	This group reads with accuracy and fluency and appropriate expression, and they are able to use inference effectively to help them understand what they have read.	This group can write in clear sentences and have a good understanding of basic punctuation. They know and consistently apply a range of spelling rules.	This group demonstrates good simple acting ability, usually with appropriate use of language, tone and gesture.

Week 2

Student's Book pages 103–107

Workbook page 55

Introduction

Explain that learners are going to read some poems with fantasy settings and characters.

You could use the reading activity as an opportunity to explore the differences between reading silently to oneself and reading aloud. Ask learners what they think the main differences might be, and share ideas about this. For example:

- In silent reading, you can jump forwards and backwards in the text if you need to, for example if you want to re-read something in order to correct your understanding of the text.

- In reading aloud, you have to read continuously without jumping about in the text, or you may confuse your audience!

- In silent reading, the sounds of the words are relatively unimportant – you don't have to think about them much if you don't want to.

- In reading aloud, the sounds of the words matter a lot, and you need to make sure that you 'perform' the text for the listener to help them understand and enjoy it.

Student's Book pages 103–104

Reading, Comprehension

As learners read the poems aloud in their pairs, circulate so you can check their understanding and answer any questions. Praise examples of good expression and intonation.

If there is time, you may want to ask the pairs to choose their favourite poem of the two to learn by heart and perform.

Answers

a *The Last Dragon* is set near a cave, in a forest, at dusk, with snow falling. Phrases that help convey this are: 'dusk-damp cave', 'first snow falls', 'he turns his face to the winter moon', 'the first owl swoops to the forest floor'.
b Open question, but learners should understand that the phrase suggests the setting is getting dark, damp and chilly.
c They nest by his feet. Because he doesn't roar or breathe fire any more.
d Open question; accept any two pairs of rhyming words.
e Verse 4 uses the half-rhyme 'moon/gone' rather than a full rhyme.
f 'Furled' means drawn in, closed or curled up.
g Open question; accept any reasonable expression of feeling and ideas for what the learner would say to the dragon.
h He finds a unicorn horn.
i 'but there are no unicorns now.' Open question about why the poet repeated this line; for example, learners may think it helps to show that the poem is about things that are different now compared with in the past, or it gives a sad/wistful feeling.
j Open question; accept any reasonable answer in keeping with the poem.
k Open question. Ways in which the poems are similar include that they are both about magical/imaginary creatures, they both have a sad feeling, they both suggest that something magical has ended or is ending. Ways in which the poems differ include that one rhymes and the other doesn't; one includes repetition and the other doesn't; the language in The Last Dragon is more literary and expressive; Lost Magic mostly uses speechlike language; The Last Dragon uses initial capital letters at the start of each line, whereas Lost Magic uses normal sentence punctuation.
l Open question; accept any preference that includes at least two reasons.

Extension and support

After learners have completed the comprehension exercise, share their answers to question part l about similarities and differences between the poems.

- Challenge more able learners to discuss the poems as a group and see if they can think of at least one additional similarity or difference to add to the ones they found.

- Less able learners may need help to articulate the similarities and differences. You could use the suggested answers to question part l above as the basis of a discussion with them.

Thinking deeper

More able learners may be able to tackle the 'Thinking Deeper' activity independently. Alternatively you could discuss it as a whole class. The question about whether the unicorns represent something else is an open one – there are no right or wrong answers and different opinions may be equally valid. One interpretation of the poem is that the unicorns might represent childhood memories – the narrator is remembering a time when he could roam freely without danger, and the world seems different now. Another reading might be that the unicorns represent friends.

Student's Book page 105

Writing

Introduce the activity using the prompts in the Student's Book. If necessary, remind learners about the different uses of verbs, adverbs and adjectives before they tackle the activity.

You could do the initial, note-making part of the activity as a whole class, if you wish – this gives the opportunity to check learners' understanding of these different parts of speech, and also to make sure they understand the difference between a 'boring' or ordinary verb etc. and a powerful one.

This writing activity shouldn't take long; depending on how difficult learners find it, they may or may not need to go through a drafting stage. Encourage them to draw pictures of the setting to go with their descriptions. When they have finished, compare the descriptions and pictures. You may be surprised how many different interpretations there are in one class!

Student's Book page 106

Spelling

You could tackle this activity as a whole class, identifying the rhyming words in the poem and using these as a basis for lists of words with similar spelling patterns. The procedure described in the Student's Book can of course be used for words with any spelling pattern, so you could extend it to include words with patterns you are currently focusing on in class.

Workbook pages 57–58

Writing

If time allows, you can follow this up with a poetry-writing exercise. Ask learners to choose their favourite of the two poems and use it as a model for their own poem about an imaginary animal. Encourage them to re-read their model poem and think carefully about how they are going to structure their own poems.

Extension and support

- More able learners can work on their poems independently. Challenge them to add extra expressive and descriptive language to create a mysterious atmosphere for the reader.
- Less able groups could be directed to write a non-rhyming poem, and use the Workbook poetry writing activity to help structure this. The Workbook activity takes learners through the planning phase of writing the poem in some detail.

Weekly review

Level	Reading	Writing	Listening and speaking
■	This group may need support to understand and read a poem with appropriate expression.	This group may need extra structure and support when completing an unfamiliar writing task.	At times this group needs support to read aloud effectively and share ideas in the group.
●	This group can normally use some appropriate expression, pace and gesture when reading a poem aloud, but they may need reminding to apply it consistently.	This group can tackle a description of a setting or a poem based on an existing structure. They may need to be reminded to think about expressive language choices and apply poetic features consistently.	This group can work on an oral performance of a poem, making some changes to improve their reading as necessary. They can share ideas in their group with some prompting and support.
▲	This group can read a poem aloud with understanding and fluency, including some appropriate expression, changes in pace and gesture.	This can write a detailed description of a setting, adding extra detail to information from the text; they can write a poem independently using a clear model.	This group can perform a poem effectively, assessing their own reading and changing it as necessary. They can share ideas independently in their group.

Week 3

Student's Book pages 107–108

Workbook pages 59–60

For the main writing activity, learners will write their own story about imaginary worlds, following the five-stage story structure they have been taught. There are several ways of tackling this, depending on the amount of support your class needs.

The story-writing exercise can be used as an end of unit review opportunity.

The prompt pictures in the Student's Book are intended to be helpful if learners don't have specific ideas of their own about the kind of fantasy setting and creatures they would like to write about. If individual learners have good ideas of their own that don't fit with the prompts, encourage them to use their own ideas.

Student's Book pages 107–108
Writing (Planning)
Ask learners to follow the prompts in the Student's Book as they plan their story. They could work in groups, in pairs or individually. Encourage plenty of discussion, and prompt learners to practise telling their story to a partner before they begin writing.

Support learners as they work on structuring their stories. They could use PCM 23 (or PCM 11) to help them collect ideas for their first draft. If necessary, model this note-taking and drafting process for them.

Learners will need to think carefully about their stories and factor in how they are going to include expressive language, dialogue etc., so it may take them more than one session to write a complete draft. It's therefore helpful to allow plenty of time for the planning and drafting stages.

Workbook page 56
Punctuation
Some learners may benefit from completing this activity on punctuating direct speech during the planning process. This activity is a revision exercise but it may be helpful to remind learners of the rules for punctuating direct speech.

Answers
1
- "Are you ready to land on the planet surface?" asked the Captain.
- "Yes," said Jenna, "I think I'm as ready as I'll ever be!"
- "Good," said the captain. "This is going to be a very difficult mission."
- "I'm sure I'm ready for it," said Jenna.
- "Don't forget your invisibility shield," said the Captain. "You're going to need it!"

(Question 2 is open; accept any accurately punctuated dialogue that fits the scenario.)

Workbook pages 59–60
This activity can also be undertaken either in class or as homework, now or at any point in this unit.

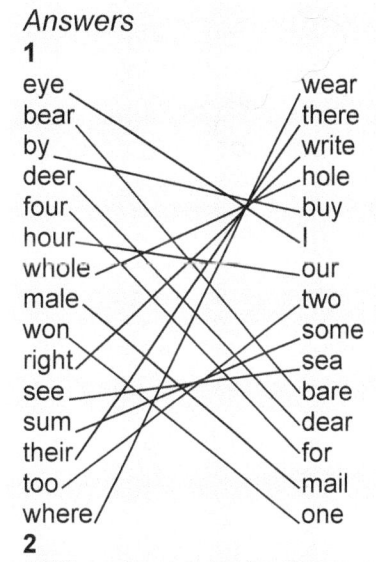

Answers
1

eye — I
bear — bare
by — buy
deer — dear
four — for
hour — our
whole — hole
male — mail
won — one
right — write
see — sea
sum — some
their — there
too — two
where — wear

2
a Where are you going?
b I left my bag over there.
c Lara can write very neatly.
d Our team won the obstacle race.
e We've got chicken noodle soup for dinner.
f The postman has just delivered the mail.
g Would you like some juice?
h The little boat was floating on the sea.
i I finished reading the whole book in one day.
j I went to the park and Ahmed came too.

Student's Book page 108
Writing (Redrafting and revising)
The prompts in the Student's Book can be used as a checklist to remind learners of the key elements they should be checking at draft stage. After an initial read-through of their own stories, encourage learners to swap stories with a partner and comment (positively!) on each other's work.

It is worth reading learners' stories yourself at draft stage too, if possible, so that you can also make suggestions.

After the redrafting stage, give learners the opportunity to write a full draft of their piece, including pictures if they wish. You could make a class book or display of the finished stories.

Extension and support
- More able learners should be able to write a longer and more complex story, using expressive language confidently to describe setting and characters, and writing appropriate and accurately punctuated dialogue.
- Less able or less confident learners may write a shorter story. Learners who struggle to write a whole story could complete the Workbook activity on alternative story openings and endings for end of unit review instead.

Weekly review

Level	Writing	Listening and speaking
■	This group needs support to understand and follow the five-stage structure when writing their own fantasy story based on a model.	At times this group needs support to listen and respond appropriately to others' ideas in discussion.
●	This group can write a fantasy story, following the five-stage structure and including some dialogue and description of setting and characters, with occasional support.	This group can normally listen and respond to others' ideas appropriately, with minimal support.
▲	This group can write a more extended story with accuracy and fluency, following the five-stage structure and including appropriate description and dialogue, with minimal support.	This group can work independently, listening and responding to others' ideas appropriately.

Formal assessment 3

Use this test to assess how well learners have managed to cover the objectives from the last three units. Hand out the sheets and let learners complete them under test conditions. Collect and mark their tests, recording the results in your class record book. Use the mark scheme below.

Assessment 2 Mark Scheme **Total 36**

Question 1

Reading

A Outside a school, in the evening. Learners should circle the bracketed section in italics under 'Scene 1: Outside school'. (2 marks, one for identifying the setting and one for circling the correct part of the text.)

B Any three from: dialogue is set out without speech marks in a play; the speakers' names go in the margin; stage directions tell the actors what to do/how to speak their lines; all the description is in the stage directions; playscripts don't tell you what people think, just what they do and say – or similar ideas in the learner's own words. (3 marks – one for each correctly identified feature.)

C One of the children: 'I thought all you children had gone home by now!' (2 marks, one for correct answer and one for correct quotation.)

D Any two from: cautiously, impatiently, urgently, thoughtfully, eagerly. Adverbs are used in stage directions to tell the actors how to move or say their words. (2 marks – half for each correct adverb, and one for correct summary of why adverbs are used.)

E Because he thinks Mr Harvey is a great peacemaker who can sort out a problem on his home planet. (1)

F Look for at least two speeches from each character, correctly set out and punctuated, and in keeping with the scenario described. (4 marks – one for each correctly-written speech.)

Question 2

Grammar, punctuation and spelling

A Speeches should be correctly set out as direct speech, for example: (4)

"Hmm," said Mr Harvey. "It's the big match this evening. If you promise to get me back home before it starts, I suppose I could come and see what I can do."

"Thank you, sir! Thank you!" said the alien. "Come with me: I promise you will be home before you know it."

Accept variations in wording as long as they are appropriate. (4 marks – one mark for changing the words appropriately for direct speech in each example, and one for putting speech marks in the correct places in each example. Do not penalise the learner for misplacing final punctuation (e.g. putting it outside speech marks).)

B

Was this some kind of prank?

I came in peace, from Planet Warthog!

This was why we needed you, sir!

It could travel great distances in the blink of an eye. (Or 'It travelled great distances ...)

(4 marks – one for each correctly rewritten sentence.)

C

We had a great day last Saturday.

I amazed Mum by doing all the washing up.

There is only one piece of cake left.

Dad gave me a big lump of cheese to grate.

The opposite of war is peace.

I went to the shop because I wanted to buy a packet of crisps.

I've nearly finished my maths homework, but I'm stuck on a difficult sum.

Some people like getting up early, but others don't.

(4 marks – half a mark for each correct use of a homophone.)

Question 3

Writing

A 10 marks – award 1 mark for each of three accurately written paragraphs, and one mark for each of the following features:

- a description of the setting
- some dialogue set out as direct speech
- some powerful verbs
- some interesting adjectives
- a beginning
- a middle
- an end.

Punctuate the story

❶ This is a passage from a historical story, but most of the punctuation is missing. Read the story carefully and add the missing punctuation marks.

It was a freezing night on the streets of London and Jim and his little sister Martha were trying to get to sleep They only had a thin blanket two old coats and a few sheets of newspaper to keep out the cold Their stomachs were rumbling loudly because they hadn't eaten a scrap of food since that morning

Are you asleep, Jim Martha asked I'm hungry I'm hungry too muttered Jim. But we've got no food left so we'll just have to hope we can find some tomorrow

Just then the children heard a very unwelcome noise A policeman was coming round the corner towards them

Hey he shouted What are you two doing here

The children looked at each other It was too late to run What could they do

❷ What do you think will happen next? Write another paragraph to continue the story. Don't forget punctuation.

Reading newspaper reports

Read this newspaper report and then answer the questions.

Stepney Gazette, 14 November 1867
NEW LAWS PROTECT CHILD WORKERS
By Ebenezer Grimes

For many years, child workers have suffered in British factories, farms and workshops. Until recently, children as young as five years old have been forced to work in terrible conditions, for almost no money. However, new laws have now been passed, which will help to improve the lives of working children.

From now on, no child under eight years of age will be allowed to work in any factory or workshop. In addition, children aged between eight and thirteen will be entitled to ten hours' education per week.

Campaigners like Lord Shaftesbury have been trying to bring about this change for a long time. They and their supporters will be delighted with the new laws, which will protect children's health and make sure that they receive some basic education. Not everyone agrees, however. Mr Granger of Stepney told this newspaper: "It is important for poor children to work and help their families by bringing in a wage. We do not need new laws to protect children – we should be encouraging more children to work!"

No doubt this debate will continue for many years to come.

1 What is the main point in the first paragraph? Write one sentence to sum it up.

_____

2 Underline these newspaper features in the report above:
- the headline
- the writer's name
- the date
- the name of the newspaper
- a quote from a named person.

3 What are the main changes for working children, as a result of the new laws?

_____

_____

4 What is the youngest age at which a child could work in a factory, under the new laws?

_____

5 Find the phrases 'entitled to' and 'in addition' in the passage. Draw circles round them, and write down what each phrase means.

a entitled to: _____

b in addition: _____

6 Do you agree with Mr Granger's point of view? Why, or why not?

_____

_____

7 Imagine you are Lord Shaftesbury, who thinks that the new laws are a good thing. What would you say to persuade Mr Granger to change his mind? Write at least three sentences.

_____

_____

_____

_____

_____

Newspaper report

Use the writing frame below to help you write a newspaper report about something that has happened recently. Don't forget to check your spelling and punctuation.

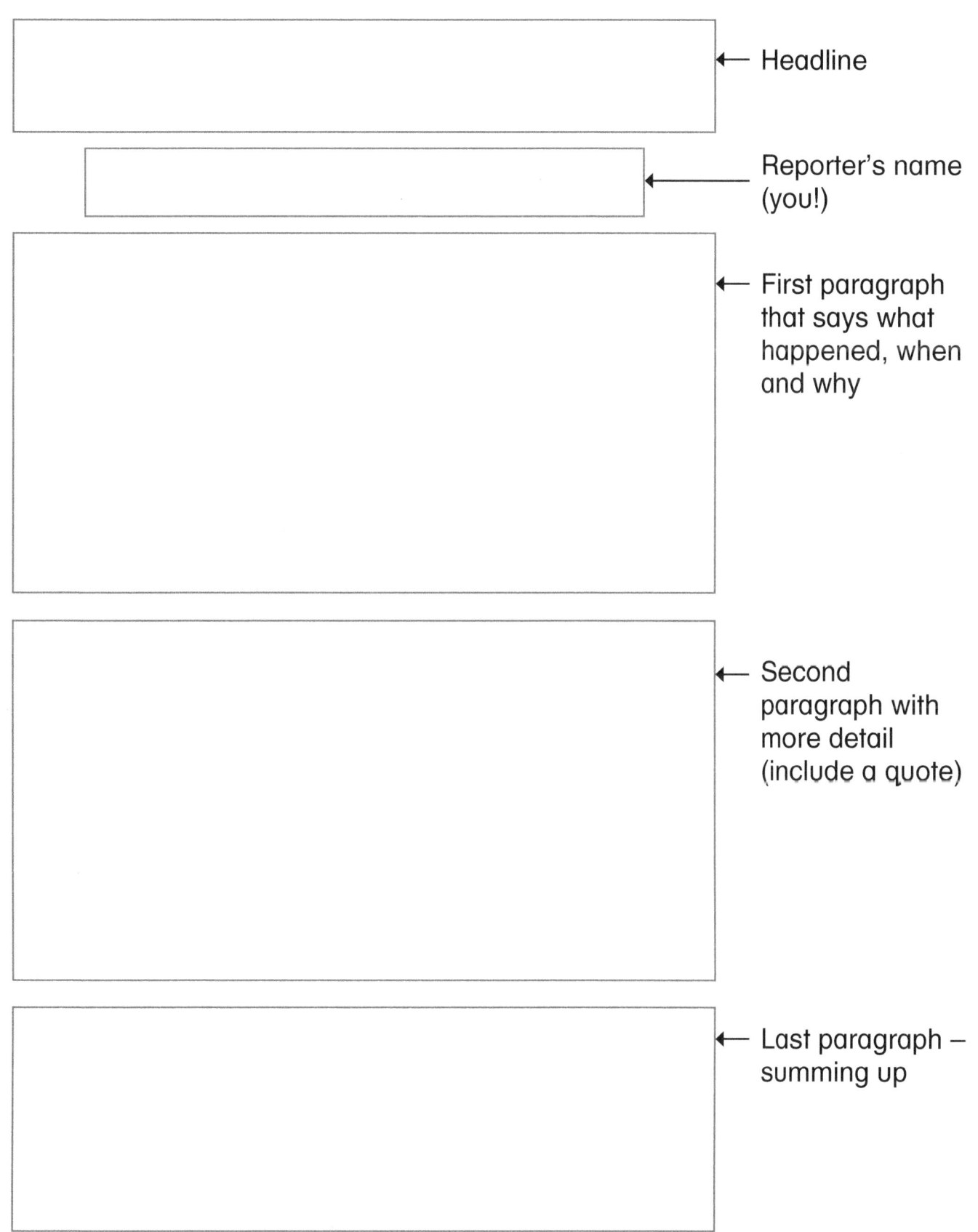

← Headline

← Reporter's name (you!)

← First paragraph that says what happened, when and why

← Second paragraph with more detail (include a quote)

← Last paragraph – summing up

Notes for a historical story

First discuss your story ideas in your group or pair. Then use the headings below to help you make some notes about the story you are going to write.

Where the story is set

When the story is set

Details to help show the reader what things were like at that time

Who the characters are and what they are like

How the story will start

Problems the characters will have

How the story will end

Paragraph plan for a story

Once you have made some notes about the characters, setting and main events in your story, use this paragraph plan to help you plan the structure of the story. Don't write the whole story at this stage – just make notes about each paragraph.

Paragraph 1: introducing the characters and setting

Paragraph 2: a problem that the characters have

Paragraph 3: the characters try to solve the problem, but something goes wrong

Paragraph 4: the characters manage to solve the problem

Paragraph 5: rounding off the story with a satisfying ending

Persuasive writing checklist

❶ Here are some of the main features of persuasive writing. Look out for these features when you are reading advertisements and persuasive arguments! Be careful, though – not all persuasive writing has all of these features.

- questions addressed to the reader (for example: 'Do you like chocolate? Then you'll **love** new Wonderbars!')
- language that stirs up the reader's emotions (for example: 'Millions of helpless puppies are cruelly mistreated every year!' or 'Enjoy the happy, zingy taste of Mintios – you deserve it!')
- alliterative language, where lots of words start with the same letter (for example: 'deeply delicious doughnuts').
- rhyming language (for example 'Don't delay – start today!')
- language that asks the reader to do something (for example: 'Hurry – sign up now or miss the chance of a lifetime!' or 'Write to the government and demand action!')
- lots of exclamation marks
- words that are big and bold or in different colours
- pictures and headings to break up the text

❷ Find some good examples of persuasive writing, and copy or stick them here. Use another sheet if you run out of space!

Using commas

> We use commas in three main ways.
>
> 1 To separate the items in a list – for example:
>   - My best friends are Chang, Jack, Noah and Emily.
>
>   We don't normally put a comma before the 'and' in a list.
> 2 When we are writing down the words someone said – for example:
>   - "Wait there a moment," said Mr Edwards, "and I'll call Ella."
>   - "I hope it's chips for lunch," said Zac.
> 3 To separate the clauses in a sentence, to help the reader understand – for example:
>   - When Mum got back from work, we showed her the lovely meal we had made.
>   - Cross the road, go past the cinema, turn left by the cafe, and the park is on your right.

1 Add the missing commas to these sentences.

a Jack's bike has blue handlebars red mudguards a black seat and a purple frame.

b Ever since our first day at school Jack Emily Chang Noah and I have been best friends.

c "I have four pets" said Noah "and I like helping to look after them."

d "My pets are a rabbit a goldfish a stick insect and a gerbil" said Noah.

e Charlie zoomed down the stairs ran out through the front door and rushed to the playground because he wanted to be there before anyone else.

f The monster's favourite foods were snail kebabs wasp sandwiches creepy crisps and jellyfish ice cream.

g Michaela could hardly wait for Saturday because she was going to spend the day with her cousins and although it was a long journey it was always fun to see them.

h "Come and have your dinner at once" said Mum "or it will get cold."

2 Write three sentences of your own – one using commas to separate items in a list, one using commas in speech, and one using commas to separate clauses.

a List:

b Speech:

c Clauses:

Word families

Use this sheet to help you record word families. Write the root word in the square box at the centre, and write as many related words as you can, around it. Add some more oval boxes if you need to!

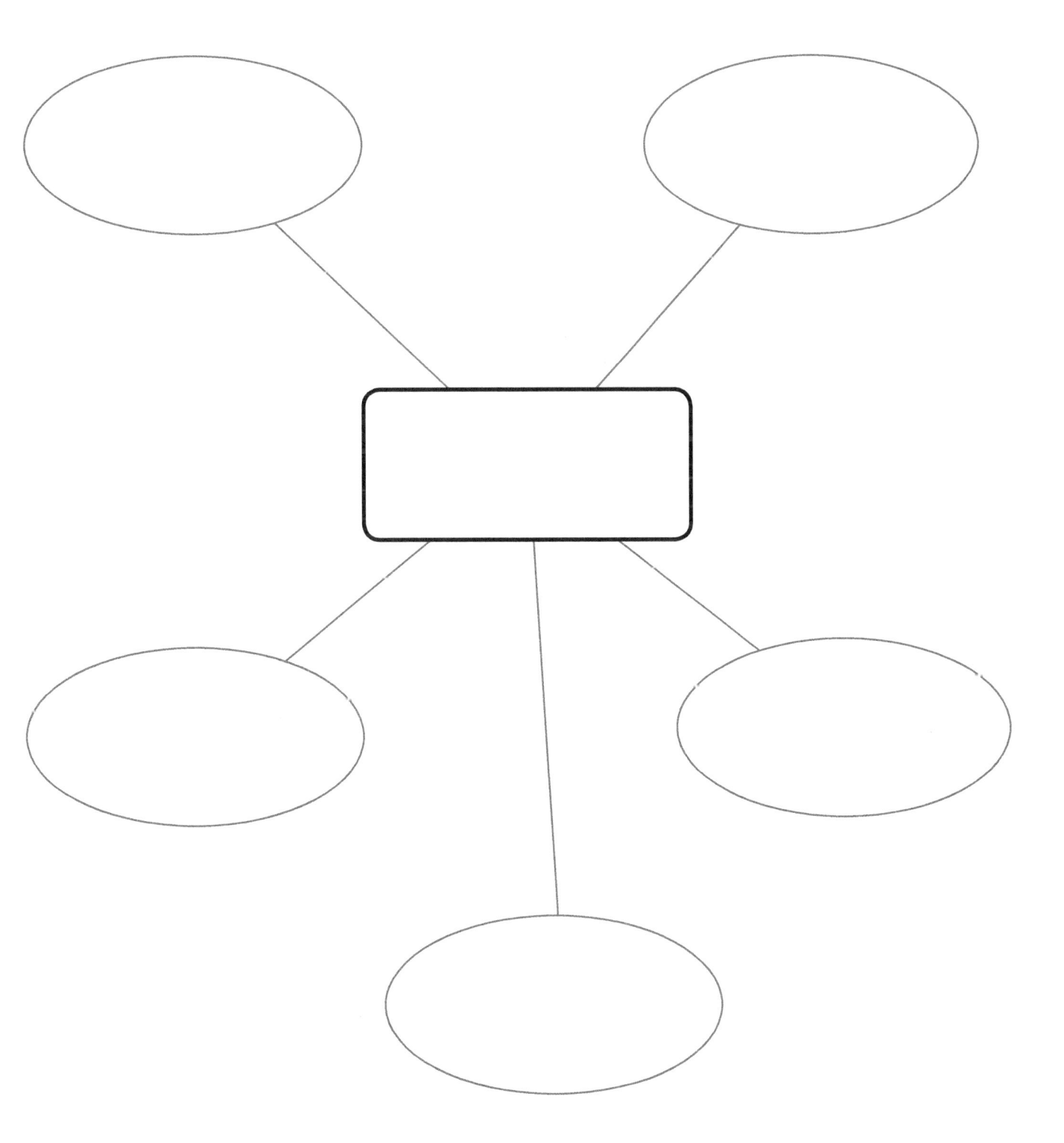

Stage 4 PCM 9

Descriptive words and phrases

Use this chart to help you write a poem or a description. Use a photo or a piece of music, and imagine you were inside the music or picture. Fill in the chart with descriptive words and phrases that show what you would see, hear, feel, taste and smell.

What can you see?	
What can you hear?	
What can you feel?	
What can you taste and/or smell?	
How does the picture or music make you feel?	

© HarperCollins*Publishers* Ltd. 2016

The Clever Farmer

A story from Eritrea

Once there was a farmer who had fallen on hard times. His fields were full of dust and stones, his water melons were all shrivelled up, and worst of all, he had had to get rid of all his cows. All except one, that is. The farmer couldn't bear to part with his last cow. She was the sweetest-natured animal you ever saw, and her name was Shikorina. As long as there was a bite of food in the house, the farmer shared it with Shikorina, and they managed to get by, somehow.

But the sad day came when there *wasn't* a bite of food in the house – not even one! What was the farmer to do? He scratched his head. "I'm sorry, Shikorina my old beauty," he said. "We can't live on air. I'll have to take you to market. Perhaps I can find a rich man to buy you. He'll look after you better than I can. And with the money I get from selling you, I can buy myself a few chickens and goats, and start again."

The farmer's heart was as heavy and empty as his old iron cooking pot. He led Shikorina sadly down the road and into town.

When they got to the market-place, the farmer spotted the richest man in the district, chatting and laughing with his friends. "Good morning, sir!" said the farmer respectfully. "Can I interest you in buying this fine cow?"

The rich man looked Shikorina over carefully. "This is a decent-looking animal," he said. "She's a bit on the thin side, but aren't we all, these days? How much do you want for her, Farmer?"

"Shikorina is no ordinary cow," said the farmer. "I won't accept less than fifty gold coins."

The rich man burst out laughing. "Fifty gold coins?" he snorted. "What kind of fool are you, Farmer? No cow is worth that price! I'll give you five gold coins – take it or leave it." And the rich man turned his back on the farmer and went back to chatting with his friends.

Well, that made the farmer angry. What gave the rich man the right to disrespect him like that? "I'm not a fool!" he shouted. "No fool knows where the centre of the world is, or how many stars there are in the sky!"

The rich man wasn't used to people talking back to him, so he got angry too. "How can a poor farmer like you know where the centre of the world is, or how many stars in the sky? I'll tell you what – I'll do you a deal. If you can answer those questions, then I'll buy your mangy old cow for *sixty* gold coins!"

The rich man's friends thought this was hilarious. They slapped the rich man on the back and guffawed with laughter. But the farmer just smiled. He lifted his wooden walking-stick and plunged it deep into the ground. "There you are," he said. "This is the centre of the world. And anyone who can prove me wrong can say so now."

There was silence. No one could prove that the farmer was wrong.

Then the farmer bent down and picked up a handful of dust. "The number of stars in the sky," he said, "is as uncountable as the number of dust grains in my hand. And anyone who can prove me wrong can say so now."

Once again there was silence. At last the rich man spoke. "You may be poor, Farmer," he said, "but I can see you are rich in cleverness! I certainly can't prove you are wrong. Since I made a promise in front of witnesses, I must keep it. Here – take your sixty gold coins, and give me your cow. She will take pride of place in my herd!"

So the farmer got his money, and Shikorina got a fine new home. And the farmer bought himself some excellent goats and chickens, and within a year he had made enough money to buy Shikorina back from the rich man – for *seventy* gold coins!

The structure of a story

Many stories follow this structure. You can use this chart to help you work out how a story you have read fits the structure, or you can use it to help you plan a story of your own.

Stage	What happens
Introduction	Sets up the story, and introduces main character and setting.
Problem/Build-up	Something starts to happen. It could be a problem, or something the main character has to do. Other characters may come into the story.
Climax/Conflict	The most exciting part of the story. The problem reaches a climax, and there may be some conflict between the characters.
Resolution	Something happens to solve the problem.
Conclusion	Loose ends are tied up, and the story reaches a satisfying ending.

© HarperCollins*Publishers* Ltd. 2016

The Selkie Wife

A story from Scotland

A selkie is half-human, half-seal. Selkies are seals when they are in the sea, but they turn into humans when they take off their sealskin coats and step onto dry land.

One night, a selkie decided to take off her sealskin and dance on the sand. As soon as she stepped out of the sealskin, she became a beautiful young woman. A young fisherman saw her and fell in love with her at once. He brought her back to his house and asked her to marry him. So that she could never leave him and go back to the sea, he stole her sealskin and hid it from her, telling her that it was lost.

The selkie was very sad, because she knew that her true home was in the sea and she longed to return to it. But without her sealskin, she could never go back.

The years went by, and the selkie fell in love with the fisherman. They had three fine young sons, and the selkie almost forgot her old home in the sea ... Almost, but not quite.

Although she loved her family, she was never completely happy, because she still yearned to return to the sea.

One day, the selkie decided to mend some old fishing nets. She looked in the shed for a length of rope, and what should she find on the top shelf but ... her old sealskin! At last she could go back home! That evening, she bundled the sealskin under her arm and ran off down to the beach, without telling her family.

At suppertime, they realised that she had gone. The fisherman guessed what must have happened, and he and his sons rushed down to the sand just in time to see the selkie slip into the waves, wearing her sealskin.

The boys and their father looked at each other sadly. They would miss her so much – but as they looked at the seal swimming away towards the horizon, they knew that at least now she was happy.

Reading aloud

Here is a checklist to help you perform a poem or story out loud.

- Before you perform the story or poem to other people, make sure that you **know it really well**. Read it through quietly, and then read it out loud to yourself at least once. The more effort you put into practising, the better your performance will be!

- Make sure that you **understand** the story or poem. If there is anything you don't understand, ask a teacher or another grown-up for help.

- Make sure that you know how to **pronounce** all the words! If there are any words that you have never heard before, ask someone to check that you have pronounced them correctly.

- Think about the **characters** in the story or poem.
    - How are they feeling? Can you make your voice show this?
    - What do they do? Can you use movement or facial expressions to help show this?

- Think about the **mood** of the story or poem. Is it exciting, funny, mysterious ...? Think about how you can use your voice to help the listener understand the mood.

- Think about making your reading interesting to listen to. Can you **vary the speed and loudness** of your reading? Some lines might work best if you almost shout them – others might need to be read very quietly or very slowly.

- **Practise** reading the piece until you feel really confident!

- **Enjoy** your performance! If you are enjoying your reading, then your listeners will enjoy it too.

© HarperCollins*Publishers* Ltd. 2016

Stage 4

Write your own poem

You are going to plan and write your own poem about having to eat your least favourite food!

1 Think about the type of food you like least. Write its name here:

_____

2 Now think of some adjectives to describe this food. Make them as descriptive (and yucky) as you can! Write your adjectives in this box.

3 If you *had* to eat this food, how would you eat it? (quickly, slowly, happily, disgustedly ...?) Think of at least three good adverbs to describe how you would eat it, and write them here.

© HarperCollins*Publishers* Ltd. 2016

Stage 4

4 Now write down some stronger verbs you could use instead of eat – e.g. *munch, guzzle, chomp* ... How many more can you think of?

---

5 Think of a good line you could repeat in your poem – for example:

Mum said, "Eat your lovely _____!"
I just can't eat it!

Write your repeating line here.

_____

_____

6 Now use your notebook or rough paper to write a draft of your poem.

7 Read your draft out loud to someone, and make any changes to improve your poem.

8 Write out the final version of your poem in your best handwriting. Draw a picture to go with it!

Stage 4 PCM 15

Who, what, when, where, why?

Most newspaper articles try to answer these questions:

- **Who** is the article about?
- **What** did they do, or what happened to them?
- **When** did it happen?
- **Where** did it happen?
- **Why** or **how** did it happen?

Read the newspaper article below, and write down the words or phrases that answer each question.

Who: _____

What: _____

When: _____

Where: _____

Why or how: _____

An alien? Fat chance!

Fishermen dragged a mystery 20-foot-long object with six tentacles onto a beach in Tasmania yesterday. At first it was believed to be an alien – but on closer inspection it turned out to be just a piece of whale blubber washed up by a recent severe storm.

© HarperCollins*Publishers* Ltd. 2016

Stage 4 PCM 16

Non-chronological reports

Use this sheet to help you write a short non-chronological report.

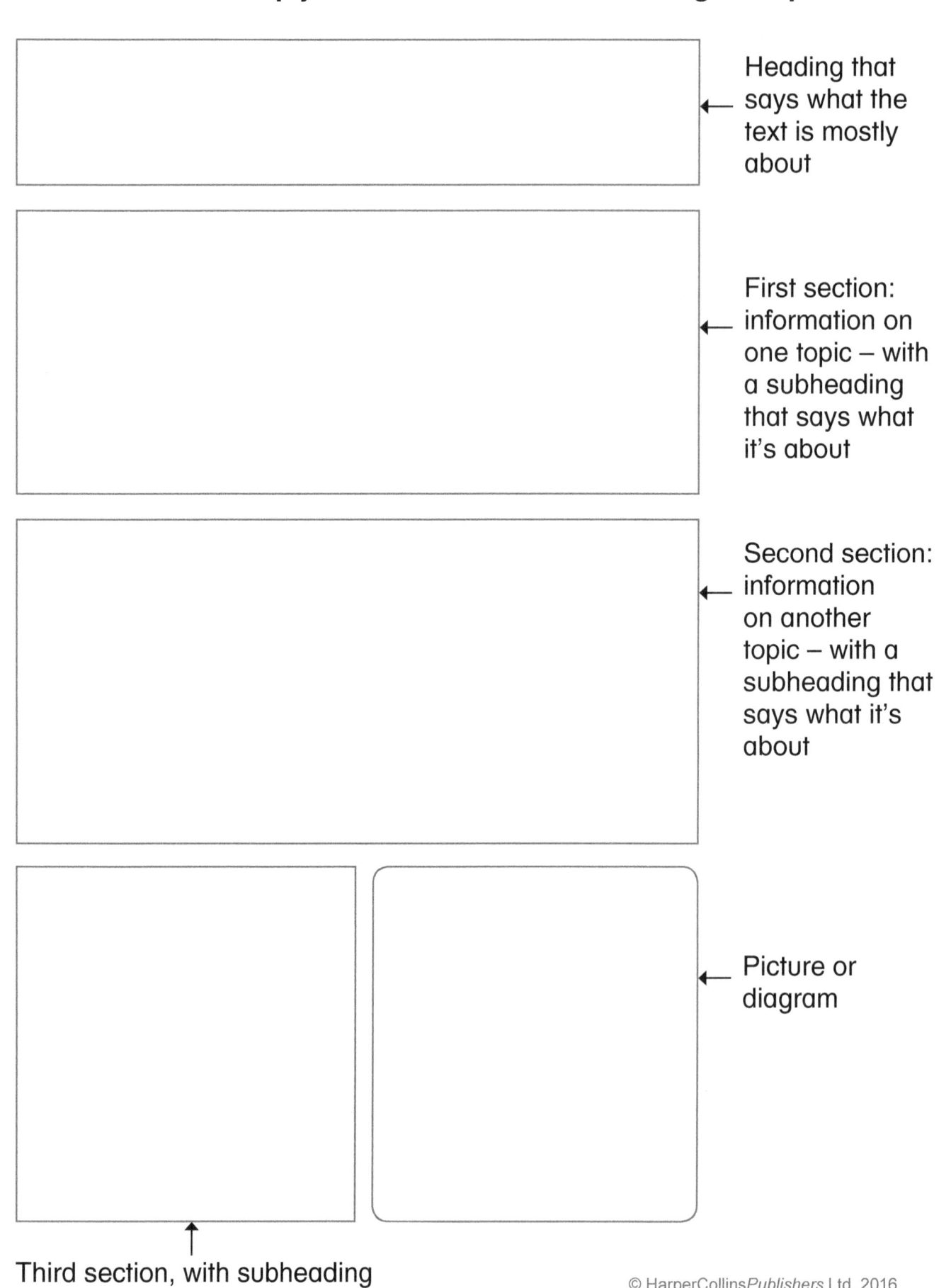

⟵ Heading that says what the text is mostly about

⟵ First section: information on one topic – with a subheading that says what it's about

⟵ Second section: information on another topic – with a subheading that says what it's about

⟵ Picture or diagram

Third section, with subheading

© HarperCollinsPublishers Ltd. 2016

Instructions

Use this sheet to help you write a short set of instructions.

⬅ Heading that says what the instructions are for

⬅ 'What you need' section – with a bullet point for each thing the reader needs.

⬅ 'What to do' section, with numbered instructions. Most of the sentences should be orders (e.g. 'Cut the paper,' etc.

Include little pictures with the instructions if that will help the reader.

Stage 4 PCM 18

Writing a letter

Use this writing frame to help you write a good letter.

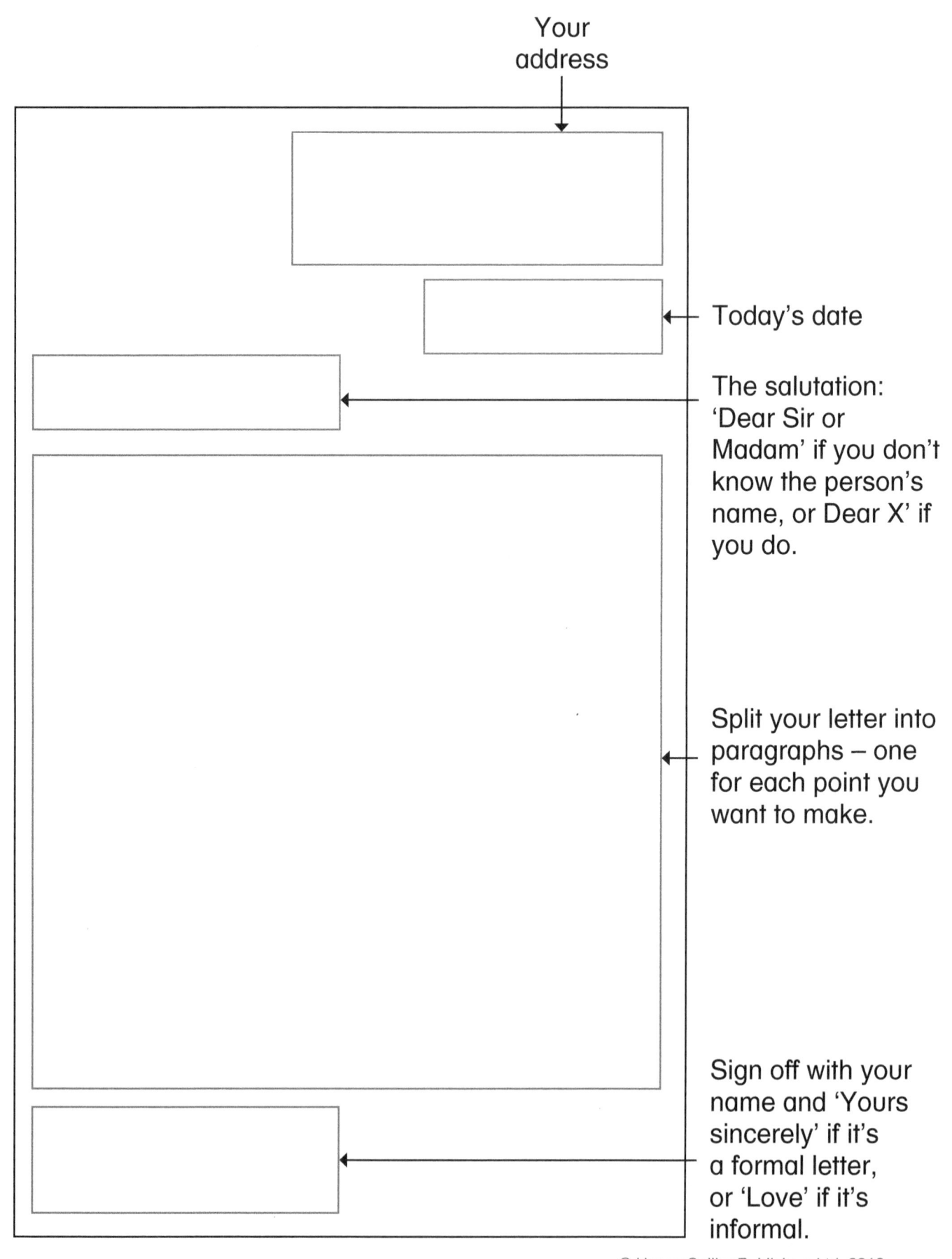

Your address

Today's date

The salutation: 'Dear Sir or Madam' if you don't know the person's name, or Dear X' if you do.

Split your letter into paragraphs – one for each point you want to make.

Sign off with your name and 'Yours sincerely' if it's a formal letter, or 'Love' if it's informal.

© HarperCollinsPublishers Ltd. 2016

Letter to a newspaper

Read this letter to a newspaper, and then answer the questions on page 44 of the Workbook.

11 Anytown View

Anytown

Anyland

6 January

Dear Sir or Madam,

I believe that the most important invention created in the last hundred years is the Internet. It is hard to believe how much our lives have changed since the Internet was invented! Here are just some of the ways in which the Internet has improved life for most people.

First of all, the Internet connects people. Families who live far apart can use video calls, so they can not only speak to each other, but see each other too. People can also use email to stay in touch easily, even when there is a great distance between them.

Secondly, the Internet contains a vast amount of useful information. If you want to know the answer to a question, just type it into a search engine. In moments you will find many different websites offering an answer. In addition, the Internet is a brilliant source of entertainment. Whatever your interest, you will find something to enjoy on the Internet.

The Internet also makes life easier. Why queue for hours at the shops, when you can order your shopping in the peace and quiet of your home – and have it delivered direct to your door?

In conclusion, I believe that the Internet is the finest human invention of the last century. I would certainly not like to go back to life before the Internet was invented!

Yours faithfully,

A Baxter

A. Baxter

Peter and the Wolf: story summary

Peter lived with his grandfather in a cottage in the middle of a forest. In front of the cottage was a green meadow, but Grandfather wouldn't let Peter play there. He kept warning Peter that a wolf was out there in the forest, waiting to gobble Peter up.

Peter wouldn't listen to Grandfather. He loved playing in the meadow, because his friends Duck and Bird lived there. Peter's Cat loved the meadow too – especially when he was trying to catch Bird!

One day Grandfather caught Peter in the meadow, playing with Duck, Cat and Bird. Grandfather was very angry and sent Peter straight to his room.

As soon as Peter and Grandfather had gone, the wolf came out of the forest and tried to catch Cat! Just in time, Cat leapt up a tree. Then the wolf decided to eat Duck, instead – and after a long chase, he caught her! He snapped her up in one gulp.

Luckily, Peter had seen what happened. He climbed out of his bedroom window and fetched a rope. Then he crept over to the tree where Bird and Cat were sitting. The wolf was at the bottom of the tree, snapping and trying to catch Bird and Cat. They were trapped!

Peter climbed up the tree without the wolf seeing him. He told Bird to fly around the wolf's head and make him dizzy. Then Peter made his rope into a lasso, and caught the wolf's tail. He hoisted the wolf up into the tree and tied the rope round a branch, so the wolf was trapped.

Just then, a hunter came along. He wanted to shoot Bird – but when Peter explained that he and Bird had just caught the wolf, the hunter changed his mind! He agreed to help Peter and his friends take the wolf to the zoo, where he wouldn't cause any more trouble.

Grandfather was very proud of Peter when he realised how brave he had been. So everyone was happy ... or nearly everyone! Duck was still trapped inside the wolf's belly. He had swallowed her whole!

© HarperCollins*Publishers* Ltd. 2016

A Difficult Decision: character cards

Stage 4 — PCM 21

Use these cards to help you get into role and decide what your character would say!

Anjali

You really, really want to go on the school trip – but you feel a bit mixed up, because you want the kitten, too.
You also feel a bit bad that Aditya would miss out on the kitten if you went on the trip.

Aditya

You feel as though everything is going wrong! First the holiday is cancelled, and now it looks as though you might not get the kitten either! You really want the kitten, and you can't see why Anjali should go on the trip if the rest of you aren't going to get a holiday.

Mum

You think it would be best to pay for Anjali's trip now, and then try and save up for a kitten next year. Anjali really wants to go on the trip; you are sure she would get a lot out of it, and this opportunity might not come up again. You feel there's no harm in waiting and getting a kitten later.

Dad

You are worried that if Anjali gets to go on the trip, Aditya will feel left out. You think that it would be best to get the kitten – that way, both children get to have something they want. Anjali will survive if she doesn't get to go on the trip, and you feel it's fairer this way.

© HarperCollins*Publishers* Ltd. 2016

Sheetal's First Landing: introduction

Sheetal has grown up on a huge spaceship that explores the galaxy. Now her help is needed to investigate a mysterious alien planet.

This was it! My first ever landing! I'd spent all the nine years of my life so far on our enormous expedition spaceship; I'd never really been outside, only on training simulations. I paused just a second at the hatch of the spaceship, getting my suit cameras to record everything. Then I stepped down, onto the planet surface, where five people in space suits were waiting. "One small step, one giant leap!" said the Landing Party Leader. That's tradition – it's what the Leader always says when someone steps onto their first planet. The Leader stuck a "Landing Party" badge on my space suit, and saluted. Then she added "Happy birthday, Sheetal." Everybody clapped and whooped. I was so excited – but I told myself to be calm and professional. The expedition had no time today for anyone messing up, or showing off, or causing problems.

We needed to finish our work on this planet quickly, because an enormous, dangerous storm was coming. So everyone who could possibly help was needed. Our main job here was to explore a mysterious alien tomb. The landing party needed a small, agile person who could get inside the tomb and put sensors there. I could do that – I had passed my tests on sensors and on planet safety yesterday.

It was the very best ninth birthday I could imagine! No birthday cake, and no presents for me today: we were all far too busy for that. But really – who cares about cake or presents if you get to go *outside*?

Stage 4   PCM 23

Story mountain

Use this story mountain template to help you plan a story.

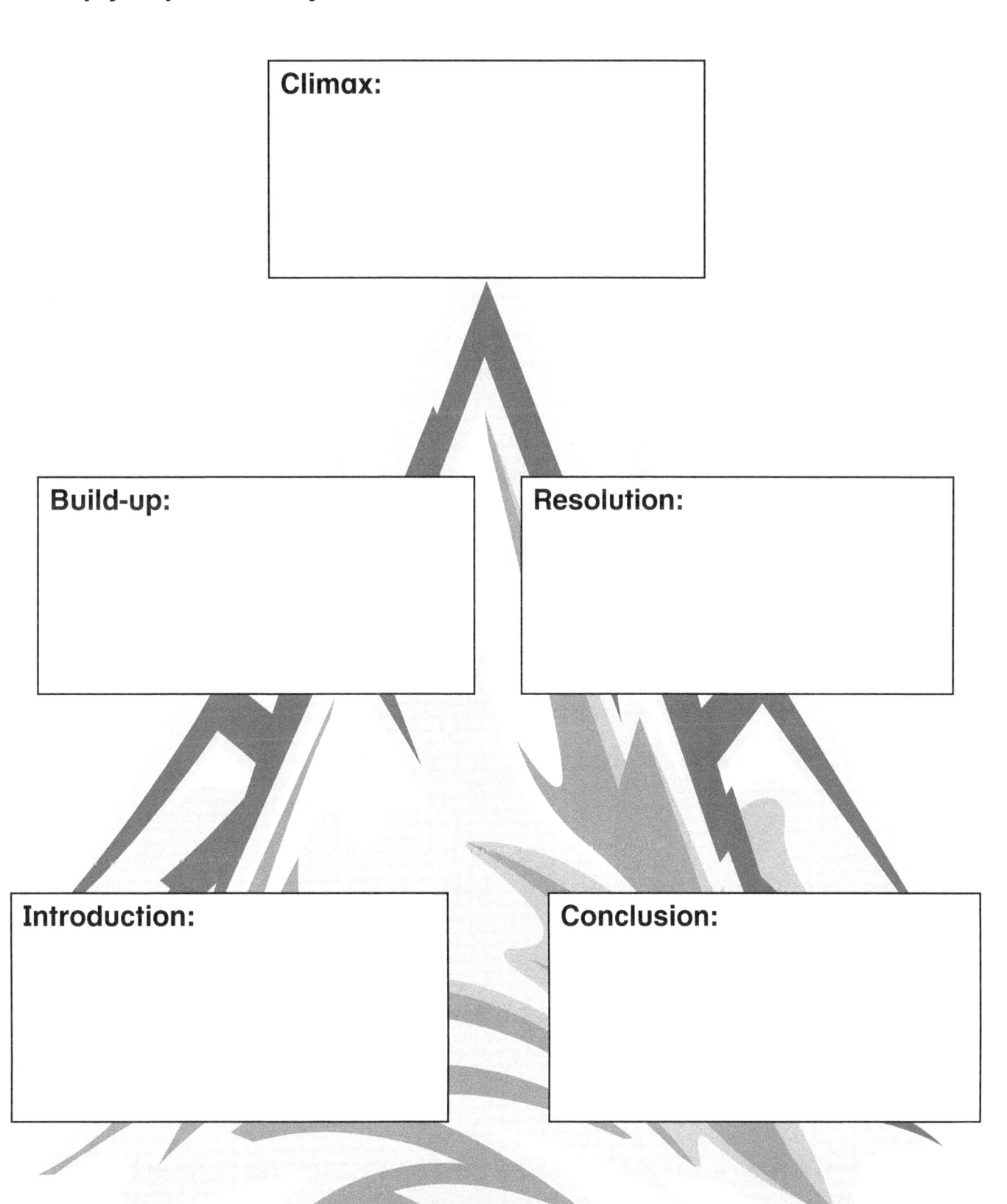

Climax:

Build-up:

Resolution:

Introduction:

Conclusion:

© HarperCollins*Publishers* Ltd. 2016

Formal assessment 1: Units 1–3

Total marks: 26

Read the poem at least twice before you answer the questions.

> **The bicycle's wrists**
>
> You must grip them carefully,
> both at the same time
> as though you were leading
> a partner onto the dance floor
>
> long slender arms extended
> into the blue air of the street,
> with just a touch of stiffness
> as though neither of you
> were sure of the steps.
>
> So you wobble then move
> on an impulse forwards
> you and the wrists
> hanging on for dear life
>
> as if dancing were all
> that kept you from falling.
>
> by George Szirtes

Question 1

Reading

A What do you think the bicycle's 'wrists' are? (1)

B What other sort of activity does the writer compare riding a bicycle with? (1)

C Find and write down two phrases that show that the person in the poem is not very confident about riding a bike. (2)

Stage 4 Formal assessment 1

D Imagine you are watching the scene described in the poem. Describe the scene in your own words. (2)

_____

_____

E How does this poem make you feel? Explain your reasons. (2)

_____

_____

Question 2

Spelling, grammar and punctuation

A Find four verbs in the poem that end in the suffix *–ing*. (2)

_____   _____

_____   _____

B Add the suffix *–ing* to these root verbs from the poem. Think about whether you need to change the spelling of the root verb when you add the suffix! (2)

grip   _____

extend   _____

wobble   _____

keep   _____

C Find two connectives in the poem. (1)

_____

© HarperCollins*Publishers* Ltd. 2016

Stage 4 — Formal assessment 1

D Re-read the first verse of the poem below, and then write it out again as if it were a sentence of direct speech, using all the correct punctuation. (2)

> You must grip them carefully,
> both at the same time
> as though you were leading
> a partner onto the dance floor

_____

_____

_____

E Put these adjectives in order, starting with the weakest and finishing with the strongest. (2)

terrified   nervous   frightened   cautious

_____

excellent   good   adequate   world-beating

_____

Question 3

Writing

A Read this description of an invention. Draw a wavy line under all the opinions and a straight line under all the facts. (4)

- This is the world's most amazing bicycle.

- It's ideal for nervous cyclists and people who are just learning to ride.

- It has a lightweight titanium frame and chunky puncture-proof tyres.

- It comes in a range of colours including black, silver, turquoise, orange and flame-red.

- It can be used on every type of surface – including roads, fields, mountains and even sandy beaches.

© HarperCollins*Publishers* Ltd. 2016

- It is every cyclist's dream.

- It stops automatically if the rider is in danger.

- If you fall off or crash, the bike's built-in crash pads activate automatically and catch you.

B Write a persuasive advertisement for this invention. Give it a catchy name, and don't forget to use facts, opinions and persuasive language in your advertisement. You can use the information in part A, and add your own ideas too. Write at least five sentences. (5)

Formal assessment 2: Units 4–6

Total marks: 27

Read this newspaper article, and then answer the questions.

One giant leap

Have you ever wondered what it would be like to jump from 39 kilometres above the surface of the Earth? Ask Felix Baumgartner – the only human being who has ever tried it.

Ever since he was a boy, Felix has dreamed of flying. He did his first skydive (jumping out of an aeroplane with a parachute) at the age of 16, and since then, he has never looked back! Felix has clocked up many daring feats and world records in his career – for example, he holds the world record for the highest BASE jump from a building, after he jumped with a parachute from the top of the 509-metre high Taipei 101 building in 2007. But for Felix, the ultimate challenge was to annihilate Colonel Joe Kittinger's record for the highest ever skydive. Kittinger set the bar high – literally – when he skydived in 1960 from a height of 31 kilometres. So when Felix came to try to beat the record, he enlisted Kittinger's help to ensure he got everything right. The adventurous duo worked with a team of experts to ensure that Felix had all of the equipment and training he needed to make a safe jump from the astonishing height of 39 kilometres above Earth. Felix even needed a specially designed protective pod to take him to the site of the jump, right on the edge of space.

After many months of preparation, the great day finally came. At 9.28 a.m. on 14 October 2012, Felix's pod was attached to a huge helium-filled balloon that slowly lifted him all the way up to the jump point. Two and a half hours later, at 12.06 p.m., Felix jumped. Less than a minute after evacuating the pod, he had reached his maximum speed of 1,358 kilometres per hour – that's faster than the speed of sound!

After four minutes, 20 seconds of free fall, Felix opened his parachute. Just nine minutes after making the jump, he touched down safely in the New Mexico desert – and smashed the skydiving world record!

Question 1

Reading

A Write one sentence to sum up the main point of this newspaper report. (1)

B Why did Felix Baumgartner want Joe Kittinger to help him prepare for his record-breaking skydive? (1)

C How did Felix's protective pod get up to the jump site on the edge of space? (1)

D What impression do you get of Felix Baumgartner from the report? Write two sentences to describe him. (2)

E How long did it take Felix to reach Earth on his record-breaking skydive? (1)

F What record-breaking feat did Felix carry out in 2007? (1)

G Re-read the first sentence of the report. Why do you think the writer chose to begin the report this way? (1)

Stage 4   Formal assessment 2

Question 2

Grammar, vocabulary and punctuation

A Find and write down one statement, one question and one order from the newspaper report. (3)

_____

_____

B Rewrite these two sentences to change them into orders. (2)

Would you like to find out about the champion skydiver Felix Baumgartner?

_____

You could tell your friends about Felix's amazing adventure.

_____

C Underline the powerful verbs in these two sentences. At the end of each sentence, write another verb that could be used instead of the one you underlined. (2)

But for Felix, the ultimate challenge was to annihilate Colonel Joe Kittinger's record for the highest ever skydive. _____

Less than a minute after evacuating the pod, he had reached his maximum speed of 1,358 kilometres per hour. _____

D Two commas are missing from each of these sentences. Write out the sentences again, adding the missing commas. (2)

Felix Baumgartner the record-breaking skydiver is the only person who has ever jumped from 39 kilometres above Earth.

_____

Felix made his amazing jump having spent many months preparing for it in October 2012.

_____

© HarperCollins*Publishers* Ltd. 2016

Stage 4 Formal assessment 2

Question 3

Writing

A Read this short description of another amazing feat by Felix Baumgartner. Use the information here to write a newspaper report about it. Your report should be at least five sentences long. Remember to include:

- a headline
- a punchy opening
- the key facts
- your own opinion of what Felix did
- at least two sentences with powerful verbs. (10)

Felix wanted to try something never done before, so in 2003 he skydived all the way across the English Channel. This was very difficult because he had to glide for 36 kilometres during the free fall, in order to get across the Channel.

To do the skydive, he wore a specially designed set of wings that allowed him to glide. He looked like a human aeroplane.

Felix's English Channel skydive

Location: English Channel

Height: 9.8 kilometres

Distance travelled: 36 kilometres

Top speed: 360 kilometres per hour

Journey duration: six minutes, 22 seconds

© HarperCollins*Publishers* Ltd. 2016

Stage 4 — **Formal assessment 3**

Formal assessment 3: Units 7–9

Total marks: 36

Read this playscript, and then answer the questions.

Mr Harvey and the Alien

SCENE 1: Outside school.

(It is evening. Only MR HARVEY, the headteacher, is still at school. He is just unlocking his bike, and is keen to go home.

An ALIEN appears behind him as if from nowhere. MR HARVEY doesn't notice at first.)

ALIEN: *(cautiously)* Er ... excuse me?

MR HARVEY: *(impatiently, still bending down and unlocking his bike so he can't see the alien)* Yes? What is it? I thought all you children had gone home by now!

ALIEN: Are you the famous and powerful leader Mr Harvey?

MR HARVEY: *(straightening up, still with his back to the alien)* Ha! Well, I don't think I've ever been called that before!

ALIEN: *(urgently)* We need your help, sir!

MR HARVEY: *(turning around and seeing the alien)* Oh, my goodness! Is this some kind of prank?

ALIEN: No, sir! I come in peace, from Planet Warthog! It is many light-years from your galaxy. My ship's computer has led me to you, sir. It tells me that you are a great peacemaker who can bring enemies together and find solutions to terrible problems!

MR HARVEY: *(thoughtfully)* Well ... I suppose I did manage to stop that fight between Jack and Zoltan this afternoon ...

ALIEN: *(eagerly)* Exactly! This is why we need you, sir! My planet is troubled with problems almost as terrible as the war between Jack and Zoltan. Only you can help us. Will you come with me? My ship is waiting. It can travel great distances in the blink of an eye.

MR HARVEY: Hmm. It's the big match this evening. If you promise to get me back home before it starts, I suppose I could come and see what I can do.

ALIEN: Thank you, sir! Thank you! Come with me: I promise you will be home before you know it.

(A space ship materialises in front of them. The ALIEN leads MR HARVEY inside, and it vanishes.)

Stage 4 — Formal assessment 3

Question 1

Reading

A What is the setting of this playscript?

Draw a circle around the part of the playscript that gives you this information. (2)

B Write down at least three ways in which playscripts are different from stories. (3)

C What does Mr Harvey think the alien is, at first?

Write down the sentence that tells you this. (2)

D Find and write down two adverbs from the playscript.

Why have these adverbs been used? (2)

E Why is the alien so keen to have Mr Harvey visit his planet? (1)

Stage 4   **Formal assessment 3**

F What might have happened next if Mr Harvey had said no to the alien? Write a new ending for the playscript where Mr Harvey says no. Write at least two more speeches for Mr Harvey, and two for the alien. (4)

Question 2

Grammar, punctuation and spelling

A Read this conversation from the playscript. Write it out again in direct speech, as if it came from a story, not a play. Remember to add the correct punctuation, and words like 'said Mr Harvey'. (4)

MR HARVEY: Hmm. It's the big match this evening. If you promise to get me back home before it starts, I suppose I could come and see what I can do.

ALIEN: Thank you, sir! Thank you! Come with me: I promise you will be home before you know it.

Stage 4 Formal assessment 3

B These sentences from the playscript are in the present tense. Write them out again, changing the words so that they are in the past tense. (4)

Is this some kind of prank? _____

_____

I come in peace, from Planet Warthog! _____

_____

This is why we need you, sir! _____

_____

It can travel great distances in the blink of an eye. _____

_____

C The following words from the playscript are homophones. Choose the correct homophone from each pair to fill the gaps in these sentences. (4)

peace/piece   by/buy   some/sum   great/grate

We had a _____ day last Saturday.

I amazed Mum _____ doing all the washing up.

There is only one _____ of cake left.

Dad gave me a big lump of cheese to _____.

The opposite of war is _____.

_____ people like getting up early, but others don't.

I went to the shop because I wanted to _____ a packet of crisps.

I've nearly finished my maths homework, but I'm stuck on a difficult _____.

© HarperCollinsPublishers Ltd. 2016

Question 3

Writing

A Re-read the playscript, and think about what might happen when Mr Harvey arrives on the alien's planet. Write a short story of at least three paragraphs about what he sees and does. Remember to include:

- a description of the setting
- some dialogue set out as direct speech
- some powerful verbs and interesting adjectives
- a clear beginning, middle and end. (10)

TRAFFORD TRAMWAYS

By

ARTHUR KIRBY B.Sc., B.A.(Com.)

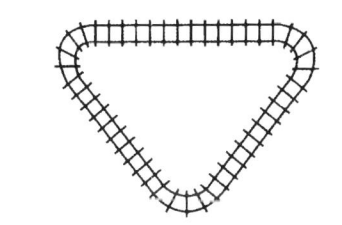

Triangle Publishing

ACKNOWLEDGEMENTS

First and foremost I am indebted to the many photographers and postcard publishers without whose work this book would not have been possible. Given the abandonment of the trams in Sale and Altrincham as early as 1931, and the absence of transport photographers, coverage in these districts is totally dependent on postcard publishers. These are credited where known, but many of those operating in localised areas produced their work anonymously. I would be pleased to hear from any reader with information on them and, indeed, additional photographs and postcards. My thanks too, to those who have contributed photographs, acknowledged with the captions.

Much of the material has been gleaned over a long period from information held by Manchester Central Library Local Studies and Archive Departments, and Trafford Libraries, to whom many thanks. Mr. R.A. Smith produced the excellent maps from my rough outlines expeditiously and efficiently.

Lastly, a big thank you to my brother, Mr. H.A. Kirby, for word processing and continuous updating of the text, and to Mr. Dennis Sweeney for undertaking publication.

Arthur Kirby,
Rhos-on-Sea, March 2003.

Plate 1. The first car to Altrincham, No.263, on 30th April 1907, seen in Stamford New Road. *Bowdon Series.*

The Metropolitan Borough of Trafford came into being on 1st April 1974 under a general re-organisation of local government in England and Wales. This publication is mainly a pictorial record of the electric tramways which operated in Stretford Borough, Sale Urban District, Altrincham Urban District and Bucklow Rural District over the period March 1903 to August 1946, and which were incorporated in Trafford.

In the last quarter of the nineteenth century the Manchester Carriage and Tramways Company had built up a network of horse tramways extending from Barton Road, Stretford, in the West, to Stalybridge in the East and from Waterhead, Oldham, in the North to Stockport in the South, operated by a fleet of 500 horse trams. Towards the end of the century, local authorities were given powers to operate tramways, whereas previously they had been permitted only to own and lease the lines. At a conference in Manchester on 19th January 1898, Manchester, Salford, Oldham and Ashton decided to acquire the company's business in their respective areas, including tracks where not already owned, in order to electrify and enlarge the operation; Stockport also decided to establish its own system. Manchester had agreed with ten adjacent urban districts to acquire the company's lines for electrification, and to operate them under lease from the individual authorities. Manchester formed a Tramways Committee on 9th November 1898, with a view to operation when the existing leases came to an end, generally speaking on 27th April 1901. Arrangements were made with the Company to minimise disruption to the horse-tram services during reconstruction of the tracks, including a guarantee of the company's rate of profit at its last full year of operation, which was equivalent to £921/7s/4d. *(£53,250 at December 2002 prices)* per mile, until 31st May 1902.

The official opening of the Manchester system, built to the standard gauge of 4ft 8½in like the horse tramways, took place on 6th June 1901, and services to Hightown and Cheetham Hill commenced the next day. The horse lines in Stretford, which were mainly opened on 1st November 1880, were a continuation of the Manchester lines in Chester Road, City Road and Stretford Road through Trafford Bar to Barton Road *(Old Cock Hotel)* with short branches in Trafford Road, Talbot Road, and portions of Chorlton Road and Upper Chorlton Road, where Stretford had a boundary with the urban districts of Moss Side and Withington. These authorities were subsequently absorbed by Manchester on 9th November 1904. In November 1901, Stretford told Manchester that reconstruction of the lines would commence in the spring for completion by the end of September 1902. It hoped to supply power towards the end of 1902, but thought it more prudent to plan on the basis of February 1903. Stretford suggested that, under its agreement with the Carriage Company, Manchester should give notice to the Company to work the tramways for a period of six months from 31st May 1902, and depending on progress, should serve a further notice for an additional three or six months' operation if necessary. In the event it was agreed that Stretford would take possession of the tramways on 1st December. As a condition, the Carriage Company required an agreement to pay interest at 5% on the purchase price of the lines and agreed equipment as from 31st May 1902, the previously agreed general deadline for the Company's operation, because the sum involved had not been agreed, and hence had not been paid. Stretford asked the Company to waive the interest until the lines had been reconstructed and Manchester had commenced operation. This was not acceptable, and an alternative suggestion by Stretford that the interest should be waived until 1st December was also turned down. The Company pointed out that every other authority concerned had agreed to pay the interest and did not see why Stretford should expect different treatment.

The matter then passed into the hands of the legal advisors and in this situation the Company declined to sell eighty horses to Manchester for working the lines, as had been done in similar situations elsewhere. Thus, on 1st December 1902 Stretford found itself without a tramway service for, the termination period having expired, the Carriage Company refrained from operating, whilst Manchester was in no position to do so. This situation was in marked contrast to that pertaining in South Manchester on that day, when electric services were introduced, including Chester Road and Stretford Road to the Stretford boundary.

Manchester immediately commenced reconstruction in Stretford Road and City Road, and on 5th December was served with a writ on behalf of the Carriage Company. On 12th December the Carriage Company was granted an injunction compelling Manchester to cease the reconstruction and a service of horse cars it had, after all, been able to provide. It was necessary to fill in the holes which had been dug for the erection of poles.

Recognising the inconvenience being caused to residents, and in agreement with Stretford, Manchester submitted to the terms which the Company had stipulated in the Court action. These were to pay interest at 5% on the purchase price as from 31st August 1902, until completion, and to pay for the cost of the upkeep of the horses from 30th November until sold. As a result the horse-car services resumed in Stretford on 10th January, when they carried 4181 passengers for receipts of £23/6s/7½d *(£1,300)*.

Reconstruction was pressed ahead, and the electrified route opened on 9th March 1903, operating from Trafford Bar to Piccadilly via Chester Road and outwards via City Road to the starting point, and reverse of this. At the same time a service was introduced between Trafford Bar and Piccadilly via Stretford Road. The horse-trams continued to operate from Trafford Bar to Barton

Plate 2. Tram No.316 makes the first trial trip over the Sale tramway to School Road on 25th July 1906.

Plate 3. Here, three days later, No.329 enters Sale; it is believed to be the first car on the service introduced that day.

Plate 4. No.316 also made the first experimental trip to Brooklands and Timperley, Park Road, on 15th August, and the service was opened two days later. The through fare was 4½d for the seven mile journey. The route board and window board both read "Special Car Private".

Road, but this section was electrified on 13th April, when the City Road/Chester Road services were extended to the new terminus. Because of the special circumstances Manchester was given a 23 year lease instead of the normal 21 years, operative from the opening to Barton Road.

Towards the end of the nineteenth century dissatisfaction by Manchester manufacturers and traders over the cost of transport of raw materials from Liverpool Docks led to the construction of the Manchester Ship Canal, which opened on 1st January 1894. Marshall Stevens, who had been one of the leading promoters of the Canal project, was anxious to develop an industrial estate in the Docks area to generate inward traffics of raw materials and outward cargoes of manufactured goods for the Ship Canal. This led to the formation of Trafford Park Estates Ltd, which bought the 1,183 acre estate of the De Traffords which typically, contained a hall, lake and open parkland, avenues of trees and a herd of deer. This deal took place in 1896.

In 1901 Manchester approached Stretford with a view to amalgamation on the basis of the latter's importance and rateable value, then expanding at a fast pace because of the industrial development taking place in Trafford Park, which lay mainly in the Urban District, because of investment made by Manchester in the Canal and the utilities. Naturally, with Trafford Park's growing importance, Stretford was also anxious to extend its jurisdiction to the private roads in the Estate. Manchester promised the Estates Company that if Stretford was absorbed the rights and privelidges of tenants in Trafford Park would be maintained; however, following an amalgamation inquiry, Stretford remained an independent urban district.

In November 1902, the Company sought tenders for the construction of an electric tramway to run from Trafford Road, along Trafford Park Road, Ashburton Road, Third Avenue and Westinghouse Road, returning along Trafford Park Road to Trafford Road. The Estate Company's line duly opened on 14th July 1903, followed two days later by a line from Chester Road along Trafford Road, but because of differences between the Company and Stretford the two systems were not connected; given this situation the Company sought Parliamentary powers.

The Trafford Park Bill came before a House of Lords Committee on 12th May 1904, when it was announced that a settlement had been made between the Company, Manchester, Salford and Stretford. The main features were that Manchester and Salford were granted running powers over the Estate line for the duration of Stretford's lease of its own lines to Manchester, and that Manchester would lay a double triangular junction on behalf of Stretford connecting the Trafford Road tramway with the Trafford Park line. This work was carried out over the period 18th August to 9th September; Manchester's trams could now run into Trafford Park because the junction had been made, but Salford's were unable to do so pending construction of the track on the Trafford Road swing bridge across the Ship Canal, the boundary with Stretford. This led the Estates Company to issue writs on Manchester and Salford in March, 1905, claiming £10,000 *(£559,000)* damages for breach of the Agreement of May, 1904. It is possible that Manchester refrained from operating because Salford was unable to do so, but another aspect of the situation was uncertainty as to whether the lines in the Park had been statutorily authorised. The Company withdrew its writs on an undertaking by Manchester and Salford to commence through running into the Park on 30th October, and Manchester withdrawing its charge of £446/14/- *(£25,000)* representing one-third of the total cost of the junction.

Meanwhile, developments had been taking place in Sale. The British Electric Traction Company Ltd. had been establishing electric tramway systems in various parts of the country since the late 1890s, including a line through Ashton and Hyde, and a system centred on Middleton. In 1902 it announced proposals for tramways in Sale connecting with the line at Barton Road *(Old Cock),* and for running powers to Manchester. Following discussions, Altrincham, Sale, Ashton-upon-Mersey (then a separate urban district) and Bucklow concluded that

Plate 5. Again on the first journey to Altrincham, 30th April 1907, tram No.263 is seen at the Downs terminus.

Bowdon Series.

a tramway from Stretford to Altrincham was desirable. On 10th November these authorities, apart from Sale, decided to oppose BETs scheme, which appeared as the North Cheshire Tramways Bill. At its meeting on 12th January 1903, Sale considered Manchester's terms for operating in the district; it decided to express to Manchester its surprise at the lateness of the proposals, and to support the BET Bill; the other districts, together with Stretford and Cheshire, decided to oppose it.

Powers were also sought in the same session of Parliament for tramways in Sale and adjacent districts through the medium of the Manchester Southern Tramways Company. Two Bills were presented; the Manchester Southern Tramways (Lancashire) Bill sought powers for lines running from Eccles through Stretford via Barton Road and Chester Road, whilst the Cheshire Bill sought powers in Sale and onwards to the Altrincham boundary, with a branch from Sale to Gatley. Sale decided, on 19th March 1903, to oppose the Cheshire Bill since it was already supporting the BET Bill. Manchester had offered a 23-year lease as in the case of Stretford, whereas BET had offered a 35-year lease. Following negotiations Sale dropped its support for the BET Bill on Manchester conceding substantially the same terms as the Company was prepared to give, and particularly a 35-year lease. BET's Bill was abandoned in favour of the alternative modified to provide a route through Chapel Road and Tatton Road instead of School Road. Ashton-upon-Mersey, whose boundary with Sale was mainly in the middle of Cross Street and Washway Road, claimed credit for the demise of the BET scheme, since it had been prepared to support only proposals which would allow a through service by tram between Altrincham and Manchester, operated by Manchester.

Manchester then opened negotiations with Altrincham which had decided to obtain its own Parliamentary powers, and heads of agreement were concluded. Manchester was to be given a 23-year lease. The question of tramways in Altrincham had been raised in 1901 by Charles E. Newton of Manchester. He financed a poll by council officials on 16th September 1902; of 2874 ratepayers, 894 were in favour of a local system and 473 against. The proposed Altrincham and District Tramway was basically a figure-of-eight system intersecting at Moss Lane Bridge (Altrincham Station) extending to Timperley, West Timperley, Hale, Bowdon and Dunham Massey. Timings for the four trams suggested for the four directions, would coincide with train arrival and departure times.

The extension of the line from Barton Road to Crossford Bridge, spanning the River Mersey, generally the boundary between Lancashire and Cheshire, was constructed largely in 1904, with completion on 7th September. The bridge was not wide enough for a double track tramway, so it was

Plate 6. For the Official Opening of the through route to Altrincham on 9th May 1907, a procession of seven trams left Manchester Town Hall via Mount Street, Peter Street, Oxford Street and Stretford Road. The convoy is here seen halted in Stretford Road, at Northumberland Road, outside Old Trafford Technical School, where members of the Stretford party boarded.

Plate 7. Journey's end in Altrincham and it is interesting to note that the front window is closed, having been open when photographed in Stretford Road - perhaps the civic worthies could not cope with the breeze from the unaccustomed speed! The decorations on the dash have also slipped during the journey. The tram standard to the right has not yet been fitted with its finial.

Neil's Series.

agreed that it should be widened. There was, however, some disagreement between Lancashire, Stretford, Sale, Ashton-upon-Mersey and Manchester over the respective contributions to the cost. These had not been resolved by February 1906, when following strong protests from Ashton-upon-Mersey about the delay in constructing the tramways, Manchester decided to go ahead with the extension to Sale. Work commenced on 17th April.

Lancashire thought it regrettable to lay a single track in view of the negotiations for widening the bridge. These were complicated by the fact that, unusually, the boundary between Lancashire and Cheshire in the vicinity of the bridge lay to the south of the river, so that the bridge was wholly in Lancashire. In July the total cost of the work was estimated at £3,000 *(£179,000)*, of which Lancashire was prepared to contribute £1,750 *(£104,000)*, the balance to be met by Stretford. Work on a single track on the bridge commenced on 4th July, laid in a position such that little alteration would be required when the bridge was widened and the track eventually doubled.

On 25th July there was an experimental trip over the new line to the terminus at School Road using open-top tram No.316. The public service started on 28th July with a through fare from School Road to Manchester of 3½d *(87p)*; the fare from Barton Road to Manchester was reduced from 3d to 2½d *(62p)* at the same time. Trams ran from School Road every eight minutes travelling to Manchester alternately via City Road and Chester Road. At Crossford Bridge cars travelling towards Manchester had right of way; later in the year a signal activated by a contact plate was introduced. The single train fare was 5½d with a return of 8d. Trams operated from School Road from 7.26 a.m. until midnight. On the first day (Saturday) takings were £117 *(£7,000)*

Plate 8. The first tram, now the last, reaches School Road as the procession returns to Manchester.

Birkenhead Series.

followed by £162 *(£9,700)* on the Sunday. The timing allowed five minutes from Barton Road to the new terminus.

On Wednesday, 15th August, open-top car No.316 also made the first journey to Brooklands and Timperley (Park Road), with the Board of Trade inspection following the next day. On 17th August the service was extended to Park Road, with a through fare of 4½d *(110p)* for the seven mile journey from Manchester. The frequency was ten minutes from 7.30 a.m. until noon, then every 7½ minutes until 10.30 p.m. As previously, the cars ran alternately via City Road and Chester Road. In late October 1906, cars running only to Stretford were re-routed to run along Stretford Road in both directions, in response to requests from shopkeepers in Stretford Road.

The branch from the main line via Ashfield Road (a better route than Chapel Road which had itself replaced School Road as originally planned) and Tatton Road to Sale Station (Sale Bridge) opened on 25th March 1907, and Manchester was granted a 42 year lease. The Ashfield Road tramway was double-track with wires supported by eight poles central to the tracks. The first tram arrived at Sale Bridge at 7.20a.m., and the service was an extension of the Stretford service operating at ten minute intervals to Piccadilly via Stretford Road.

On the afternoon of 30th April 1907, a Tuesday, balcony car No.263 made the first journey over the Altrincham lines. Its appearance caused some surprise since work on the overhead had taken place earlier in the day, and the Press had indicated that the new section would not open until 9th May. The official opening of the route to Altrincham took place on this day, a Thursday, when seven special trams, several of which were decorated with evergreens, journeyed from Manchester Town Hall to Altrincham, stopping in Stretford where members of Stretford Council and representatives of other public bodies boarded the cars, and also at Crossford Bridge where invited guests from Sale and Ashton-upon-Mersey joined. Meanwhile, the Altrincham representatives left the Town Hall at 3.30p.m. in wagonettes and drove to the Altrincham boundary where a silk tape had been stretched across the road. The Manchester contingent arrived shortly before 4.00p.m., and as the first car stopped at the tape the assembled company gave a welcoming cheer. The cars remained only for a few minutes at the terminus, commencing the return journey at 4.20p.m., the first car arriving back in Albert Square, Manchester, 45 minutes later. The procession then continued to Heaton Park, reached at 5.50p.m., where some 300/400 guests were entertained to tea. An illuminated tram left Heaton Park at 8.00p.m. reaching the Altrincham terminus at 9.50p.m. This had been decorated with 1,800 coloured lights and was followed by five other double-deck trams.

Work started on 13th September to widen Crossford Bridge from 40 feet to 65 feet, which entailed setting back the Bridge Inn at the southern approach. The track was eventually doubled in January 1908 and came into use about the 23rd of that month. Following widening of a portion of the bridge at Sale station and other road improvements, the Sale tramway was extended to Sale Moor, an additional 1346 yards of which 1023 yards was single-track and 323 yards double, comprising two passing loops and a terminal spur. This service opened on 4th July 1912 with car No.673; Manchester's lease for this extension was, as the section to the station, for 42 years.

Plate 9. This tram, seen in Hyde Road Works with some of the employees involved, was decorated to mark the opening of the jointly operated through route to Waterhead, Oldham, on 21st January 1907, following connection of the tracks at Hollinwood, the Failsworth - Oldham boundary.

With slight alteration to the headboard it was probably used to mark the opening of the extension from Seymour Grove (West Point) to Chorlton. On the evening of 8th May 1907 the decorated tram left Piccadilly at 8.30p.m., reaching the Chorlton terminus at High Lane at 9.05, thence returning to Piccadilly at 9.40p.m.

The following day the same vehicle visited Altrincham in the evening as detailed in the text.

Route numbers were introduced in 1914:

12/13	Hightown-Chorlton
27	Trafford Bar-Clayton
29	Trafford Park-Guide Bridge
30	Trafford Bridge-Fairfield
45	Piccadilly-West Didsbury-Chorlton-Piccadilly
46	Piccadilly-Chorlton-West Didsbury-Piccadilly
47	Altrincham-Manchester via City Road in, Chester Road out
48	Altrincham-Manchester via Chester Road in, City Road out
49	Sale Moor-Piccadilly
58	(from 12th Sept 1926) Barton Road-Pendleton

After an approach by the Post Office, arrangements were made for a posting box to be carried on one journey on each of 14 Manchester and 7 Salford tram routes commencing on Monday, 5th November 1923. These were timed to arrive in Manchester around 9.30p.m., thus providing a later posting facility for the districts covered. They included the 9.04p.m. departure from Trafford Park on the 29 route arriving in Manchester at 9.30p.m., the 8.26p.m. from Altrincham on the 47 route arriving at 9.25p.m. and the 8.46p.m. from Sale Moor on the 49 route arriving at 9.30p.m. Because of initial confusion, these cars were soon identified by the stencil "POST CAR" instead of the usual route number. Commencing on 6th December 1926 an additional facility was available from Barton Road and from 7th January 1929 another was brought into play from Marsland Road. In August 1930 the timings were such that the post cars were passing through Stretford at 8.56, 8.57, 9.05 and 9.06p.m. The Trafford Park box was additional to these.

In the 1920s Manchester developed a number of suburban bus services which acted as feeders to the tramway routes. A significant development took place on 11th April 1927 with the introduction of an express "limited stop" service between Heywood to the North of Manchester and Cheadle in the South, running along tramway routes for part of its length. The fares were somewhat higher than those on the trams, and on the tramway sections the service stopped only at stage points. A service between

Plate 10. The first passenger car to Sale Moor seen at the terminus on 4th July 1912. The notice in the second window along in the lower saloon indicates that the tram passes the White City entertainment centre near Trafford Road, formerly the Royal Botanical Gardens.

Neil's Series.

Plate 11. En-route to Manchester in the Stretford portion of City Road, this tram has probably started from Barton Road *(Old Cock)* as the photograph was taken in 1905.

Plate 12. Again in the early days, No.160 is about to turn from City Road into Chester Road on its way to Stretford.
Courtesy N. Ellis.

Littleborough, north of Rochdale, and Altrincham opened on 16th May 1929, thus introducing a service over the Manchester 47 and 48 tram routes for the first time. Manchester introduced a service between Altrincham and Piccadilly on 14th March 1930, and on 31st March restricted the tramway service. On 10th April buses commenced to operate between Sale Moor and Piccadilly at peak periods.

Following a resolution of Altrincham Council on 5th August requesting "Removal of the trams in the District entirely", Manchester announced proposals to discontinue the Sale and Altrincham tramways. Negotiations then took place with Altrincham, Stretford and Sale (which merged with Ashton-upon-Mersey on 10th October 1930) regarding the financial aspects given that the lease in Altrincham had expired, those in Sale expired at various dates to 1954, the Stretford lease terms had been miscalculated, and that there were other tramways in Stretford operated by Manchester.

The Altrincham services required 12 trams throughout the day plus a further nine at peak periods; for Sale Moor the figures were 12 and 6 respectively. The journey time to Altrincham had been reduced from 58 to 53 minutes. Annual loadings were 10.2 m passengers for the Altrincham service and 10.8 m for Sale Moor.

On 3rd November, Manchester introduced double-deck buses on the Altrincham-Piccadilly express service and told Altrincham it would "take off as many trams as possible as soon as you have granted licences for the double-deck buses". Buses took over the regular service on 19th January 1931 with trams operating at the peak periods until Saturday, 6th June when the last tram departed Altrincham at 1.00p.m. Buses took over the 49 service to Sale Moor on 19th July, two weeks later than originally expected, and also the 58 route which had been operated by Salford (previously joint) from 17th January 1927. The tram tracks south of Warwick Road and in City Road from Chester Road to Great Jackson Street were then abandoned. On 11th May the Altrincham - Manchester railway had been electrified, with a schedule time of 24 minutes from Altrincham to London Road (now Piccadilly) station. This now forms part of the Metrolink tramway system, diverging from the original trackbed at Cornbrook at the Manchester boundary to enter Lower Mosley Street via one of the viaducts to the former Central Railway Station (now G-Mex) and running along the side of this building to street level. The journey time to G-Mex, the equivalent to Knott Mill (now Deansgate) station on the original route, is 18 minutes, and to Piccadilly 26 minutes.

In 1921 a double-track tramway was laid in Seymour Grove linking Trafford Bar to the Chorlton tramway at West Point, and in 1924 the Talbot Road stub terminal was extended along Talbot Road, linked to a double-track tramway in Warwick Road which served the Lancashire County Cricket Ground and Manchester United Football Ground. Seymour Grove was served by route 54, initially operating between Albert Square and Chorlton via City Road, but the route was varied over the years.

The 29 service latterly operating from Trafford Park to Fairfield ran for the last time on 17th

Plate 13. A busy scene at Trafford Bar about 1906. On the left, tram No.305 is inward bound to Deansgate, and is about to pass a tram which is probably on its way to Stretford. Tram No.493 is destined for Trafford Park whilst No.375 has just started its journey from Trafford Bar to Clayton via Piccadilly.

Courtesy, N.Ellis.

Plate 14. Stretford Road, showing tram No.344 on its way to Sale. The building with the dome on the right beyond the tram is the Technical School.

Plate 15, and opposite, Plate 16. An interesting pair of photographs, since close study shows that the photographer's camera has not been moved. In *Plate15*, a point boy, whose hut is on the left-hand pavement, stands with the point iron at the ready, his eyes apparently on an approaching tram. Behind him tram No.271 awaits departure for Clayton. A few moments later tram 263, which was at the end of the line, has now reversed and in *Plate 16* awaits departure to be followed eventually by tram No.158. The date is about 1906.

The Brooks-Watson Daylight Camera Co., Ltd.

February 1934, and was replaced by buses, trams continuing to operate in the Park at peak periods. Full-day operation of the 30 service to Trafford Bridge appears to have ceased about January 1936. Route 27 was converted to trolleybus operation on Ashton New Road, and to bus operation between Ancoats and Old Trafford on 31st July 1938.

The Chorlton Road service 13 gave way to buses on 12th June 1939, and the 23, which had replaced route 12 on 29th April 1929, was converted on 2nd July. The 45/46 services had been truncated to operate as 46X between Piccadilly and Chorlton via Brooks's Bar on 5th December 1938. The 23 and 13 (replacing the 46X) finally ceased on Saturday 4th May 1946, having been reinstated during the war.

Following revisions to services on 31st July 1938, Seymour Grove had been served by route 37, and this continued to operate throughout the war, the last all-day service in any part of Trafford. This service had been scheduled for conversion to bus operation in September 1939, but this did not go ahead given the outbreak of the war. It finally went over to buses on 26th August 1946, and on this day the Trafford Park lines were also abandoned, marking the end of tramway operation in Trafford 15 years after the first closures.

Plate 17. In this Trafford Bar view the Clayton tram is obscured by the horse drawn vehicle on the left, but on the main line trams are bound for Altrincham and Trafford Park, No.152, whilst the open topper No.379, is destined for Openshaw, from Trafford Park, about 1909.

Plate 18. A warm day, judging by the open windows of the top covered cars. Apart from No.343 waiting to start its journey to Clayton, the trams are very heavily loaded; presumably the crowds are also waiting for trams. Possibly there is an event at Old Trafford - the destination of the enclosed tram.

FARES*

Fare (d)	May 1907	Oct 1913	Dec 1917	July 1918	June 1920	Oct 1920	May 1922	Dec 1924**
1	Trafford Bar	Trafford Bar	Trafford Bar	Princess St./ Lucy St. (Erskine St.)	Egerton St./ York St. (Gt. Jackson St.)	Gt. Jackson St (Higher Cambridge St)	Egerton St./ York St. (Gt. Jackson St)	Northumberland Road (Cornbrook St)
1.5	Warwick Rd	Taylor's Rd	Warwick Rd	Trafford Bar	Northumberland Road (Henrietta St)	Princess St./ Lucy St. (Upper Moss Lane)	Northumberland Road (Henrietta St.)	Trafford Rd
2	Derbyshire La.	Barton Road	Derbyshire La.	Warwick Rd	Trafford Rd	Trafford Bar	Trafford Rd	Cavendish Rd
2.5	Barton Rd	School Rd (Sale Station)	Barton Rd	Derbyshire La.	Cavendish Rd	Warwick Rd	Cavendish Rd	King St.
3	School Rd (Sale Station)	Marsland Rd (Sale Moor)	School Rd (Sale Station)	Barton Rd	King St.	Taylor's Rd	King St.	Crossford Bridge
3.5	Marsland Rd	Park Rd	Marsland Rd (Sale Moor)	School Rd (Sale Station)	Crossford Bridge	King St.	Crossford Bridge	School Rd (Sale Station)
4	Park Rd	Barrington Rd	Park Rd	Marsland Rd (Sale Moor)	School Rd (Sale Station)	Eye Platt Bridge	School Rd (Sale Station)	Raglan Rd (Sale Moor)
4.5	Barrington Rd	Altrincham	Barrington Rd	Park Rd	Raglan Rd (Sale Moor)	Dane Rd	Raglan Rd (Sale Moor)	Park Rd
5	Altrincham		Altrincham	Barrington Rd	Pelican Hotel	Roebuck Lane	Pelican Hotel	Barrington Rd
5.5				Altrincham	Navigation Rd	The Avenue (Sale Moor)	Navigation Rd	Altrincham
6					Stockport Rd	Pelican Hotel	Stockport Rd	
6.5					Altrincham	Broadheath Station	Altrincham	
7						Hazel Rd		
7.5						Altrincham		

December 2002 equivalent (p) of 1d at the above dates

22.6	*20.7*	*11.1*	*10.2*	*8.3*	*7.9*	*11.5*	*11.5*

December 2002 equivalent (p) of the Manchester-Altrincham fare

113	*93.2*	*55.7*	*56.2*	*53.9*	*58.9*	*74.6*	*63.1(50.6**)*

* Stages on the Sale Moor route are shown in brackets where different from those on the Altrincham route.
** A maximum fare of 4d was introduced in February 1930.

Plate 19. The Trafford Bar terminus in Talbot Road of the Clayton cars looking towards Manchester. Car No.348 awaits departure in 1906.

Plate 20. Looking down Trafford Road from Chester Road, a sharp contrast to the present day dual carriageway and traffic volume.
The Brooks-Watson Daylight Camera Co. Ltd.

Plate 21. Trafford Park Road with, in the foreground, the triangular junction with Trafford Road, leading on the right to the Trafford Road swing bridge and the Salford system, seen about 1915.
Abel Heywood & Son.

Plate 22. The decorations in Trafford Park mark the visit of King Edward VII on 13th July 1905, to open the Ship Canal Company's Number 9 Dock. Tram No.6, showing the Destination "Trafford Road", belongs to the Trafford Park Estates Company, whose fleet was acquired by Salford in November 1905, following the introduction of through services by Manchester and Salford on 30th October.

H.L.P.

Plate 23. Westinghouse Road, Trafford Park, about 1910 showing in the distance a Manchester tram outside the premises of British Westinghouse Electric and Manufacturing Company Ltd., from which the road took its name. The insulators carrying the overhead on the Trafford Park system were attached directly to the arms of the standards.

Barber.

Plate 24. "Balloon" car No.572, photographed on 21st January 1916, approaching Trafford Park Road. There were 34 locations where tram tracks crossed railway tracks in the Park. Two of these can be seen in the foreground of this photograph.
F. Ingham, courtesy Ted Gray.

Plate 25. Perhaps this is a lunch break outside the "Westinghouse" which later became Metropolitan Vickers. The tram's destination is Openshaw and the route board on the side reads "Openshaw Piccadilly Exchange & Trafford Pk. for Docks". The square plate with circular design on the building behind the tram stop indicates a parcel receiving office for the tramway delivery service.
T. Pinder, courtesy Ted Gray.

Plate 26. Special cars for cricket at Lancashire's Old Trafford ground await returning passengers at the *Dog and Partridge* loop near Warwick Road.
Courtesy, N.Ellis.

Plate 27. This early view of Chester Road, Stretford, probably taken from the then UDC offices, shows clearly the portion of road maintained by the tramways, extending to 18 inches on the outside of the outer rails. Between the trams a flock of sheep is occupying most of the road width.
Horatio Grundy.

Plate 28. Shortly after the opening of this section, tram No.111, with original cow-catcher type lifeguard, picks up passengers outside the Stretford Urban District Council Offices.
Speed's Series.

Plate 29. Inward bound tram No.600 on the 48 route is seen at King Street, Stretford.
Horatio Grundy.

Plate 30. The Stretford terminus, with tram No.390, at Barton Road before the extension to Sale showing the *Old Cock Hotel,* extreme left. Adjacent are the premises comprising the former horse tram depot.

Plate 31, (right.) Crossford Bridge before widening, looking towards Manchester. This (widened) roadway forms the Manchester-bound section of the present dual carriageway.

Courtesy J.M.Lloyd.

Plate 32, (below). Tram No.472 bound for Sale encounters flood water from the River Mersey in Cross Street, Sale, in the 1920s.

Plate 33. This photograph was taken about 1908 and shows tram No.338 en route to Piccadilly, probably from Sale. Dane Road is on the right, slightly to the rear of the photographer

Isaac Richards.

Plate 34. Open-top tram No.264, complete with a dent in its dash, is returning to the depot. The tramways hut on the right and the personnel on the tram suggest that its journey is connected with the tramway construction

Plate 35. Timperley-bound tram No.165 stands at the junction with Ashfield Road about 1907.
Whittaker & Co.

Plate 36. A view looking towards Sale showing the tracks leading into Ashfield Road.
Grosvenor Series.

Plate 37. The short branch from the main line to Sale Station opened on 25th March 1907. This view of the Library and Technical School shows tram No.187 turning from Ashfield Road into Tatton Road in the opening months. Prominent in the foreground is one of the eight ornamental tram standards which, unusually central to the tracks, supported the overhead in Ashfield Road. *Modern Series.*

Plate 38. The Sale terminus, seen shortly after the opening to this point with tram No.308 displaying an oil lamp on the dash. These lamps were provided in the event of a power failure at night; one such incident occured on Saturday 31st August.

Isaac Richards.

Plate 39. Another early view of Sale bridge terminus looking from School Road shows a bogie tram turning into Tatton Road at the start of its journey to Piccadilly. The original proposal was for trams to travel via School Road.

Isaac Richards.

Plate 40. The Sale terminus seen from another angle, about 1907. Tram No.471 carries the route board "Manchester, Stretford, Sale". The bogies (Brush B maximum traction) were an unusual type for Manchester, and contrary to normal practice ran with the smaller (pony) wheels outwards. They were more prone to derailment than bogies with the driving wheels outwards.

Plate 41. The extension from Sale Station to Sale Moor opened on 4th July 1912, following various road widenings including the bridge at Sale Station. About this time tram No.673 is waiting to enter the single track in Northenden Road. *Isaac Richards.*

Plate 42. Further along Northenden Road, tram No.677, one of eleven trams (669-679) built by Manchester in 1909, is returning to Piccadilly.

J. Valentine.

Plate 43. Northenden Road, showing tram No.217 halted at the stop in the passing loop at Irlam Road for passengers to board and alight.

Neil's Series.

Plate 44. The other passing loop on Northenden Road was at Clarendon Road, where tram No.676 is waiting, shortly after the extension was opened. The message on the card states that this is "where the cars stop for such a long time while the others come up". These delays were unnecessary, as the terminus had a double track, part of a passing loop on an authorised extension to Gatley where it would have met the Stockport system.
Neil's Series.

Plate 45. A view at the Sale Moor terminus shortly after the extension to this point. Tram No.484 is similar to No.471 seen *(Plate 40)* at the earlier terminus, with reversed bogies. The route board still shows Sale rather than Sale Moor. On the right is one of Manchester's works cars, equipped with a tank for watering the tracks in hot weather, when melting pitch was liable to impair electrical contact on the rails.
Grenville Series.

Plate 46. Route numbers had just been introduced when this view of St. Anne's Sunday School Procession was taken in 1914. The tram is nearing the terminus but the indicator has already been turned to denote Piccadilly for the return journey.

Plate 47. Tram No.675 ready to start its journey to Manchester from Sale Moor. The inward bound track appears to be unused judging by the photo, but the trolley has perforce to be put on the inward wire.

Plate 48. The approach to the terminus, taken in the late 1920s, showing a fully enclosed Manchester tram. *Horatio Grundy.*

Plate 49. The view beyond the terminus, showing the overhead wires terminating at a pole outside the *Legh Arms Hotel*. The authorised extension was along this road. *J.L.Brown.*

TRAFFORD TRAMWAYS 1929

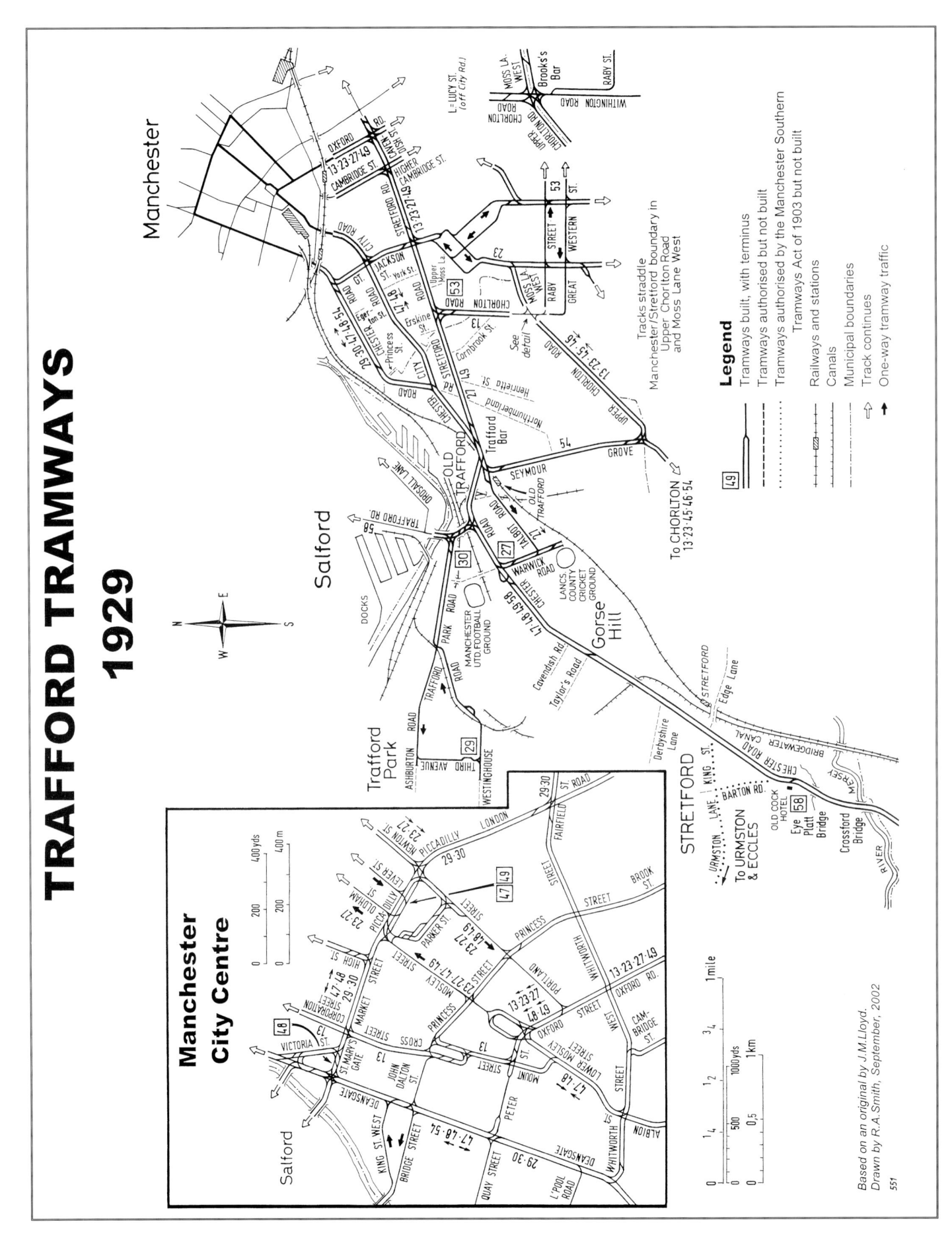

Horse Tramways
Same scale as main map

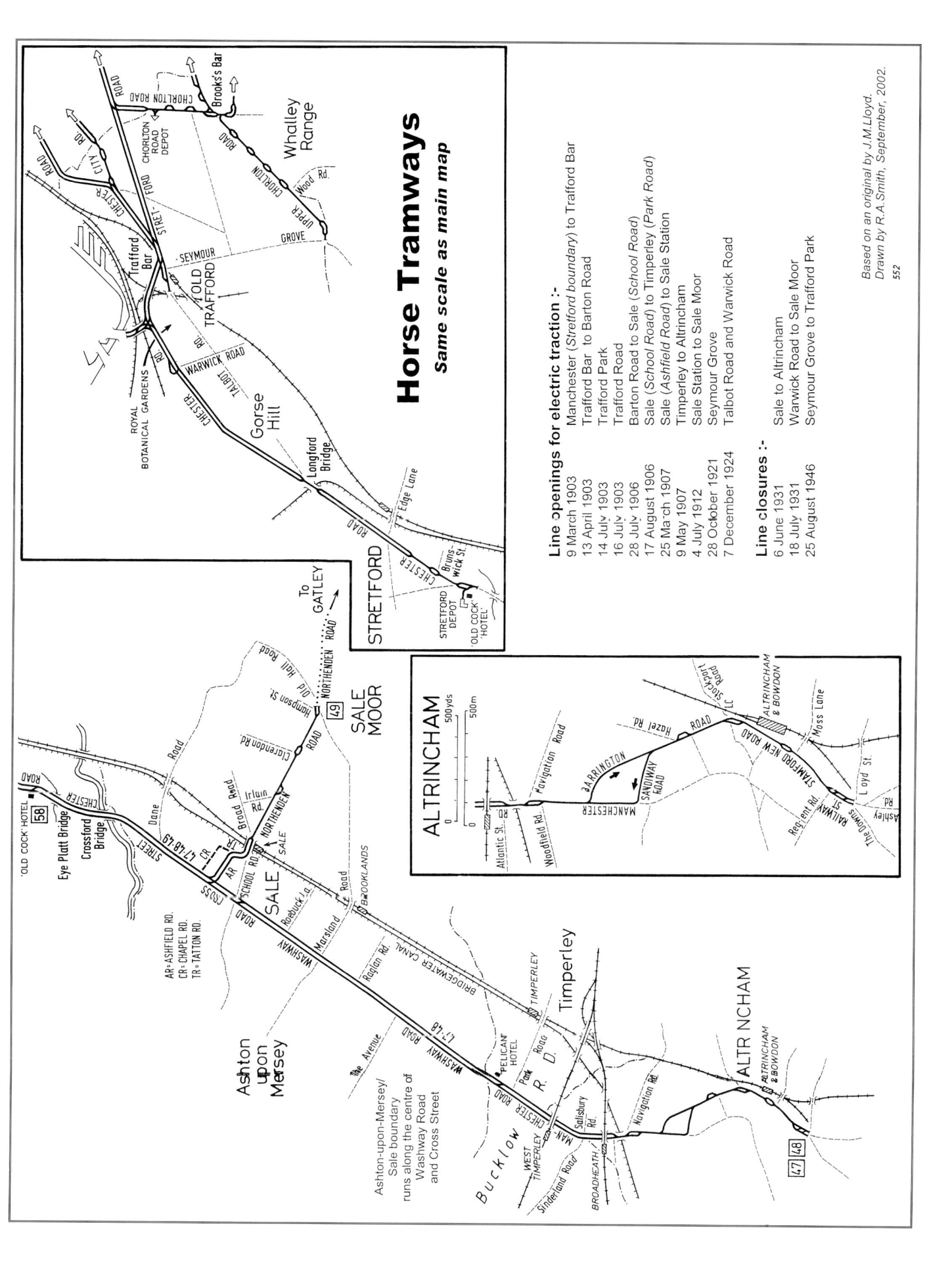

Line openings for electric traction :-

9 March 1903	Manchester (*Stretford boundary*) to Trafford Bar
13 April 1903	Trafford Bar to Barton Road
14 July 1903	Trafford Park
16 July 1903	Trafford Road
28 July 1906	Barton Road to Sale (*School Road*)
17 August 1906	Sale (*School Road*) to Timperley (*Park Road*)
25 March 1907	Sale (*Ashfield Road*) to Sale Station
9 May 1907	Timperley to Altrincham
4 July 1912	Sale Station to Sale Moor
28 October 1921	Seymour Grove
7 December 1924	Talbot Road and Warwick Road

Line closures :-

6 June 1931	Sale to Altrincham
18 July 1931	Warwick Road to Sale Moor
25 August 1946	Seymour Grove to Trafford Park

*Based on an original by J.M.Lloyd.
Drawn by R.A.Smith, September, 2002.*

552

AR = ASHFIELD RD.
CR = CHAPEL RD.
TR = TATTON RD.

Ashton-upon-Mersey/
Sale boundary
runs along the centre of
Washway Road
and Cross Street

Plate 50. Passing the *Volunteer Hotel,* Sale, about 1910, tram No.608 is one of a hundred "Balloon" type trams, of which fifty were converted from open-top, introduced over 1904 - 1907.
Grosvenor Series.

Plate 51. An early view in Ashton-upon-Mersey shows tram No.121 on its way to St. Mary's Gate as implied by the Deansgate destination displayed. Unusually this is shown on a four-sided rotating indicator fitted to the early trams, but generally replaced by roller blinds by 1906 when the Sale tramway opened.
Wrenwood.

Plate 52. Halted at the tram stops at School Road, Sale, open-top tram No.193 is outward bound to Timperley whilst covered-top No.608 is destined for Piccadilly, about 1907.

Fielding's Series.

Plate 53. A quiet scene in Washway Road, by School Road, about 1910.

S.Walker.

Plate 54. Tram No.607 bound for Timperley is seen near the junction of Washway Road and School Road, Sale, in 1907.

Birkenhead's Series.

Plate 55. This fine postcard was posted in Swansea on 18th May 1907, but the scene predates the opening of the extension to Altrincham. Tram No.552 on the left, originally open-top, shows Deansgate as the destination and will therefore travel via Chester Road, whilst No.191 is about to pass on its way to Timperley. The route board on the enclosed car reads "Manchester-Stretford-Sale" to which has been added underneath "Timperley". This last name was replaced by "Altrincham" when the route was extended.
Birkenhead's Series.

Plate 56. Open-top car No.468, which was rebuilt totally enclosed after the 1914-18 war, is seen in Washway Road approaching School Road in 1913 headed for Piccadilly, in which case it will travel into Manchester via City Road, returning via Chester Road.
J.Valentine.

Plate 57. A very rural and peaceful scene in Washway Road, Ashton-upon-Mersey, in stark contrast to the present, but where exactly? The sender of this card, in September 1910, referred to thousands going to the show. "Every tramcar is full when they get here...we can't get on a car to go anywhere towards Bowdon today.

Plate 58. Fully-enclosed car No.470, rebuilt from open-top about 1920, on its way to Deansgate and seen in Washway Road in the 1920s. The overhead at the nearest pole suggests that there was a section-breaker installed at this location. In May 1922 the Ministry of Transport granted an increase in the speed limit from 14 mph to 16 mph, despite strong objection from Sale.

Horatio Grundy.

Plate 59. Car No.296 is passing from Sale into Bucklow Rural District and just ahead can be seen the *Pelican Hotel*. The tracks in Bucklow, which were of unequal length because of the configuration of the Altrincham/Bucklow boundary, were owned by Manchester, whereas those in the other districts were leased. The extension from Sale to Timperley, Park Road, opened on 17th August 1906.

E.P.Cooke.

Plate 60. Car No.559 seen outside the Pelican Hotel, a somewhat different structure from the present day building. The sender's message included "I hope you will like this photo of the much talked about Sale cars". The card was posted on 15th September 1906, and thus within a month of the Timperley opening. *Fieldings Series.*

Plate 61. The crewe of car No.582 pose for the photographer in Washway Road, at Brooklands Road.
Grenville Series.

Plate 62, (below). Car No.628, previously of the 'Balloon' type, rebuilt to fully-enclosed state in 1923, seen in Manchester Road, Broadheath in 1925. It is approaching the over-bridge at West Timperley Station, as the convergence of the overhead wires indicates.
Valentines Series.

Plate 63. The railway bridge referred to in *Plate 62* can be seen in this view of Manchester Road taken from the Altrincham side, at the bridge over the Bridgewater Canal where the tram-track became single. In May 1930, Manchester was told by Altrincham that it was intended to replace this bridge with a 64 feet wide structure which would enable the track to be doubled. The Ministry of Transport suggested that Manchester should contribute to the cost, given the perceived benefit. Mr. R.S.Pilcher, the tramways manager, said that a double track would be of no advantage and suggested that Altrincham should tell the Ministry that Manchester did not wish to double the track, and was not prepared to contribute to the cost of the works. The new bridge was completed in 1935.
Neil's Series.

Plate 64. A further section of single track in Manchester Road, seen about 1920. *H.Davis.*

Plate 65. The outward route to Altrincham diverged from the inward route at Barrington Road, where in the early days of operation an open-top tram, possibly No.306 - waits for passengers to alight.
Neil's Series.

Plate 66. A road bereft of traffic in the 1920s shows tram No.904, built by Manchester in the 1920s, on the 47 route turning into Barrington Road on its way to Altrincham.
Courtesy, D.Rendell.

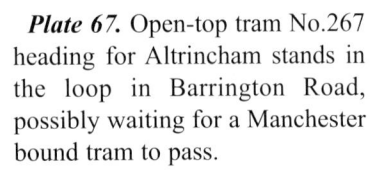

Plate 67. Open-top tram No.267 heading for Altrincham stands in the loop in Barrington Road, possibly waiting for a Manchester bound tram to pass.

Plate 68. Car No.609 has just passed Sandiway Road as it heads for Altrincham along Barrington Road.
C&NWPC Co.

Plates 69 (right) & 70 (below). Two views in the early days of the tramways in Altrincham show an open-top tram Manchester bound in Sandiway Road and emerging from Sandiway Road onto Manchester Road in 1907. In those days there was apparently no risk to the youngsters standing in the roadway to be more central to the photograph.
Neil's Series.

Plate 71. This view shows Sandiway Road in the 1930s shorn of its tram standards but with the track still in situ in a widened road. *A.M.Gunn.*

Plate 72. Here we see a 'Balloon' car travelling along Manchester Road having just turned from Sandiway Road.
Grosvenor Series.

Plate 73. From Barrington Road the trams turned into Stamford New Road; Stockport Road on the left crossed the railway by a level crossing and, at the time of this photograph - pre- 1914 - the passage of trains was hardly likely to cause much inconvenience to road users. However, the steady growth of road traffic eventually led to the construction of a road bridge over the railway leading to Barrington Road, to the rear of the photographer.
Courtesy, D.Rendell.

Plate 74. On the stroke of noon, open-top car No.212 passes the station on its way to the Altrincham terminus.
Courtesy, D.Rendell.

Plate 75. The clock tower at the station seen from the opposite direction, with balcony car No.279 heading for the Altrincham terminus, although the indicator shows Deansgate for the return journey.
Neil's Series.

Plate 76. There was a passing loop just beyond the station and it is apparent from this view that little road space remained for other traffic when two trams passed at this location.
Kingsway Series.

Plate 78, (opposite). In contrast to the previous view open-top car No.224 is travelling towards Manchester on what became the 48 route, since it displays Deansgate as the destination and shows Chester Road in the bulkhead window.

Plate 77. Back on the single track section again, yet another open-top tram, No.402, heads for the terminus at Altrincham.

Plate 79. On its way to Manchester a 'balloon' car is seen in Stamford New Road, Altrincham, about 1910.

Grosvenor Series.

Plate 80. In contrast this tram is Altrincham bound on the 47 route when photographed about 1925.

J. Valentine.

Plate 81. The single track in Stamford New Road became double in Railway Street for the last leg of the journey to the terminus. The single track section was controlled by lights activated by the trolley running over a skate in the overhead, seen on the right-hand wire. This cleared the line for traffic in the opposite direction by displaying a white light in the box on the left-hand tram standard. When the way was not clear a red light was shown. *Courtesy, Ted Gray.*

Plate 82. A few yards further on, tram No.562 has entered Railway Street and is approaching the crossover further from the terminus, about 1910. The destination has already been set for the return journey via City Road. *Courtesy, Ted Gray.*

Plate 83. An early view of car No.121 shortly after departure from the terminus, seen in Railway Street.

Plate 84. This church procession has brought the Manchester bound car on the 48 route to a temporary halt. Unusually it shows the destination "Exchange via Deansgate". The tram stop sign "All cars stop here" can be seen suspended from a span wire above the front of the tram.

Plate 85. About 1924, balcony car No.684 nears the terminus, with its 47 route number showing above a broken piece of opal glass. A hamper containing parcels for delivery in the Altrincham area can be seen on the front platform. *Horatio Grundy.*

Plate 86. The following views are a selection of scenes at the terminus. First, above, we have four wheel open-top car No.493 which will be travelling via Chester Road and Deansgate, given the indication of "Chester Road" in the rear window of the lower saloon. The photograph was probably taken shortly after the opening, because the route board on the side has "Altrincham" added below the original wording of "Manchester-Stretford-Sale". *Neil's Series.*

49

Plate 87. By way of contrast open-top car No.210 is a bogie car travelling to Piccadilly, in which case it will traverse City Road, as is confirmed by the card in the saloon bulkhead window. Again, the layout of the route board on the side suggests that this is an early photograph, and unusually the photographer records the view beyond the terminus.

Plate 88. Car No.576 stands at the Altrincham terminus about 1910 bound for Deansgate. The destination "Deansgate" is not very explicit since it will travel along that thoroughfare, turning right into St. Mary's Gate which was regarded as the terminus, before continuing its journey along Market Street.

Grosvenor Series.

Plate 89. The trolley is being turned as passengers alight from car No.578, which has just arrived on the 48 route, probably in the early 1920s. At this time the route board had been simplified to "Manchester & Altrincham".
Courtesy, D.Rendell.

Plate 90. Another view of the terminus at Altrincham with tram No.626 ready for departure about 1920. *Grenville Series.*

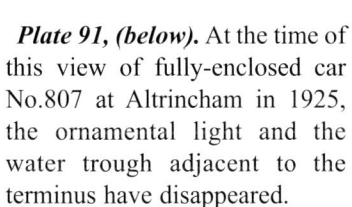

Plate 91, (below). At the time of this view of fully-enclosed car No.807 at Altrincham in 1925, the ornamental light and the water trough adjacent to the terminus have disappeared.
J.Valentine.

Plate 92. This last terminus view at Altrincham shows car No.810 on a warm summer's day, judging by the open windows, possibly about 1929. There was a stretch of 165 yards of double track at the terminus with a cross-over at each end. Perhaps the one further from the terminus was used at times of congestion. One wonders when the inward bound track from the terminus to the first cross-over was used.
Horatio Grundy.

Plate 93. Piccadilly bound, in Stretford, tram No.182 was photographed on 10th November 1930, a week after the introduction of double deck buses to the route. This tram had entered service about three months earlier, having replaced the original single-truck car of this number.

Plate 95. The last day for operation on the 49 route to Sale Moor was 18th July 1931. This photograph, taken on the evening of that day, shows tram No.866 passing through Stretford, showing Sale Moor as the destination rather than Sale.
Stephenson.

Plate 96. The Sale trams travelled along Stretford Road to the City centre, entering via Oxford Road and Portland Street to Piccadilly, and returning via Mosley Street (where car No.209 is seen outside the Art Gallery about 1907) St. Peter's Square and Oxford Street

Plate 94, (opposite). The last tram in Altrincham departed at 1.00 p.m. on Saturday 6th June 1931. The regular service had been replaced by buses on 19th January, leaving the trams as supplements at peak periods. Generally these were the older trams operating without route numbers. This photograph, taken in the last few days of operation, shows one of the 28 surviving cars of this type (the remainder had been rebuilt into fully enclosed cars in the 1920s).
E.J.Horley.

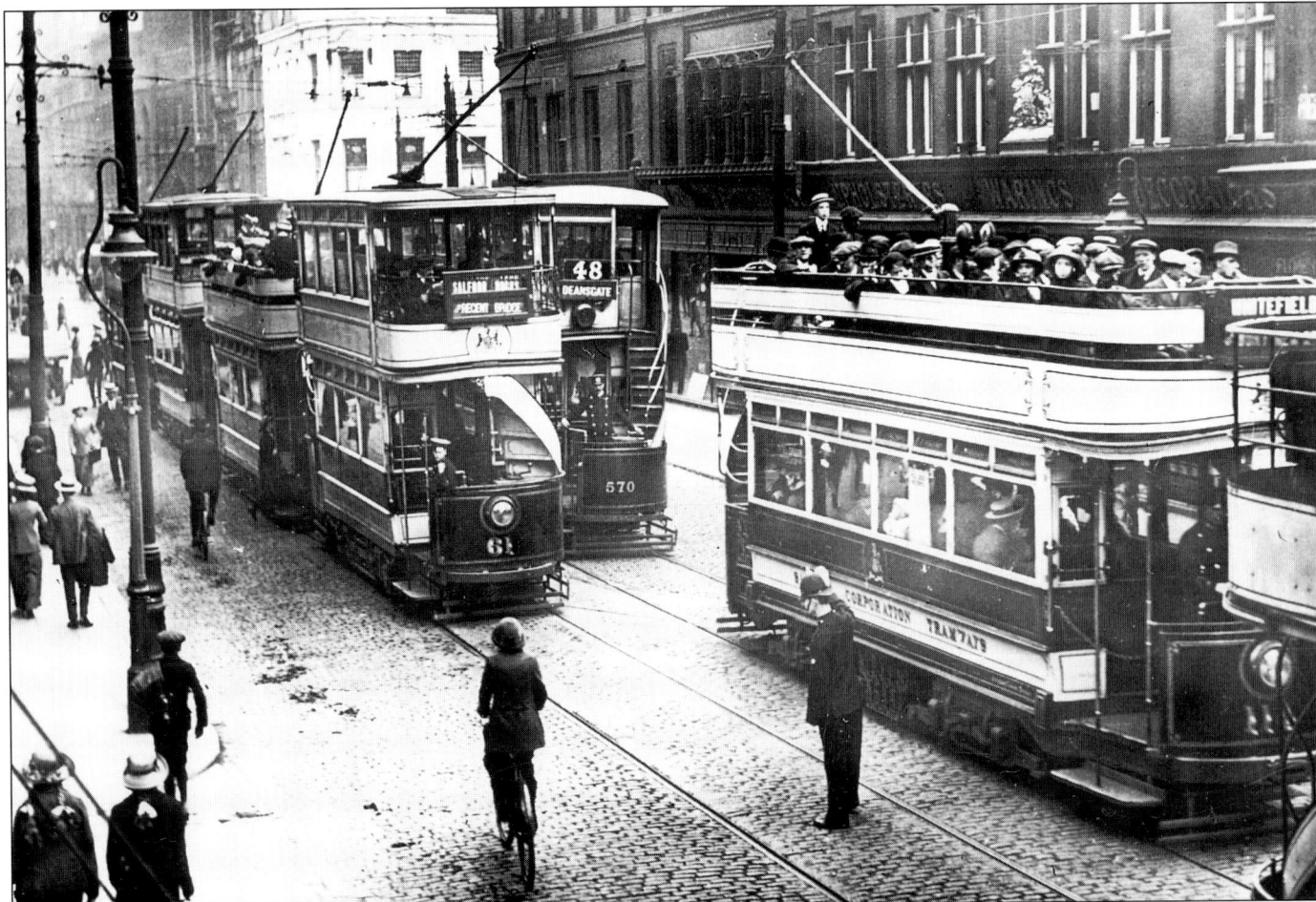

Plate 98. In 1914, tram No.570 is surrounded by Salford trams as it makes its way along Deansgate to its terminus in St Mary's Gate.

Plate 97, (opposite top). Interruption to service! Car No.323 has derailed in Mosley Street as it is about to enter St. Peter's Square, and has attracted the interest of passers by; already two trams are held up.

Plate 99, (right). Also in 1914, a congested scene in Mosley Street near York Street delays tram No.673 on the 49 route.

Plate 100. A photograph taken in 1914 shows car No.478 in Oxford Road on route 49 shortly after route numbers were introduced in that year. It is passing the Palace Theatre of Varieties, but somewhat surprisingly shows Sale rather than Sale Moor as the destination. Perhaps the latter had not been added to the roller blind indicator. The tower of the Refuge Assurance Company dominates the skyline.
J.Valentine.

Plate 101. At the time of this photograph, about 1926, the route 47 trams entered Manchester from City Road via Portland Street to Piccadilly, which was regarded as the terminus, before continuing down Market Street, where car No.800, built by English Electric in 1919/20 is seen on the return journey. From 17th June 1828, when tram traffic flows were reversed, they entered via Mosley Street. Tracks leading to High Street can be seen in the foreground.

J.Valentine.

Plate 102. Probably taken on the same day as the previous photograph, car No.942, newly in service from English Electric, has left its terminus in St. Mary's Gate and will turn from Market Street into Mosley Street. When the directions in Mosley Street and Portland Street were reversed it left via Portland Street to St. Peter's Square and thence to City Road.

Plate 103, (below). This magnificent view, taken during Manchester's Civic Week, 2nd-9th October 1926, shows over twenty assorted trams, including a Salford vehicle in the distance, passing through Piccadilly on various routes. Prominent in the middle is a tram on the 47 route which has turned from Portland Street and is headed for Market Street. The track nearest to the camera carries trams which have arrived via Portland Street, due to leave via Mosley Street.

A.Walsh.

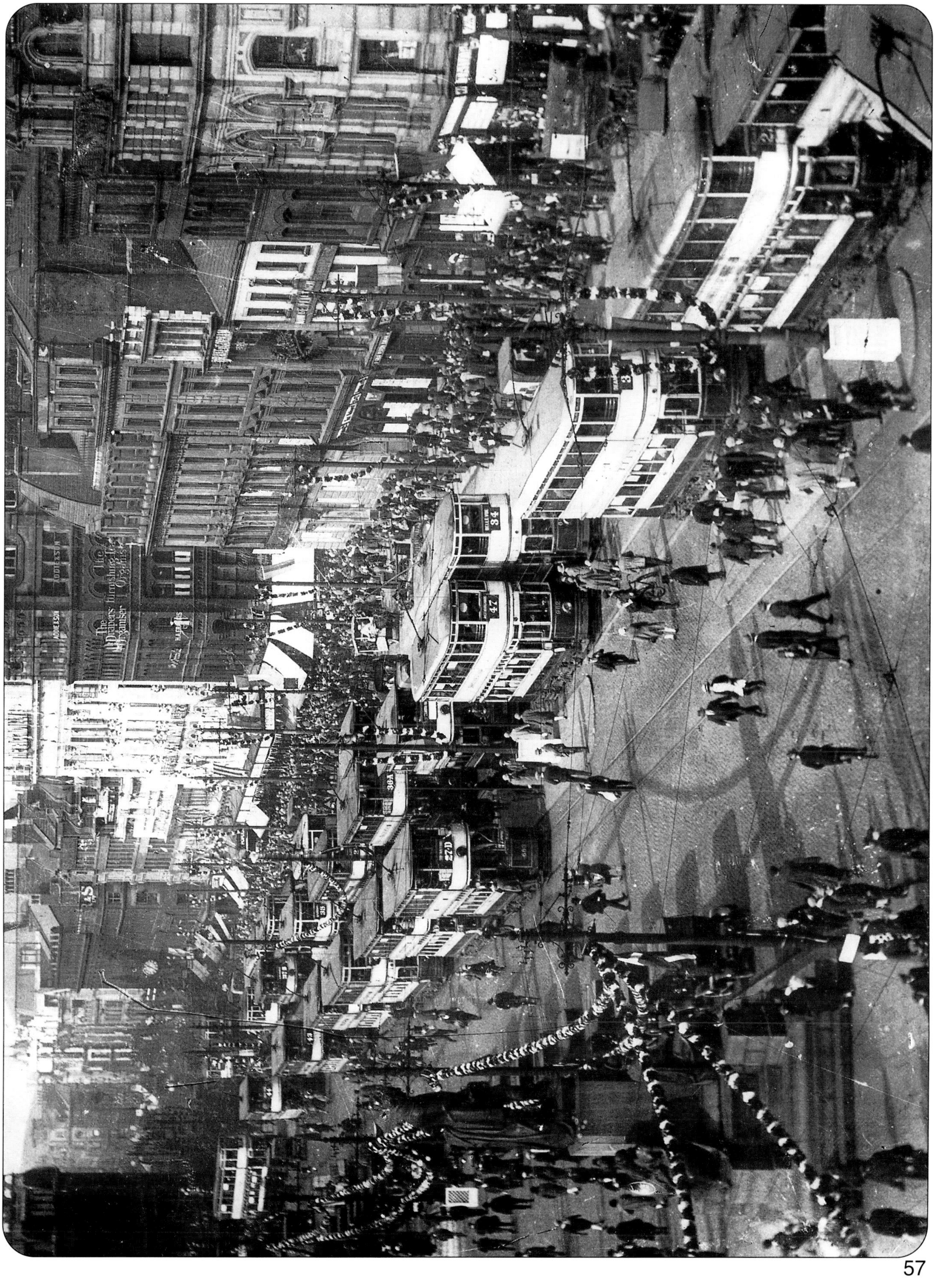

Plates 104, 105 & 106. During Civic Week a procession of trams toured the City covering a different portion of the system each day. It included a horse tram ex-Morecambe, open-top No.101, newly built enclosed tram No.988, a skeleton tram then under construction at Manchester's works at the Hyde Road complex, and an illuminated tram. Because of the success of this initiative, the skeleton and illuminated trams visited the outer districts during the following week, including Altrincham on the evening of Monday, 11th October 1926. These two vehicles left Hyde Road depot at 7.15 p.m. via Grosvenor Street and Stretford Road to Old Trafford and then via Sale to Altrincham, departing from Altrincham at 8.10 p.m., reaching Warwick Road at 8.45 p.m. The skeleton tram (possibly No.112 which entered service in January 1927) incorporated some design details featured in 50 trams (1004-1053) ordered from English Electric in May 1926 and delivered between April 1927 and April 1928.

Both trams are seen at the Hyde Road works, the skeleton vehicle apparently straddling the tracks.

B.Pearson.

Plate 107. The late 1920s, and tram No.198, built by Brush Electrical Engineering Co. with open-top in 1901, given a balcony top cover about 1915 and rebuilt to its fully enclosed state after the war, is seen on route 49 in Oxford Street, at the junction with Portland Street. Again, even more surprisingly, given the elapse of time since the extension to Sale Moor, it shows Sale as the destination. The route board on the side reads "Manchester, Stretford & Sale"

A.Hill.

Plate 108. This photograph was taken about 1906 looking down Chorlton Road, most of which, from Brooks's Bar end where the photograph was taken, was in Stretford. In contrast to the Manchester tramway system generally, the poles in Stretford were topped by a ring and spike rather than a ball and finial. It is evident from the trolley that tram No.138 has just emerged from Moss Lane West on the right. Services from Hightown were operated on a circular basis through Brooks's Bar, outwards from Albert Square via All Saints, Hulme and Moss Lane West and inwards via Chorlton Road, Stretford Road and All Saints, and the reverse of this. A service along Moss Lane West to Brooks's Bar opened on 1st December 1902, and one in Chorlton Road on 13th April 1903, which date also saw the extension of the circular route (later 53), operated by single-deck tram, along Upper Chorlton Road, to the left of the photographer, to Seymour Grove.

A.C.Series.

Plate 109. The Upper Chorlton Road tramway was single-track with passing loops, one of which is shown here. The Hightown trams began running to Chorlton (High Lane) on 9th May 1907, when the tramway was extended from the then terminus at Seymour Grove. Stretford claimed that Manchester had no powers to make this connection and informed Manchester that, "A physical disconnection has been made of the junction formed by the Corporation with the Council's Upper Chorlton Road tramway, without consent of the Council, by removing a short length of rail crossing the point of termination of the old line in this district. The removed rail is placed behind a seat on the footpath leading to Chorlton-cum-Hardy beyond the district, convenient for reinstatement." In the picture, taken shortly after the extension, both trams are in Stretford since the boundary included the whole of Upper Chorlton Road at this location, crossing the road again, at a point just ten yards beyond the original terminus at Seymour Grove.

W.Fry & Co.

Plate 110. This view of Upper Chorlton Road in 1909 shows tram No.614 on its way to Hollinwood. The left hand side of the tram is in Stretford and the right hand side in Manchester, given that the boundary ran between the rails. The housing on the left has been set back from the road with a view to future widening, and this led to the doubling of the track during 1920 and 1921, as a result of which the three left hand rails lay in Stretford and the right hand one in Manchester.

Plate 111. A double-track tramway in Seymour Grove opened on 28th October 1921, serviced by route 54 operating between Chorlton and Albert Square via City Road. Car No.241 seen here in 1922 is on Stretford territory but will move into Manchester where the tracks converge. The destination reads "Chorlton via Seymour Grove", but the route number is not clearly discernible, apparently because the opal glass is dirty.

Plate 112, (above) and Plate 113 (left). These two views of trams in Seymour Grove date from about 1925 by which time the 54 route had been amended to operate along Deansgate instead of to Albert Square. Tram No.130, above, is en route to Deansgate whilst tram No.747, left, is outward bound to Chorlton. *Charles Downs.*

61

Plate 114. Earlier photographs showed open-top trams on the short terminal stub in Talbot Road adjacent to Trafford Bar, displaying the destination Clayton. This became route 27 in 1914. Here we see car No.288 in the 1920s on a short working on the 27E to Piccadilly with the wires from Seymour Grove trailing in from the right. *Charles Downs.*

Plate 115, (above). In 1924 the Talbot Road track was extended as a single track on its own side of the roadway, given the width, to link up with a new double track tramway in Warwick Road which gave access to Chester Road. This view shows the initial part of the Talbot Road extension. As with the other Stretford lines they were leased to Manchester, the lease permitting the storage of trams in Warwick Road but not Talbot Road

A.H.Clarke.

Plate 117, (left) and Plate 118, (below). These views at Trafford Bar, possibly taken on 30th July 1938, the last day of operation of route 27, show tram No.229 (left) on the last stretch of its journey from Droylsden to the terminus in Warwick Road and (lower) returning to Droylsden. The double-deck bus displaying 49 is operating on the former tram route.
A.M.Gunn.

Plate 119, (right). Warwick Road's main use was for storing trams during matches at the Lancashire County cricket ground and at Manchester United's football ground. This 1932 view is taken from the end of the tracks looking away from the railway (now Metrolink), with the cricket ground on the left.
Dr. R.S.B.Hamilton.

Plate 116, (opposite). On the opening of Talbot Road, trams outward bound on the 27 route were extended along these tracks to terminate at the junction with Chester Road. Car No.499 is seen here in Chester Road approaching the Trafford Bar junction on the return journey in the 1930s. It had replaced the original single-truck car of this number in June 1925. With the conversion of the 49 tram service on 19th July 1931, the 27 service was re-routed the next day for journeys before 9.00 a.m. to travel anti-clockwise along Chester Road, Warwick Road and Talbot Road, thus travelling on the wrong side of the road in both Warwick Road and Talbot Road.
A.H.Clarke.

Plate 120. This view, taken in the opening months of 1939, shows trams awaiting the home-going crowds from a fixture at the football ground and displaying 'United Grd' (Specials for Manchester City displayed 'City Grd'.) The photographer is standing with his back to Chester Road, and the trams are standing wrong road, having presumably entered from Chester Road. On departure they will use a cross-over near Chester Road to regain the correct track before turning right into Chester Road. If the track here was insufficient to accommodate all the trams, then presumably the later arrivals would reverse over the cross-over and travel wrong road on the nearside track. *F.D.Rourke.*

Plates 121 & 122. On Monday 26th August 1946, the 37 route operating between Chorlton and Levenshulme via Trafford Bar was curtailed to operate only between St. Mary's Gate and Levenshulme. These photographs were taken on the last day of operation from Chorlton and show (left) car No.632 about to turn from Seymour Grove towards Trafford Bar and (bottom left) a car in the reverse direction approaching Seymour Grove. The track in the foreground leads to Talbot Road for Manchester United football ground and the Lancashire County cricket ground, and the overhead is still in place. All these tracks were abandoned at this time, bringing to an end tramway operation in Stretford and hence the present day Trafford Metropolitan Borough. The last Manchester tram ran on 10th January 1949.

F.D.Rourke.